The Secrets To Making Love *Happen!*

Mastering Your Relationships Using Handwriting Analysis & Neuro-Linguistic Programming

By Bart A. Baggett

Empresse´ Publishing

http://www.myhandwriting.com

The Secrets To Making Love... Happen!
Mastering Your Relationships Using Handwriting Analyis &
Neuro-Linguistic Programming
by Bart A. Baggett

Previous subtitle of earlier editions:
How to Find, Attract, and Choose Your Perfect Mate Using
Handwriting Analysis and Neuro Linguistic Programming

Published by:
Empresse' Publishing
P.O. Box 720355
Dallas, TX 75372
1-800-398-2278

http://www.myhandwriting.com

Copyright © 1993, © 1994, © 1998 & © 1999 by Bart A. Baggett
First Printing 1993
Second Printing 1994
Third Printing 1998
Fourth Printing 1999

Library of Congress Cataloging in Publication Data
Baggett, Bart A.
The Secrets To Making Love... Happen: How to Find, Attract, and
Choose Your Perfect Mate Using Handwriting Analysis and
Neuro Linguistic Programming / by Bart A. Baggett—3rd ed.

Bibliography: p.

1. Relationships—Dating, Single, Love, 2. Graphology —
Handwriting Analysis, 3. Psychology, 4. Neuro Linguistic
Programming, I. Title

ISBN # 1-882929-24-1
Library of Congress Catalog Number: 93-70750
Printed in India

What Other Readers Have To Say...

"I've been liberated; I'll never have a bad relationship again!"
— Melanie Graham, Tampa, Florida

"If you want to add handwriting analysis to your toolbelt of vast personal resources, this book will set you in the right direction. Bart does an outstanding job of making the subject practical, fun, easy to understand and apply to your life."
— Rex Steven Sikes, NLP and Mind Design ™ trainer

"No one should ever be in a relationship again before reading this book. It should be required reading for young people. It should be in every school curriculum in America."
— Tex Taylor, Lubbock, Tx

"It is the perfect book for my friends; they are always dating the wrong guys! It's a great way to help others grow, a fun gift, and a great conversation piece!"
— Diana Morrow, Oklahoma City, OK

"Italians line up to get their handwriting analyzed too! Thanks for giving me a tool that is changing my life ! "
— Paolo Alguriez, Student, Italy.

"I think your book is great! I have read it once and am half-way through again! I am so inspired with this new tool for reading and understanding people."
— Sharon Sparks, Dallas,Texas

"This is the most fascinating thing that I have done, and I have done a lot of different things in my life!"
— John Adams, Senior Sports Executive, Australia.

"Everytime I dated a woman with Trainwreck Handwriting, she ended up being a Total Trainwreck. The handwriting doesn't lie. Now, I depend on it."
— Stan Hayes, Dallas, TX Video Producer

"I have gained wonderful insights to myself and my co-workers and what makes them tick. In my new job at Federal Express, I can get to know my new co-workers on a different level. It has made a huge impact on how well I get along with others ! "
— Angela Deatrick, Systems Engineer, St. Louis, MO

"No one that shares my appreciation, thankfulness and excitement from your teachings more than me. Your books and courses have changed my life."
— Daniel Arola, Houston, TX

"It is as if you were a reincarnation of Milton Bunker, except, this time 'round you apply all that knowledge to practical, no-nonsense objectives."
— A. Grauman, Brooklyn, New York (Master Certified Graphoanalyst)

"When I first saw your book in the bookstore I thought, 'Ehhh, It's probably worth $16.' I had no idea! It has opened up a whole new world for me. Its value is at least a 100 times the price! Thank you."
— Dennis Rudolph, Sierra Madre, CA

"Exactly what I've been looking for! I'm already reaping benefits from changing my T bars and Y loops. In just a few weeks, my wife and I have noticed changes that are quite profound in our marriage! "
—John Grey, Publisher, Houston,TX

Table of Contents

Foreword

I am honored to be writing the foreword to Bart Baggett's "Asian" edition of this remarkable and useful book.

It is a rare privilege to meet someone who is inspiring, enlightening, and entertaining. As you read this book, I think you will agree that Bart Baggett is all that and more.

When I first met Bart in person, I only expected to learn about handwriting analysis and bring something different to my seminar clients in India. But, to my pleasant surprise, Bart took my mind on a whirlwind adventure that has forever changed my life. I was immediately curious and perplexed with this new form of personality assessment. What's more, the concept that I could actually change my life by changing my handwriting intrigued me. As Bart was touring India in the Spring of 1998 conducting live seminars, I watched as hundreds of people's lives were transformed by Bart's words, activities, and exercises. Even in my own life, my ambition and confidence has increased substantially - as the height of my t-bar has risen to the top of the stem!

The book you hold in your hands is Bart Baggett's breakthrough work about using handwriting analysis in the context of relationships. Although Bart originally wrote this book with a non-married reader in mind, the information contained within its pages can be applied to any gender, any race, any marital status, at any age. Who couldn't benefit from learning more about themselves and how their fellow human beings think?

This is a guidebook for attracting, selecting, and choosing your ideal mate. And, if you are already in a relationship, you will find this book a "toolbox" of skills, techniques, and exercises to dramatically improve the degree of compatibility and happiness in your life. The techniques taught in this book are powerful, accurate, and immediately applicable in everyday life.

The great thing about handwriting analysis is you can apply it to every area of your life. This book focuses on your interpersonal relationships. But, you can use the same material and make yourself more money, get along better with co-workers or even become a better parent. The applications are unlimited.

I think you will discover Bart is funny, intelligent, provocative, clever, and most of all, inspiring. Don't be surprised if the curiosity to learn more increases with every turn of the page. You may even find yourself calling my office to ask how you can get access to more of Bart Baggett's books, tapes, and even his live seminars. I am pleased to endorse this book fervently. Read it again and again.

Sincerely,

Pradeep Agarwal

Dedicated to my family, whose love, support, and faith in me helped create who I am today.

> *"Love looks not with the eyes,*
> *but with the mind;*
> *and therefore is winged*
> *Cupid painted blind. "*
> *— William Shakespeare,*
> *A Midsummer Night's Dream*

Introduction

Finding the perfect mate can be a long and confusing process. In fact, it can drive you crazy. I used to be confused as to what opening line I should use, or how I could convert a new friendship into a romance. I used to be apprehensive around the opposite sex. I used to say, "I just don't understand." I used to believe fate was my only ally in finding the right romance. But I don't think that way anymore. Things have changed.

Purpose

The purpose of this book is to take the frustration out of meeting and selecting people to date and improve all your current relationships. It will also help you make better choices and be more effective at accomplishing your relationship goals. Whether you're looking to settle down with Mr. or Mrs. Right, or you think it would be exciting to know that anytime, anywhere, you could walk right up to an attractive person, develop rapport, create chemistry, and if you choose, get a date. If you apply what you learn in this book, you can do just that. I can. My friends and clients who use the skills outlined in this book can do it –anytime, anyplace, regardless of circumstances. I have met and started relationships in elevators, parking lots, movies, grocery stores and even had women give me their phone numbers...in front of my own date! Not only is it gratifying to know people find you interesting, but it is a lot of fun too!

You may have had failed relationships in the past, and you may even have been burnt once or twice. Whatever your past experiences were, they will now improve. What you will learn is a method of understanding people which will help you avoid painful mistakes and help you create the kind of pleasure in relationships that you deserve.

Don't Judge A Book By Its Cover

Everyone knows the cliche; yet people start relationships based mostly on physical appearance—hardly even looking to see what is inside. Some people still try to get to know someone the old, long, hard way. Maybe you've been doing this. You could spend a lot of time, money and emotional energy to get to know someone only to discover that you have incompatible needs or desires. All the while, you were hoping they really were as beautiful on the inside as they were on the outside—and yet you had no way of opening them up and just taking a look! And what if you get emotionally involved, and then hurt, and then it takes you six months to recover from the pain? Have you ever had that happen? Do you know any cosmetically beautiful people who are neurotic basket cases? I know a few of them. You need a way to know in advance what makes a person tick.

How do you find that ideal relationship? The answer is not simple. In fact, it takes this whole book to explain my answer. But there are a few basic elements of the procedure that will help you in your quest: *initial contact, recognizing the right person, and creating chemistry.*

Initial Contact

This book will help make meeting people both fun and easy. There is no way you can meet the person of your dreams if you stay locked in your room daydreaming. Many of you have met so many losers, users, scum, drunks and neurotics that you feel it is better just to stay home. The reason you may feel that way is because you haven't mastered one of the most important parts of dating: recognizing the right person and screening out the others.

Recognizing The Right Person

You probably know what you're looking for—physically. But is that all that matters to you? Haven't you had a partner who was physically attractive but their personality was a dud? If you want successful relationships, you need to start looking for the personality characteristics that you like. Then you can start using both your heart and your head to make decisions.

Emotions vs Logic

Emotions are powerful motivators; we sometimes follow our heart ignoring what our head tells us. This is especially true when we have plenty of emotional information ("he is soooo hot!") and very little logical information ("I'm not sure if he lied to me or not"). Unfortunately, this scenario is typical of new relationships.

I can speak from experience from a man's point of view. More than once I've been a sucker for a beautiful woman and I know that this is a common problem. It's happened to me...her physical beauty overtakes my emotions and my emotions overtake my actions. I find myself daydreaming about her. I can picture us kissing on a beach at sunset while the theme to *Love Story* plays in the background of my mind like some "B" movie. I forget to eat, can't sleep, and find that nothing really matters except being with her. The scary thing is that these feelings happen before I even get to know her!

Then, I analyze both sides of the equation. On the emotional side: she is beautiful, she makes me feel good, she kisses nice, I feel warm fuzzies in my belly when she holds my hand, and my friends think she is hot. On the logical side: she isn't too bright, her laugh is irritating, her mom is more irritating, she is too picky about her food, and she doesn't like Jimmy Buffett concerts. What is happening? The logical side of my brain is presenting a strong case for changing my phone number and not telling her what it is! Does any of this zaniness sound familiar? As time goes by, I begin to be bothered because she doesn't understand my jokes, she's stubborn, and she is not a good dancer. Suddenly, she isn't as attractive as she was in the beginning. Slowly, the logical side of my brain comes back to life saying, "Bart. Wake up!" Once I do wake up, the relationship dissolves. We part as "good friends" and I start the cycle again. Does this sound familiar?

I am not suggesting that you discard your emotions and become a stoic philosopher. But if you investigate more deeply on a logical psychological level, your heart can have a bit of logic to balance out those important decisions. Use your logic to avoid the losers. As you become more selective and know what you're looking for, you will be able to find what you want. Some people are then totally amazed when they begin to actually *attract* the kind of people they want! Picking up this book was the first step in attracting the person you want. Congratulations!

What you must learn to do is *recognize* the good prospects and eliminate the bad prospects *before* you get *emotionally* involved.

Once you get emotionally involved, your logic becomes fuzzy and not very useful. That is why I recommend you take every opportunity to know the person's personality in detail. This book will show you how. Besides, the techniques you will learn are also great for breaking the ice with strangers. What you are really doing is eliminating the bad apples before you spend time, energy and money. What you must remember is that if he or she has some serious bad traits, you must be able to say "No, thank you," right off the bat. If you can't allow your logic to control your actions at the beginning, you will be helpless once you get involved. The key to this process is selectiveness. Once you begin to recognize the good traits and invite compatible people into your life, your life will suddenly be filled with choices of which good prospects you want to date or mate.

Why Don't They Make Cliff's Notes On People?

Do you remember literary classes in school where instead of reading the whole book, you read the Cliff's Notes? Those little black and yellow miniature books gave you a summary, an outline and all the meat of the book, in about ten minutes. I used them because I always wanted to find the easiest and quickest route to achieving my goals. Who wouldn't? Wouldn't it be nice if you were given the Cliff's Notes of every person in which you were interested?

You can! In relationships it's not called Cliff's Notes, it is called *Neuro-analysis*, more commonly known as the combination of handwriting analysis and NLP (neuro linguistic programming) for interpersonal relationships. You can use neuro-analysis to determine if someone is compatible with you within the first five minutes after you meet, maybe even sooner. It is fast, accurate, and allows you to get a complete summary instead of *choosing a lover by the cover.*

What Is Neuro-Analysis?

Neuro-analysis is the combination of modern neuro-sciences with the empirical study of personality. Over the years, behavioral scientists and handwriting experts have categorized neuro-muscular tendencies as they are correlated with specific observable personality traits.

Each personality trait is represented by a common neurological brain pattern in each individual possessing that trait. Each common neurological brain pattern has an associated neuro-

> *" Any sufficiently developed technology is*
> *indistinguishable from magic."*
> *- Arthur C. Clarke*

mechanical micro-movement tendency. Therefore, every person, regardless of sex, race, ethnic background, or language with that personality trait will share the same neuro-muscular tendency.

In plain English, this explanation of handwriting simply means that there are very small neuro-muscular movements that are the same for every person who has a particular personality trait. The movements are so tiny that they have to be graphically frozen to be identified.   Handwriting is an example of this graphically frozen movement. Analyzing and interpreting that data is the science of neuro-analysis. It takes handwriting analysis and the neuro-sciences one step farther.

You may be asking yourself, "How is handwriting going to help me get the man or woman of my dreams?" By the time you finish this book, you will not only understand how to find and choose the right person, but you will know how to make the person you choose like you as well. Handwriting will help do both.

Creating Chemistry

The third step to finding the ideal relationship is *creating chemistry*. This means that you have passed the first two hurdles, you met and you recognized each other. Now what? You must develop chemistry or, as some say, fall in love. There are various ways to create this love chemistry. The best way is to create rapport as quickly as you can. When you connect with people in an intimate way, something happens. The attraction you feel is not only emotional but chemical. These chemicals are part of your body's natural neurological make-up. As you feel certain emotions, your body combines certain chemicals. There is a scientific explanation for that state called chemistry. In fact, the specific procedures to create these states at will are the topic of my next book and current live seminars. It is absolutely amazing how quickly you can discover the secret to creating an intense magnetic attraction with someone instantly! Later, in the section on creating chemistry I will take you through the process of creating this rapport instantly with anyone you choose. After you learn the basics of creating rapport and analyzing personality, you may begin wondering about ways to learn more. Simply turn to appendix C for the most current information on these advanced methods.

One of the best ways to develop instant rapport with people is to discuss an intimate topic in a serious way. By analyzing handwriting, you can immediately bypass superficial fluff and have meaningful conversations with people about what is really important: relationships, ideas, or feelings. After someone has shared a part of his life that only a few know, he feels *close* to you. This is another key to connecting with people.

When embarking on the search for a new romantic relationship remember the three fundamental steps: 1-Initial contact, 2-Recognize the right person, 3- Develop chemistry. Sounds simple, doesn't it? This book explains how to accomplish each step. What's more, you will have fun doing it!

> *"Great spirits have always encountered*
> *violent opposition from mediocre minds."*
> — *Albert Einstein*

Chapter 1

Top Secrets

Your Secret Weapon : Handwriting

If you had a secret weapon that allowed you to see inside the enemy's headquarters to see all their files, documents, and war plans, would your chances for winning be improved? Absolutely. We aren't at war, but we do have a secret weapon to win over the heart of the one you want. It is the science of handwriting analysis.

If you were ever curious why handwriting reveals so much about a person, just ask a baby. Did you ever wonder how a baby knows to smile when she is happy or pout when she is sad? A baby knows how to smile naturally. Just like crying is a natural reaction to being uncomfortable. She is born with that instinct. If you think about the essence of a smile, a cry, or a pout, you realize these are simply neurological reactions to a specific emotion. Across all cultures, a baby's smile signifies the same thing. Therefore, the link between a person's psychological state of mind and his muscular reactions exists beyond any doubt. Over centuries, muscular reactions to emotions have been categorized and become more specific. From the smile to the very useful skill of reading a person's body language, man has improved on learning about the mind from the body. Handwriting is a definite expression of muscular motions that was often overlooked as a tool for under-standing personality. But, when you think about it, you realize handwriting contains the same minute specific muscle contractions and expansions as a baby's smile. So, with the help of research scientists, handwriting reveals to us much more than the feelings of happiness or sadness.

Since you will use handwriting to create rapport with new friends and understand their personalities at a deep level, it will help you to have an understanding of why handwriting reveals so much pertinent information about a person. A person's subconscious mind dictates the way he writes. This writing reveals various aspects of the subconscious mind. Cursive handwriting is the preferred method of writing because of the consistent use of upstrokes. Upstrokes in handwriting represent the subconscious mind, while the downstrokes yield information stemming from the conscious mind. Since the subconscious contains such important information, we need to take special note of the upstrokes in handwriting. Therefore, analyze cursive handwriting when it is available. However, if only printing is available, analyze it. The personality will still reveal itself in each stroke of the pen. One of the most common questions I am asked is, "What does it mean if I always print, I don't write cursive?" Since we evaluate character on a stroke-by-stroke method, I need to look at one's individual handwriting to give an in-depth answer. However, because upstrokes, found mostly in cursive, reveal subconscious thoughts, it is fair to answer that question about printing with the following: "People who always print tend to put up barriers so others cannot easily see who they really are." From that general basis, look at the individual strokes.

It makes no difference whether the writer is male, female, Italian, French, Russian, right or left handed. The handwriting never lies. In all honesty, I have been wrong about someone's handwriting before. When I was learning I made mistakes. The mistakes I made in my character analysis were always a result of overlooking some aspect of the handwriting. In my experience, the handwriting has never been wrong.

Everything you learn about handwriting will apply equally to men or women, regardless of race, culture, or even language. This book is designed with both sexes in mind. Don't be surprised if a member of the opposite sex is analyzing your handwriting, checking you out, too!

Handwriting analysis is one of the most non-discriminatory tools available. It cannot deduce race, gender, culture, age, etc. That is one reason it is widely accepted in the corporate business world. However, you and I are going to use it for interpersonal relationships. After all, if it is good enough for multi-billion dollar companies to use it to evaluate prospective executives, it is good enough to choose your next date.

Research scientists have categorized neuro–muscular movement tendencies as they are correlated with specific observable personality traits. These personality traits have been categorized and labeled (human behavior patterns and thinking patterns). Each personality trait is represented by a neurological brain pattern and each person who has a particular personality trait shares a common human neuro-mechanical micro-movement tendency. These tendencies reveal themselves in muscular movements such as body language, thought processes, and handwriting. In a nutshell, this is the science of neuro-analysis. See the appendix for further in-depth explanations and summaries of statistical clinical research on neuro- analysis.

Handwriting is actually brain writing. It is an expression of small electrical impulses from the brain to the hand. A thought, a movement, even a feeling is a result of such electrical impulses dictated from the brain. Knowing this simplifies the process of understanding how an electrical neuro-muscular activity like handwriting could hold the secrets to many of the associated elements of our personality. Some people do not understand how we know which movements or strokes represent which corresponding characteristics of the persona. How did we put a man on the moon? Research and testing, research and testing.

Handwriting analysis dates back to the Roman Empire. However, the modern form of handwriting analysis dates back over 200 years. Researchers have tested each theory and deduced a specific scientific basis for interpreting personality from handwriting. Now it is so accurate, you can study just the basics and know a person better than if you had known him for years. I will explain the basic handwriting traits in a simple and visual format. I understand how boring some technical writing can be. This is why I don't write in a boring fashion. Instead, you will notice that my writing style is more enjoyable because I chose a loose but professional style packed with humor, sarcasm, and good juicy stories!

Psychological research has exhaustively categorized personality traits into easily identifiable strokes in the handwriting. I have presented these in a simple easy–to–learn format. All you have to do is enjoy the stories I tell and look for the corresponding specific strokes in the handwriting. But again, don't take my word for it. Prove it for yourself. Einstein said, "Ultimately, all development is self-development." Until you see it for yourself, you have a right to question it. So, pay attention and get ready to learn what may be one of the most valuable tools you will ever possess.

Human beings are much like the classic impressionistic paintings by Monet. From a distance, we see all the beauty of the subject captured so perfectly in brilliant color. We love the whole picture. As we walk closer, we realize that it is made of individual strokes of the brush. If you stand right next to the painting, all you can see is dots of color scattered in every direction. As we back away, the thousands of small dots blend to create a dynamic, clear portrait.

Analyzing personality through handwriting is much the same way as viewing a Monet painting. It is easy to look at just the individual strokes of the pen and get lost in the myriad of meaning. But as you complete the picture and put all the strokes in their proper place, the entire painting of the person comes out to look as interesting as piece of classic art.

Handwriting simplifies the personality into individual traits identifiable in specific handwriting strokes. The trait dictionary and the Grapho-Deck (see Appendix) give great examples of individual strokes in handwriting. People are obviously more complex than their individual traits. However, it is incredibly valuable to understand the *specific* traits. Afterwards, you will learn how they fit together to create a *complex personality*. When you look at someone's face, you can see the eyes, nose, and mouth. But, it is the way these are put together that makes each face unique. The same is true about a personality. Eventually, you will be able to paint a picture in your mind of a person's personality just by looking at his/her handwriting. All you have to do is ask yourself how each individual trait affects the other characteristics. It might be helpful to understand a little of the overall psychology behind each stroke's meaning. This is not difficult to learn and will aid in the accuracy of your analysis. This book will give you the necessary psychology.

Research indicates that as much as fifty–eight percent of all communication is non-verbal. This means you perceive reality through other means than the words someone chooses to speak. Such avenues of communication include body position, voice tonality, eye movement, breathing patterns, and even hand gestures. Your subconscious recognizes these signals whether you are consciously aware of them or not. Handwriting analysis takes body language many steps farther. Your handwriting reveals your exact state and mood at the moment it is written, much like your personality being frozen on the paper. Some say it is an advanced form of body language on a micro-scale. You will be surprised to find it is so accurate.

This book is not about handwriting. It's about people, human behavior, you and me, relationships, emotions, fears, defenses, motivations, and even sex. But the real topic of this book is choices.

That's right, *choices*. When you finish reading this book, you will realize that you have the choice of who to date, with whom you spend money, love, and time ... and who to marry. It is completely up to you. And the formula for picking that ideal mate is as clear as the writing on the wall. The tools you need are in this book. Once you have finished reading it, the fun part begins... doing it!

The Economics of Love

What creates value in our society? From an economic perspective, value is created by the law of supply and demand. When discussing the value of a person, does this hold true? What creates more value in your eyes for one person and less for another? The answer can be as complicated as the U.S. Treasury system or as simple as a penny. Different people value different things for different reasons. However, one of the most fundamental principles of value is the supply and demand of that commodity. And yes, this includes people.

You will find this obvious when you think about dating and seeking out new people to date. Have you ever noticed you tend to be attracted to those people who are already taken? Do you see yourself as a "geek magnet" while the guys you like don't give you the time of day? Have you ever been told that you try too hard? Are the good ones always taken? These examples illustrate the philosophy, "The more difficult to acquire, the more value is perceived."

It is in light of this principle that nice guys often get walked on. Many women perceive men who are too nice as being too easy. Therefore his value is diminished. Likewise, a woman who sleeps with a man on the first date is too easy and her value is decreased accordingly. (Of course, some men will sleep with her, they just won't call her the next day. Those kind of guys usually have a certain value predetermined for this type of woman anyway.)

How does this principle affect you when you are trying to find a new relationship? It took me many years to understand what my friends were trying to tell me when they exclaimed, "Bart, you can't go looking for a girlfriend. You're trying too hard." Being a self-starter, I assumed girlfriends were like commodities, if you want it, go out and get it. But I learned this is not the case. When you put a "FOR SALE" sign on a car, people immediately know that you don't want the car anymore. If you put an "available" sign on your forehead by aggressively seeking out a boyfriend or girlfriend, people often assume someone doesn't want you, therefore something must be wrong with you. (Is this convoluted logic? Maybe, but people think this way.) For this reason, when I used to chase girls, they always ran away.

One day I realized that the women I actually dated were women that I met without the pretense of getting romantic. In other words, I wasn't terribly interested in dating them when I met them. In fact, my attitude was, "I could take it or leave it. If she calls, great. If not, so what?" This may sound aloof, but it conveys a meaning of "I'm not easy. I have value. If you want my attention you must demonstrate your worth to me." By the way, I am not suggesting you take this literally and actually verbalize these words to a potential lover. It is enough just to possess the attitude. Most people see being cocky as a negative personality trait. Modest confidence is the best attitude to display.

When one person throws himself at another, without a just invitation, the balance of control is lopsided. Once one partner gains more control in the relationship, it is downhill from there. Sadly enough, the one that desires it more holds the weaker position. Sometimes, the level of interest reveals the amount of control, or lack thereof. Have you ever heard the wisdom of a poker player: you must know when to fold? Being too anxious gives the other person leverage. You have to be able to walk away from the table, or you are sunk! The same holds true with dating.

> *"You've got to know when to hold' em,*
> *know when to fold' em, know*
> *when to walk away, know when to run!"*
> *— Kenny Rogers, The Gambler*

I have heard people say women are only attracted to jerks and men only like beautiful women. Fortunately this is not always true, but it does apply in many cases. Again, the explanation involves the economics of love. Because there are fewer beautiful women in the world and beauty is a valued commodity, beautiful women are in higher demand. Face the facts. Men often say many pretty women are bitches. These women give off that attitude because most men look only at their beauty and are too forward—these men act like losers. Men become easy when struck by beauty. Therefore, the beautiful woman has more choices with regard to men. She is choosy. What does she choose? Based on supply and demand, she wants a man who is a challenge. She can get attention all the time from men who throw themselves at her. What she wants is a man who has enough value in himself so he doesn't throw himself at her. Being selective is often interpreted as a sign of self-worth and confidence. These are very attractive qualities. Unfortunately, this formula sometimes represents a jerk. Not only is the guy she ends up with a challenge, but he really doesn't care about her. Ideally, she wants a sweet, generous, sensitive man who doesn't drool over her. But realistically, she wants a man whom she perceives as valuable. Back to the theory of supply and demand, the harder he is to get, the more she values him.

I believe men have it easier than women. A man doesn't have to be overly attractive to attract beautiful women. In general, women aren't as obsessed about good looks as men tend to be. Perhaps you could call men more superficial. However, it goes deeper than this (I hope). Men, in general, have a tendency to be more visual than women. For men seeing is believing. For women seeing is important, but feeling is often just as significant in creating the emotions we call love or infatuation. (These are often confused, but never interchangeable.)

These are generalities, but they are useful. Studies show men rank visual stimuli, such as beauty, as a higher priority in a partner than females rank it. (This may relate back to the fact that, on average, young boys have better spatial/visual perception than young girls.) Women, on the other hand, tend to rate attractiveness behind other personality characteristics such as confidence, honesty, or classiness. (It should be noted women are swayed by good looks. Anyone who has ever observed the way women behave at a male strip review understand women can be very attracted to men based on looks. The gyrating hips don't hurt.) Both sexes are attracted to a combination of looks and personality. However, it is useful to understand these tendencies.

> *"Women become more attracted to the one they love. Men become more loving to the one they are attracted to."*
> — *Stacy Hamaker, M.A., C.N.L.P*

Therefore, if you are a man, know your appearance is <u>not</u> the most important factor in your persona. If you are a woman, or are dating someone who needs to *see* things to appreciate them, you may have to work to provide visual verification that you are special. By visual, I mean creating visual impressions like wearing make-up, giving Hallmark cards, and taking him to visually stunning places.

If you feel your physical beauty is less than average, you must create value in other ways: humor, intelligence, talent, etc. Then, market these talents so *people of value* take notice. In either case, the person you want most will be in less supply.

It amazes me how many phone numbers bartenders get. My bartender friends get more offers than any other profession I know.   Why?   Most bars are scenes for people to meet new prospects. The only person in the bar who is obviously *not* looking for a new lover is the bartender.   He or she is just working. However, after an entire night of sleazoid scumbag men hitting on them, the average woman looks at the nice bartender and thinks, "There is a nice guy, wouldn't it be nice if he asked me out instead of all these meat market jerkos?" Why does she think this? The bartender isn't necessarily better looking, wealthier, or even wittier than the others. But he didn't make an offer, therefore his value is perceived as higher. Think about this the next time you are in a bar.

I was on a T.V. talk show with a very attractive female bartender from New York City. She said she got hit on at least fifty times a day while at work. In fact, she had started laying the change on the counter because each time she handed the change to the guys, they would actually grab her! I asked her if she had a boyfriend and she said, "Yes." I said, "He is another bartender, isn't he?" She said, "Yes." I knew of all the guys in the bar, the other bartenders were the only ones not hitting on her. Men need to learn to look past the physical appearances to see what most women want in a relationship: friendship, love, affection, trust. You must establish value in yourself up front in order to gain access to a person's more intimate values. Most successful couples say their spouse is their best friend. Therefore, begin with a solid foundation of friendship and you can't lose.

The principle is very simple: "Create value in yourself by not being too easy!" A woman who says, "I am kind of seeing someone," seems more attractive than a woman who says, "I don't have a boyfriend, but I'm looking!" The best attitude to display is, "I'm not here looking for someone, I'm here enjoying my fabulous life. If you're not what I like, I have no problem walking away because I have plenty of choices." This may sound haughty, but it will display an attitude of your intrinsic self value. You don't have to feel superior to others, just don't ever subordinate yourself. By being friendly, but not anxiously aggressive, you balance the level of control between the sexes. It is on this level playing field a successful relationship can be initiated.

Curiosity and Mystery

One of the essences of romance is the concept of mystery. Do you think the great Italian lovers ever charted out the evening of lovemaking? One of the greatest thrills of a person's life is not knowing whether the person he is attracted to likes him or not. The anticipation of what might be makes the heart palpitate. It is the predictable men in this world who make good accountants but not great romantics. Also, women tend to be drawn to the untamable male. Often, the more a man tends to be spontaneous, uncontrollable, and strong, the more the woman yearns for his attention. Also, a man who has a sense of mystery about him is very sexy -- much like the modern day movie heroes Maverick (Tom Cruise) in *Top Gun* and Riggs (Mel Gibson) in *Lethal Weapon*. They were unpredictable, courageous, and mysterious. Most women would love to be swept off their feet by a charming confident James Bond-agent 007. It is from the spirit of these great lovers and heroes that we derive a conceptual formula for what makes a man romantic. These rules apply to both men and women. If you are not perceived as a romantic, ask yourself if you fit any or none of the following characteristics of a romantic:

Spontaneous	Unpredictable	Sexy
Courageous	Strong	Passionate
In Demand	Independent	Untameable
Confident	Mysterious	Has a Purpose

One more trait which could be on the list is a "Sense of urgency" or "Last chance." A man or woman is more likely to feel romantic and give in to passion if he/she believes it may be the last opportunity to do so. This is why vacations are notoriously filled with flings and short romances. The lovers know if they procrastinate, their desires will go unfulfilled. Imagine telling a prospective lover, "You don't have to sleep with me tonight. I'll be here tomorrow, the next day, and next month waiting for you. There's no hurry." On the same token, can you imagine a car salesman saying to you, "This is the lowest price I can go. It is a great bargain! But, if you don't want to buy right now, I will hold it for you indefinitely at this low price!" It won't happen. Romance, like sales, takes advantage of the urgency of the moment and the state of passion. *Logic is not a part of romance.* This is why someone with a high degree of logic, predictability, and self-centeredness is not very romantic. The spontaneity of eloping in Las Vegas is romantic; a logical pre-nuptial agreement is not.

Relationships & Compatibility

Relationships are one of the most popularly discussed and written about topics. Look at the covers of magazines and tabloids, especially women's magazines. When they put the word "sex" on the cover, sales increase. I'm not sure who is worse, women or men. Women have sex and then want to read more about it. Men have sex and want to look at pictures when they're not having it! I suppose some people out there don't have any sex at all and that must be the worst.

Psychology offers a rich source of information on relationships. Research areas include mate selection, marital success, and dysfunctional relationships. I will be brief in relating the appropriate results of psychological research to your life. Two helpful approaches regarding relationships are: 1) similarity and 2) complementary.

The theory of **similarity** states that *The more like a person you are, the more likely you are to like each other.* In other words, the more similar another person is to you, the more likely you are to choose him or her and to enjoy success in a relationship. Think about the question, "What do we have in common?" Similarity includes such factors as attractiveness, values, wealth, culture, religion, education, and even geography. An example of such a couple would be my friends Edward and Lori. They both are conservative, religious, quiet, reserved, and kind. An analysis of their handwriting reveals that they are both at the middle of the road emotionally, each exhibits a good self-image, and both are stubborn. Both of them have very similar basic dispositions. Based on the similarity theory, their relationship has a higher probability of long-term success.

Using neuro-analysis, you can identify individual personality traits between two people and then predict their compatibility from their writing. The most common example of incompatibility is an extreme extrovert trying to date and relate to an introvert. The extrovert openly expresses her feelings and requests that her partner be emotionally expressive as well. The introvert, a person who rarely expresses feelings, could go weeks without ever saying, "I love you." Since the extrovert needs to give and receive emotional expression more often than the introvert, conflict arises. Thus, it becomes a case of different emotional outlays giving rise to relationship problems. Once identified and understood, the conflict can be resolved using various techniques. Compatibility profiles become much more complicated when all the traits are added together.

The second theory is **complementary**. One trait of one person complements a strength or weakness of the other one. An example of compatible personality traits are a very sensitive insecure woman that dates a very expressive, talkative, generous man. He constantly reassures her and tells her how much he approves of her. Because she is happy receiving this kind of attention, she works very hard to please him in return. Their two personalities complement each other.

Here is another example that is quite common. A man with a highly sarcastic tendency (sharp pointed t-bar), impulsiveness (hard right hand slant) and a temper (t-bar on the right side of stem) would hurt a woman with a high degree of sensitivity to criticism (large looped d stem) and a low self-image (low t-bar) because she is overly sensitive and he is overly caustic. Although he may feel that he loves her, she will be walking around with her ego bruised most of the time because his expressions of frustration are often mean and caustic. If he would choose a girlfriend with a good self-image, sarcasm, and a lack of sensitivity, she could fight back and not be hurt as easily.

The problem with using these traditional psychological theories is that it is difficult for you to pinpoint which personality traits a prospective lover possesses. You could ask your next date to take a 600 question written personality test, but that method has its drawbacks. Traditional personality tests are impractical for you and me to use. Some are accurate, but they are time consuming, costly, and confusing. What you need is a fast, accurate, simple, and covert method of analyzing each other's personalities. As you now know, neuro–analysis is that method. Simply look at the handwriting, ask a few questions, and observe. You will get the answers you need.

Although it may seem complicated, it is actually quite simple once you practice. You don't have to know about all the traits in someone's personality. You don't need to be an expert on all types of people. All you need to know is how to recognize the personality traits that you want in a mate. Every time you meet a potential mate, you look at his/her personality traits and compare them to yours. If the next prospect you meet has two personalities, lies pathologically, and is paranoid, you simply ask yourself if those qualities will be compatible with your qualities. In this case, I hope you say no. But, if you have two people living inside of you, believe that the whole world is against you, and enjoy making up lies for the fun of it.... you two probably have a lot in common. I wish you the best of luck and the four of you should be very happy together.

Therefore, just look at the individual traits of someone you are interested in and ask yourself how similar or complementary they are to your own. Yes, it's that simple. When you doubt how the traits will reveal themselves in the context of your life, analyze your past relationships. Did any of your ex's have certain traits that drove you nuts? I know I've developed a list of specific traits in other people I call "Hell Traits!" I'll share them with you later in the book. Your list may be completely different. So get out those old love letters and analyze those past mistakes for a roadway to a better tomorrow!

Know Thyself

The first step to using neuro-analysis effectively in relationships is to take an objective look at yourself. Are you insecure, oversensitive, or afraid of being rejected? You need to know these things about yourself. If you are oversensitive and introverted, you do not want to get involved with an extroverted, sarcastic, hate-filled person. Your ego would be crushed.

The easiest way to take inventory of your true personality is to analyze your own handwriting. Simply look at your own handwriting and compare it with the traits found in this book. You can also use the information found in the trait dictionary or a Grapho-Deck, if you have one. Discover those traits about yourself that a partner would find attractive or repulsive. Check out the trait dictionary and compare the results for a reality check. Before looking at your own writing, how would you describe yourself? You will take an inventory of your own perceptions in a moment.

Be honest. Are you stubborn or domineering? Do you have to have it your way? Are you a loner? Do you prefer to sit in your room and read than be around people? Are you emotionally withdrawn, sarcastic, vindictive, or mean? Are you generous, good at keeping secrets, friendly, enjoy people, or optimistic? Are you ambitious or confident?

Most people's perceptions of themselves vary slightly with reality. Handwriting has always been a good reality check for me. I can't tell you how many times I have looked down at my own handwriting only to cover it up and hope no one was watching!

To make your personality list easy and painless, I have designed a Personality Inventory in which you can just fill in the blanks. This checklist is designed to outline what you think your personality is like and what you want in a relationship. The instructions are very simple. Check any box you feel applies to you or your ideal mate. Check both boxes if it seems right to you. Be sure to include both positive and negative traits. This will give you an inventory of where your strengths and weaknesses lie. After you have completed the Personality Inventory, make a written list of your most prevalent traits and the traits you want in a mate, as you chose in the inventory. Keep this list handy so you will know what to look for when you start looking at handwriting samples of prospective lovers.

When developing a profile of your ideal mate, attempt to structure the list in individual traits, opposed to generalities of behavior. Some men would like to say, "Uh, subservient, good cook, keeps her mouth shut, good in bed, and serves me and the boys beer during the football game!" (No, we won't have any of those vast chauvinistic generalizations!) Instead, break those desires into traits. It is perfectly okay to want a mate that can keep a house organized and clean. In that case look for *organizational ability* and *perfectionism*. Be aware that you may be giving up the ability to throw your jeans across the chair when you get home!

No matter what you want in an ideal mate, you are the real issue in this game. The person you attract will only be a reflection of who you are. If you are a loser, you will attract losers. If you are an interesting, sincere, and neat person, once you begin to use neuro-analysis effectively, you will attract more good people like yourself.

Take a look at your own personality and decide what type of person best suits your needs. Be objective. You also may *need* something completely different than you think you want. If you are a weak, domineering, manipulative, violent scumbag that hits women... you need a woman with a low self-image (low t-bar) and a desire to be punished (pointed backward t-bar). That way, your psychotic criminal behavior complements her insecure self-castigating weaknesses. (Sick, but true.)

Hopefully, that example doesn't apply to you. Take a good look at yourself before you start looking at others. You might want a strong person because you are passive. You might want someone equally as strong as you. Make this distinction when filling out the Personality Inventory. You may not know what you want. Understanding what you need is a process. It takes practice, learning, and fine-tuning. Use your imagination and best judgement. Remember, you can always change your mind.

Much of this book is dedicated to understanding people so you can avoid bad apples and recognize diamonds. However, I strongly believe that you will (and always have) attract to you those people that match your needs on some level or another. Therefore, if you are not completely satisfied at the moment, you need to evaluate carefully all your needs. So, get a writing utensil. Find a place with few distractions. Complete the Personality Inventory on the following pages. The box marked " Me" is your own traits, "Mate" is for what you want in a mate.

> *"The person you attract*
> *will be a reflection of who you are."*
> *— Bart A. Baggett*

Personality Inventory

Me Mate

<u>Emotional Outlay</u>
☐ ☐ Keeps feelings inside
☐ ☐ Expresses emotions impulsively
☐ ☐ Internalizes some feelings, expresses others
Middle-of-the-road expressiveness

<u>Emotional Intensity</u>
☐ ☐ Passionate. Intense: remembers emotional experiences
for a long time
☐ ☐ Lets emotions go easily, forgives and forgets quickly

<u>Thinking Patterns</u>
☐ ☐ Procedural, slow, cumulative
☐ ☐ Sharp, quick, impatient, takes in everything at once

☐ ☐ Digs deeply and thoroughly for all facts
☐ ☐ Makes quick surface decisions, based on others
investigations

☐ ☐ Intense ability to concentrate and focus on one thing
☐ ☐ Can do many things at once, easily distracted

☐ ☐ Intuitive
☐ ☐ Just the facts, logical

<u>Goals</u>
☐ ☐ Ambitious
☐ ☐ Practical
☐ ☐ Afraid of change

☐ ☐ Persistent– works hard until a goal is achieved
☐ ☐ Sets own goals, determined to achieve them
☐ ☐ Gives up easily, lazy

☐ ☐ Fears success
☐ ☐ Fears failure

☐ ☐ Prefers to follow
☐ ☐ Prefers to lead
☐ ☐ Takes the initiative

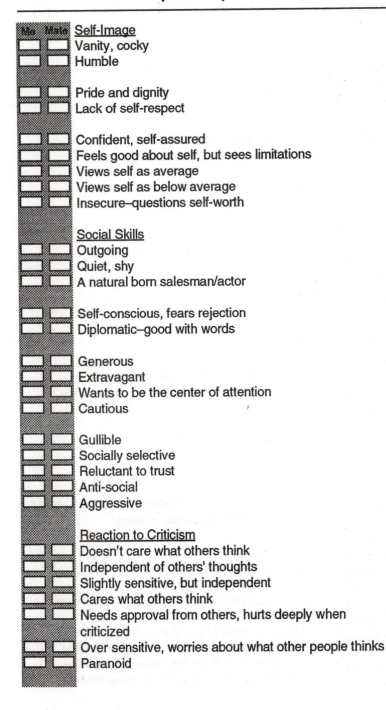

Me   Mate

Self-Image
- Vanity, cocky
- Humble

- Pride and dignity
- Lack of self-respect

- Confident, self-assured
- Feels good about self, but sees limitations
- Views self as average
- Views self as below average
- Insecure–questions self-worth

Social Skills
- Outgoing
- Quiet, shy
- A natural born salesman/actor

- Self-conscious, fears rejection
- Diplomatic–good with words

- Generous
- Extravagant
- Wants to be the center of attention
- Cautious

- Gullible
- Socially selective
- Reluctant to trust
- Anti-social
- Aggressive

Reaction to Criticism
- Doesn't care what others think
- Independent of others' thoughts
- Slightly sensitive, but independent
- Cares what others think
- Needs approval from others, hurts deeply when criticized
- Over sensitive, worries about what other people thinks
- Paranoid

No	Mate	
☐	☐	**Attitude**
☐	☐	Optimistic
☐	☐	Pessimistic
☐	☐	Open-minded
☐	☐	Close-minded
☐	☐	Open mind to philosophies
☐	☐	Locked down code of ethics and philosophies
☐	☐	Critical of others
☐	☐	Understanding/supportive of others
☐	☐	Enthusiastic
☐	☐	Short-lived excitement/lack of follow-through
☐	☐	Perfectionist
☐	☐	Loose and versatile
☐	☐	Needs stability
☐	☐	Likes change
☐	☐	Attentive to detail, structure, procedure
☐	☐	Loose, unstructured, detail secondary importance
☐	☐	Desire to be different
☐	☐	Conventional
☐	☐	Direct - gets to the point
☐	☐	Lives in the moment, enjoys today, doesn't plan ahead
☐	☐	Plans for future, philosophically probing
☐	☐	**Physical/ Sex Drives**
☐	☐	Not important
☐	☐	Low need for activity
☐	☐	Average sex/ physical drives –needs physical exercise/ sex occasionally.
☐	☐	Strong drives–needs physical exercise/ sex often
☐	☐	Insatiable physical drives–needs constant activity
☐	☐	Gets too many irons in the fire (activities, people)
☐	☐	Huge imagination regarding sex, average drives

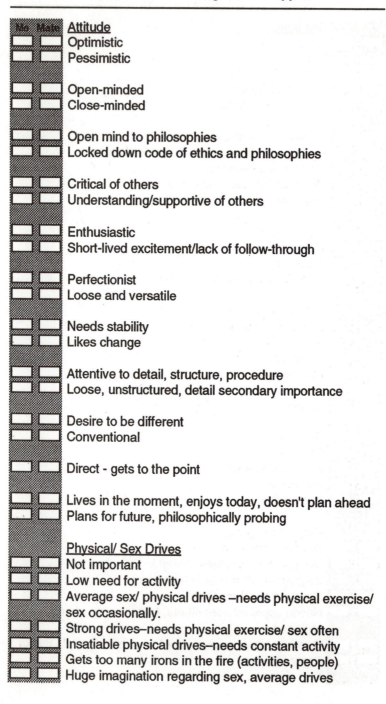

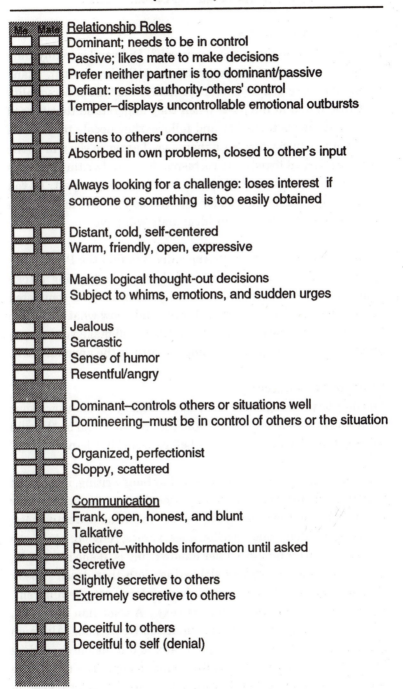

Relationship Roles

- ☐ ☐ Dominant; needs to be in control
- ☐ ☐ Passive; likes mate to make decisions
- ☐ ☐ Prefer neither partner is too dominant/passive
- ☐ ☐ Defiant: resists authority-others' control
- ☐ ☐ Temper–displays uncontrollable emotional outbursts

- ☐ ☐ Listens to others' concerns
- ☐ ☐ Absorbed in own problems, closed to other's input

- ☐ ☐ Always looking for a challenge: loses interest if someone or something is too easily obtained

- ☐ ☐ Distant, cold, self-centered
- ☐ ☐ Warm, friendly, open, expressive

- ☐ ☐ Makes logical thought-out decisions
- ☐ ☐ Subject to whims, emotions, and sudden urges

- ☐ ☐ Jealous
- ☐ ☐ Sarcastic
- ☐ ☐ Sense of humor
- ☐ ☐ Resentful/angry

- ☐ ☐ Dominant–controls others or situations well
- ☐ ☐ Domineering–must be in control of others or the situation

- ☐ ☐ Organized, perfectionist
- ☐ ☐ Sloppy, scattered

Communication

- ☐ ☐ Frank, open, honest, and blunt
- ☐ ☐ Talkative
- ☐ ☐ Reticent–withholds information until asked
- ☐ ☐ Secretive
- ☐ ☐ Slightly secretive to others
- ☐ ☐ Extremely secretive to others

- ☐ ☐ Deceitful to others
- ☐ ☐ Deceitful to self (denial)

Analyzing the Results

Did you learn anything about yourself? Did you learn anything about the type of person you want to settle down with? Many people who take this Inventory see clearly the type of personality that they dated in the past. When they understand that type of personality leads to misery and failure, they decide to choose a personality which works with their own. I am sure you will do the same. Each trait listed has a corresponding handwriting stroke to assist you in recognizing it in your next romantic prospect. As you read through this book, look for the strokes you have in your own writing as well as those your ideal mate will have.

To make this easier, turn to Appendix B to find the Personality Inventory Chart expanded to include the handwriting stroke which identifies each trait. Therefore, you can use your completed chart to create a list of your ideal traits and know what strokes to look for in someone else's handwriting. It will make your search for the perfect mate perfectly simple. Turn to the appendix now.

Choosing Intelligently

You may be thinking to yourself, "Bart, would you really pick your girlfriend by her handwriting?" And the answer would be, "I would *never* get involved with someone before seeing her handwriting!"

Although the personality, as revealed by handwriting, is the most important factor, there are many other factors in picking your mate. You can't overlook such factors in life as attractiveness, finances, location, education, heritage, values, religion, etc. Let's face it, no matter how great her handwriting is, if she is a 600 lb, grotesque, mustache-toting slobbering sloth that doesn't speak English... I'm not dating her! Your standards may be different. Everyone has a profile of what is sexy. A comedian once said, "There are no impotent men, only unattractive women." Although his analogy is chauvinistic, inaccurate, and a bit harsh, it does illustrates one aspect of a healthy relationship. You must have some physical attraction toward your mate. Therefore, keep in mind all the factors that create a compatible mate for yourself, including personality and physical attractiveness.

Values

When picking a new relationship, I want to make sure that her basic core values and beliefs are similar to mine. For example, you don't want to get involved with a Jehovah's Witness if you are equally dedicated to Catholicism. These core values and beliefs might be too different to blend together. It would be difficult for me as an American to fall in love with a die-hard Communist. It wouldn't be impossible, but it would take tremendous effort on both our parts to live together with such fundamental differences in politics and life goals. But as I think about it, if she looked anything like the Russian spies in the James Bond movies, I'd become a Communist for the evening in a New York minute. Individuals can adapt to most cultural differences over time. You can get used to someone eating matzo ball soup relatively simply. However, the individual personality idiosyncrasies are not as easily adapted to in an intimate relationship. In other words, a stubborn Russian or a stubborn American is still stubborn.

The reason for looking for similarity is simple: **rapport**. The more similarities that two people have, the more they will like each other. As humans, we tend to find familiar territory more comfortable. We may venture out for excitement, but we are always more comfortable at home. Would you have tea with the Queen of England dressed in your underwear, without combing your hair or taking a shower? I hope not. The point is *the more similar we are to each other, the more we feel we understand one another.*

Three simple questions to establish values

Although our personality traits may be similar, our dispositions and/or our belief structures may be entirely different, causing problems. Handwriting is the key to revealing the most relevant elements of compatibility with the least investment of time and effort. However, don't overlook the most obvious method for eliciting someone's values: <u>ask.</u> In a short conversation you can ask questions to discover if someone's highest values are in line with your own. One simple question to discover someone's values and criteria is "What's important to you about _____." Fill in the blank with whatever topic you are talking about. My most common word used here is "a relationship." They might answer with "TRUST." Then I ask, "How do you know when you have <u>TRUST</u>?" The answer to this question reveals what it takes for that person to know TRUST is their (criteria.) If you asked these questions *three times*, you can then rank them to get that person's highest values in order of priority

For example, if someone says career and love are important in life, ask, "If you had to choose just one right now, which would you choose, career or love?" The answer, "I love my career," isn't exactly what you're looking for. Ask which one is absolutely necessary. Below is a list of values that you need to rank the in order of importance. Make sure your highest value isn't ranked as the lowest on your partner's list. You should also realize that simply mentioning your partner's values will increase rapport dramatically. Keep your highest values in mind when searching for your ideal mate. Feel free to add to this list if your values aren't listed.

Value List

Achieving	Honesty
Adventure	Intimacy
Career	Investment
Comfort	Knowledge
Contribution	Learning/Growing
Creativity	Love
Family	Loyalty
Freedom	Making a Difference
Friendship	Passion
Fun/Happiness	Power
God	Security
Health	Spirituality
Strength/Vitality	Success
Helping Others	Trust

Look Before You Leap

Have you ever been on a blind date? Imagine the insight you would have had if you looked at her handwriting before you met her. Imagine the embarrassment if you told her everything you know from her writing before seeing her face–to–face, "I see here that you are overly sensitive to criticism, you lie a lot, and you are obviously sexually frustrated!" Actually, I've been that blunt before and it's quite a coup. I don't recommend it. This approach doesn't have a positive, rapport-building effect. If the blind date was the one above, I would just keep those things to myself, compliment her, not believe a word she said, and attempt to solve her sexual frustration problem without calling attention to the fact it is a problem. You can do the same.

I've had many past relationships in various forms. Some were good, some were not so good. I've also interviewed many others and documented their experiences. I've included many of these experiences as prime examples of the principles I am teaching. Hopefully, you will learn from others' past mistakes.

> **"Experience is not the best teacher,**
> **Someone else's experience is the best teacher!"**
> **— *Curtis Baggett***

One experience I had was with a lively, vivacious, bouncy, and happy, redhead named Marsha. She talked very fast and used her hands to express herself. I talk fast and laugh a lot, therefore rapport was developed through our similar communication style. It wasn't until after our first date that I got the chance to see her handwriting. Uh oh! She had insatiable sex drives (huge y's), low self esteem (low t-bar), hidden anger for men (hook in a d), and a dual personality (variable slant). I would normally have ended it right away, but I had already allowed the physical attraction to affect my emotions. My logic was not in control. That was my first mistake. Don't let your sex drive do your decision–making for you!

I thought it would be wise for me to investigate this girl further. As I listened to the grapevine, her past was just as tumultuous as her handwriting. It turned out that she had already slept with many of my friends and did not have the greatest reputation for stability or self-respect. In this case, the stories I heard about her verified what I saw in her handwriting. In most cases, you won't have access to his or her case history because they may not tell you the truth. Good news: the handwriting will tell you the truth every time.

Now that you know who you are and what kind of personality you want in your next mate, it is time to prepare yourself to be successful in your next love affair. The next chapter prepares you for that wonderful experience called romance.

Chapter II

Preparing Yourself For a New Romance

Do You Really Want To Be In Love?

Before you decide you want to find your perfect lover, ask yourself what love is. There are probably a thousand different definitions for the concept of love. It is important to know what you are looking for so you will know when you've found it. Webster defines love as a deep and tender feeling of affection for or attachment or devotion to a person or persons. I define love in a slightly different way:

Love is an electromagnetic bio-chemical bond.

As you can see from my definition, love is more than just a mental bond between two individuals. Love is physical. Anyone who has ever had a loved one leave or break up knows what I mean. Have you ever had a wrenching pain in your gut caused from the emotional pain of loss? That is the result of a very real chemical reaction called emotion. It is the development of these strong emotions that connect two people in the state of euphoria called love.

We know a connection exists between people on a much more physical level than just thought. The human body is much more than flesh and bone. We are completely electrical in nature. I once saw my doctor make a tiny light bulb work with just the electricity from his fingers. If you aren't familiar with amazing electrical aspects of our body, check out the Chinese art of Chi. It is the foundation of acupuncture. Not only is the body electrical, it is chemical. It contains thousand of different chemicals that, among other things, create thoughts and emotions.

An experiment done on rabbits illustrates the powerful electro-chemical bond two animals have with each other. A mother rabbit and two of her baby rabbits were used in the experiment to discover what kind of bond existed between the family members. The three animals were separated for about a week. The mother rabbit was connected to heart monitors and blood pressure gauges. Then, in front of the mother, one baby was killed. In obvious distress the mother's body reacted with increased heart rates and blood pressure. You can imagine how any animal, including humans, would react to their baby being killed in their presence. About a week later, the other baby was taken about a mile offshore in a ship. The mother was again connected to the monitors. At a specified time, the second baby rabbit was killed by the researchers. At the same time, the mother rabbit's heart and blood pressure went crazy. She had the same reaction as she did the week before. Her body, emotions, and electric systems reacted as if she knew her baby was in trouble. Obviously, she did.

Have you ever had similar blood pressure and heart increases when you were either falling in love or losing a love? Falling in love is a state we all yearn for while losing love is a state we dread. Yes, there are risks involved in being in love. If love is some kind of physical bond, it might be painful if the bond is broken. I have had a few heartbreaks in my time. But now, as I look back, I usually got over the pain in a short time. I remember a particularly painful breakup after a nine month romance. I spent about a month in the dumps. However, I realize now I had nine months of pleasure that definitely outweighed the one month of pain. Some of you have had a nine year, nine month, or nine minute romance that you still

haven't gotten over. It is time to let it go.   My friend Blanco
Navarro once told me "I'd rather have my heart broken than to
never have known true love at all." Below is my visual illustration
of the risk and rewards of love.

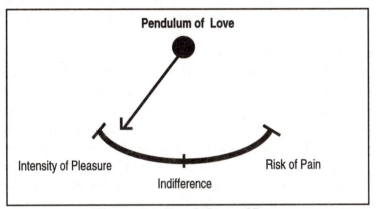

Figure 2.1: Pendulum of Love

Before you read this book any further you have to ask yourself the
following question. Is the pleasure of being in love worth the
possible pain of losing that love? If you say yes, congratulations.
You are in for a wonderfully fulfilling life. Read on.

If you say no, you need to evaluate how much pain **not** having love
brings you. If you are content being alone now, what about the
future? How much pain will being alone bring you in the next year,
five years, ten years? Visualize yourself on your death bed alone.
Realize how much pleasure you have missed because you weren't
willing to take the risk of being in love.

As you see that image, realize it is only one possible timeline of
your life. You can choose now to open up your heart and be willing
to love. When you choose love, the future becomes much different.
After making the decision, you see yourself one year, five years, ten
years down the road, in your happy home surrounded by the
person or people who love you. What color is this scene? That is
your color of love. Loving and being loved will make you happy the

rest of your life. As you now look back on your life, you realize the decision to accept the risk of being in love brought you so much more pleasure than it did pain, you would make the same choice again. As you can see clearly from looking through the eyes of your future self, <u>deciding now </u>to open your heart is the decision which will bring you love and happiness the rest of your life.

Finding Your Next Lover
One of the most common complaints I hear is, "I can't find anyone I like." Have your ever said that? Out of 4 billion people on this planet, can you honestly say there isn't anyone you like? If you say yes, you have one of two problems: 1) You have your eyes closed. In other words, you aren't *noticing the prospects* you meet on a daily basis. 2) You are not letting the other 3.99999999 billion people know you are available. In other words, you need to *market yourself* better.

How to Open Your Eyes
Somewhere in your subconscious mind, you have decided not to give anyone else a chance. *You may have hope, but not trust.* I say trust because it takes trust to open up enough even to begin a relationship. In handwriting analysis, trust and relationships are revealed in the letter's lower zone loops. The smaller the loop, the less the person trusts other people. If you are one that has trouble attracting new people into your intimate life, you may have the anti-social loop. That is, the lower case loop that is very small and practically retraced. Since there is no loop, it signifies very little trust. Therefore, you are closed off to new relationships. Usually, I will find a small loop on some letters and completely

> *"You may have hope, but not trust.*
> *It takes trust to find love."*
> *— Bart A. Baggett*

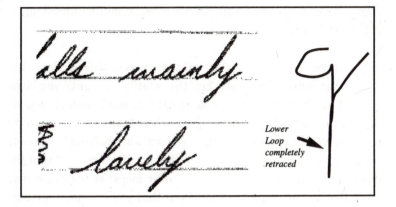

Figure 2.2: Lack of trust

Figure 2.3.a   **Figure 2.3.b**   **Figure 2.3.c**

**Figure 2.3: Lack of trust and imagination reveals itself
in narrow lower loops of the lower zone letters
such as y's,g's, and j's.**

retraced on others. This variation tells me there is hope. The writer probably trusts one or two people, but intimacy is still an issue. This person probably has been emotionally burned and is reluctant to open up again.

If you have this trait, pay special attention to this section. You cannot get involved in a new healthy relationship until you begin to trust and have the courage to take the intimacy risk. If you are saying to yourself, "I'll trust again when someone proves to me they are worthy of my trust," then you will keep talking to yourself, because you may never have a companion. The mere fact that you don't trust people (have retraced lower loops) sends out a non-verbal signal to all those around you that you are not approach-able. Believe me, those who might be interested will detect this signal and avoid a relationship with you. Or haven't you noticed? What you must do is change your way of thinking so you begin to send out signals that you *are approachable*. It is even possible your next relationship will be with someone you already know, but you never before noticed the possibility of a romance. Check to see if your "y's" are closed. You don't want to overlook the obvious.

> **"Trust, but verify"**
> — *Ronald Reagan*

Sometimes I refer to a stroke in handwriting as being synonymous with a personality trait or behavior. The handwriting is not the cause of the personality trait. Rather, the handwriting is merely a symbol directed by your specific brain waves which is translated into more specific neuro-muscular patterns revealing themselves in handwriting. One way to consciously interrupt this communi-cation pattern is to change your handwriting. By changing the form of your lower case y's and g's, you are interrupting that old pattern of *not* trusting on a neurological level. Then, each time you

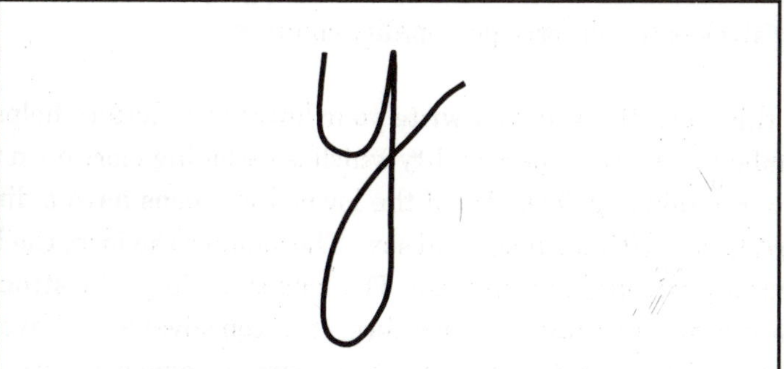

Figure 2.4: A Healthy, Average "y" loop.

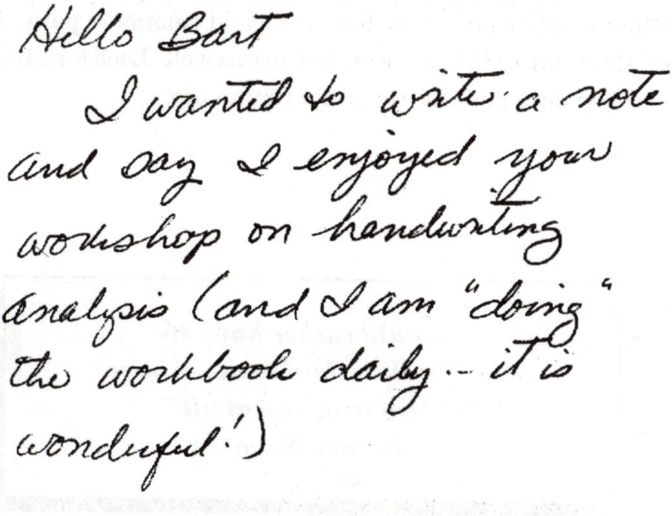

Hello Bart
I wanted to write a note
and say I enjoyed your
workshop on handwriting
analysis (and I am "doing"
the workbook daily -- it is
wonderful!)

Figure 2.5: Healthy Physical Drives

Figure 2.5: Sample of handwriting of someone whom trust, lack of imagination, and anti-social behavior is *not* an issue. Notice the full loops in the g's and y's.

notice yourself writing a lower case y or g loop, you can change the way you and your body react to the issue of trust. By removing that symbol of not trusting (retraced lower loops) you reinforce all of your conscious efforts to open up your subconscious mind to be prepared for a relationship. This is actually a very effective behavioral modification technique — changing specific handwriting strokes to reinforce personality changes.

In this case, the way you write your lower zone letters helps to symbolize your new personality which is becoming more open to a new relationship. The size of the lower zone loops have a direct correlation with intimacy and sex. The smaller the loop, the less intimacy is being experienced. The longer the loop, the stronger the sex drive or libido. Therefore, it is conceivable to have an antisocial, aggressive, or loner-type person engage in sex, but never allow intimacy to happen (a very long y without a normal loop.) This is very sad because a healthy sex life includes a deep level of intimacy with one's partner. Many men and women turn off their emotions in the bedroom to avoid emotional pain. However, this reduces the physical pleasure as well. Look for a healthy lower loop for a healthy sex and intimate life.

> *"I would rather have my heart broken than to never have known true love at all."*
> *— Blanca Navarro*

Marketing Yourself

The previous section about lack of trust might not have applied to you at all, yet you are still alone. Why? You may fall into the second category of unsatisfied people. You are simply *not marketing yourself.* You may be the type of person that isn't choosing the wrong mates, but you are not doing any choosing at all. It may seem that if you go out with anyone, it is because they chose you. This limits your choices considerably. The quality of your love life is at the mercy of whomever asks you out.

What if you shopped for food only by waiting for the delivery boy to come by your house once a week? You asked what he had in his bag this week. He tells you he has some prunes, lemons, garlic, canned spinach, bacon, and a can of beans that Mrs. Smith upstairs didn't want. What about the apples, the sliced turkey, the custard pie you ordered? He says, "Sorry, it was bought by someone else before I got to your door. If you want the pick of the market, get up early and go down yourself. First come, first served." You decline and decide to wait until he comes by next week in hopes he will bring something you like. After all, you couldn't actually *get out of the house and go after what you want!* Or could you?

This is essentially the way many people approach new relationships. They simply hope the perfect one will fall into their lap. Ha! I have news for you. Even when you do get up early and go to the market, you must squeeze four or five tomatoes before you find the ripe one!

If you are suffering from a lack of people to choose from in your life then you probably have one of the following three personality traits. By recognizing these in yourself, you can take steps toward overcoming your self-imposed limitations.

1. Self-Consciousness

This is a fear of dissapproval from strangers / acquaintances. It is a fear of being ridiculed or looking bad. This fear causes the person to compare herself and fears not being good enough. She always feels people are looking at her. Self-consciousness stops the initiative to approach unknown people, leaving you lonely in the corner wishing you had approached someone new. This is the fear which motivates some people to say "I can only have fun when I am drunk." (See Trait Dictionary in Appendix A.)

2. Low Self-Esteem

Someone with a low self-image will have a fear of change. You may not be happy where you are, or about who you are with, but you don't want to change it and risk the possibility of making it worse. Also, deep down inside you don't believe anyone would really be attracted to you if they get to know the real you. Some people with a low self-esteem do not believe they deserve to be happy. (See Trait Dictionary in Appendix A.)

3. Emotionally Withdrawn

Emotionally withdrawn people have a natural tendency not to trust people or be expressive. Because emotional expression is difficult, letting people get to know them is challenging. Since this person is content to keep his thoughts inside, he lacks the outgoing "market yourself" personality which would make people notice him.

If you have one of the three personality traits described above, recognize it and take steps to overcome the limitations they bring. Notice I didn't include "shy" on the list. Shyness is a result of unnecessary fears which probably include one or more of the three traits listed above. Being shy is no excuse. Look at yourself using trait names to put the shyness into perspective: you're scared!

The first step is to find someone without these traits to take you out and force you to meet new people. The second step is watch for it in your handwriting and change it. Each time you change the way you write, it becomes a reinforcement that you are changing that particular element of your personality!

You must get out and let people know you are there. Businesses must advertise, why don't you? You must market yourself. Remember the saying, "If you build a better mousetrap, the world will beat a path to your door?" It is a lie! You must market that mousetrap. *People cannot choose you if they do not know you exist.*

One More Way to Market Yourself

Since marketing yourself is one of the biggest obstacles to finding new relationships, I designed a new way to utilize handwriting analysis to help you meet new people. It was the invention of the Grapho-Deck®. It is a deck of cards with different personality traits on each card. It is like a deck of flash cards for personality. Anyone can use it to analyze handwriting, anywhere. This is the perfect way to break the ice with strangers. It is fun, simple, and accurate. All you have to do is ask someone for his handwriting. The cards do all the work. I have met hundreds of people this way, and started dozens of relationships! One man, Bill Kemple, says, "I think the Grapho-Deck is so wonderful, I rarely leave home without it!" It has been called the ultimate icebreaker. See the appendix for information about how you can order a Grapho-Deck and appear like an expert today.

Ask And You Shall Receive

The world has a way of giving you exactly what you ask for. Your subconscious mind is like a computer. When you input a program, it will perform that program exactly. The key is to be aware that you are *always* programming your internal computer. Every doubt and fear has just as much an influence on your future as your prayers. Your subconscious mind doesn't know the difference between the two. If you send it a clear picture of something your mind envisions, it makes it a reality, *even if you are seeing clearly what you don't want to happen.* This has been statistically proven in real life cases involving victims of rape . A leading New York university research team recently revealed, on average, once a woman had been raped, she was three times as likely to be raped again. Why? Partly because her mind replayed the event repeatedly making the rape such a part of her reality that would happen again. In addition, once her confidence is broken, a rapist can spot her as an easier victim. Her entire physiology reacts to the pictures she plays in her mind. She walks, stands, and speaks with fear. This relates to you in many ways. If you *want* to have a relationship but you consistently see yourself alone or in a bad relationship, your mind will create that reality. You must visualize what you *want*, not what you *don't want*.

I've seen this happen many times in my life. I simply and clearly instruct my subconscious mind as to what I want, what to expect, and when it is going to happen. And as if by magic, it happens. I've used this technique successfully with cars, friends, money, etc. It usually comes from unexpected sources, chance encounters, or luck. In other words, I didn't necessarily work really hard and pay cash for it. Is it luck or chance? I don't think so. My definition of luck is: *preparation meeting opportunity*. So, make clear pictures in your mind of your future lifestyle with a successful relationship.

The Dog Theory

I have a fun theory about a sure-fire way to change someone's relationship patterns. There are many solutions to relationship problems outlined in this book. Therapists have a hundred and one different ways to help you overcome your relationship barriers. My dog theory is the simplest of any cure out there. It goes something like this:

The Problem: You can't seem to get involved in a new relationship. Solution: Buy a dog.

That's right. Buy a dog. Now, if you were to actually go out and purchase a puppy right now, you could learn a few valuable lessons about relationships. Let's analyze this example. As we grow older, our bodies and mind adjust to whatever environment we are in. We become comfortable with what we have. We may not be happy, but we get by. If a person has lived for a while without a serious relationship in his life the person's mind, body, and environment have become accustomed to being alone. Therefore, what he must do is stir up his environment and his mind. We must force him to step out of his comfort zone and learn some new tricks. Until the unconscious conditioning changes from *alone* to *together*, he will never be ready to accept a relationship even if one is standing on his doorstep wagging its tail, panting, and flashing its big brown droopy eyes.

In handwriting we see this visually in the retraced lower loops. In order for someone to trust another, there must be imagination (loops) inside the relationship area (lower zone). This relates to the puppy pal relationship in many specific psychological ways.

When you get a dog, we'll call it Poochi, you must do the following to make the relationship work*:

1. Give Poochi a place to stay in your home.
2. Spend money for food, collar, tags, etc.
3. Feed it on a regular basis. (Which means you can't go away for weeks at a time like you did in your swinging single days!)
4. Let Poochi inside so it doesn't get lonely and cry at the door.
5. Pay the vet big bills so Poochi isn't sick.
6. Take Poochi places, like for a walk in the park.
7. Clean up the crap in the middle of the living room floor.
8. Avoid kicking the crap out of Poochi when he does #7. (This hurts the dog, your foot, and means more crap for you to clean up!)
9. You must learn to forgive Poochi for #7 and still love him.
10. You must learn to forgive yourself for breaking rule #8.
(It is purely coincidental if any of these things relate to a romantic relationship.)

If all this sounds like a real responsibility, it is. In fact, it could change your entire daily routine. It may even open a part of your "loner" psychological makeup to start allowing love for someone else besides yourself. This is the key. Once you take on the responsibility of a new dog, change your routine, and show affection for the puppy, you will notice your heart will be ready for a human to fill in the gap which has just developed in your "y's"! Of course, you don't have to go through all the crap cleaning hassles to learn this lesson, but hey, some of us are slow learners!

After presenting my theory to many experts in the field, they agreed it was most ingenious. However, they proposed the following scenario:

The Problem: What if you already have a dog?
My Solution: Get rid of the dog.
Reason: If you a have dog, you have developed a routine around having that relationship. When you get rid of it, you leave a vacant space in your heart that will have to be filled. Hopefully a person will fill the hole in your heart, and if you are lucky maybe that person will already have a dog!

I'm not suggesting you go out right now and buy a cute little puppy dog, but I should also mention taking a puppy into a public place is the second best way ever developed to meet people (the first is the Grapho-Deck). They come running to pet your puppy. It's amazing. (When I was in high school I used to borrow a friend's puppy or my neighbor's baby just to pick up girls in the mall. It worked! Pet-sit for a day, check out the attention you get.)

Are you ready?
Now that you know how to overcome those fears of trust and any reluctance to love, it is time to learn about your emotions in more detail. There is someone out there, right now, waiting to create a deep bio-electrochemical bond with you. Are you paying attention? The next chapter will help you know when you have found a lover who has the same electrical emotional outlay as yourself. You don't want to fall in love with a 110 amp person if your circuits are wired on 220.

Chapter III
Emotions in Handwriting

Introduction to Slants - Emotionality

One of the most important aspects of personality is emotionality: how people respond to their feelings. We all have emotions. However, the handwriting reveals the intensity and expressiveness of those emotions.

People's emotional responses can be accurately estimated from their writing. Is the person basically ruled by logical, practical judgement (left slant) or by feelings, expressiveness, and impulsiveness (right slant)? How do you make most of your decisions, with your head or your heart? The answer to this question is revealed in the slant. A vertical slant reveals logic and restrained emotion. These writers keep their emotions inside, they are reserved and emotionally distant. It's not that they don't have emotions, because they do, maybe as deeply as anyone. It's just that they don't express their emotions easily. A leftward slant signifies someone who would rather hold their emotions inside. To get along you must understand how they react. Don't expect them to be consistently giving and expressing how they feel toward you.

Human emotions are very complex. One wonderful aspect of using handwriting to understand emotions is that handwriting graphically freezes emotions on the page. Unfortunately, emotions are often momentary feelings rather than continuous states. However, in neuro-analysis, we group the overall emotional outlay as a basic enduring state of responsiveness. For example, it is more common to say "She is very outgoing," rather than say, "When she is at a party, she enjoys talking and socializing with people." It is for this reason the emotional outlay categories may seem general in scope. They have very specific tendencies which are very accurate and need to be understood. There are six basic emotional outlays (FA, AB,BC,CD,DE, or E+). Obviously, there are more than six types of people. When you use one of these six general dispositions as a foundation for the personality, the other traits become bricks to build the unique structure we call personality. We can build very different houses using the same foundations. Hence, the emotional outlay, the slant, is the foundation of the personality.

A hard right-handed slant signifies an emotionally driven person. These writers need people. They express their emotions outwardly. They respond emotionally and sympathetically to outside stimuli and situations. The farther to the right the slant becomes, the more emotionally expressive the writer will be. Advertisers like this type of person because they respond well to the beer commercials with the pretty girls and rock-n-roll. Products advertised merely have to relate to social life, excitement, or adventure or sex in order to sell to the emotionally-driven person. It doesn't have to be logically the best product. Intellectually, we know a can of beer will not get us the life of excitement a commercial displays. But emotionally, it seems more realistic. Therefore, these people develop a *feeling* of fun every time they see that specific brand of beer. Conversely, those writers that write with a vertical slant usually do not buy products strictly on emotion. If they buy a can of beer they can tell you logically why it is the best choice based on price, taste, origin, etc..

In a relationship, the right-handed slant man or woman will fall for someone on a whim. There may be no logical reason for the infatuation she feels, but it is very real. However, anytime someone buys on emotion, there is a high degree of buyer's remorse. Therefore, in relationships, when the truth comes out and the person turns out to be not–so–great, the buyer would like to return him for a full refund. Think about that when someone says "love at first sight."

If you would like to attract an emotional person, DE or E+ writer, sell him or her with emotions and moving stories. Tell stories about how you were so sensitive or emotionally moved by some experience you had. If you meet a person who is emotionally expressive, you will want to tell a story which will pull at the heartstrings. Maybe a "how I was so sad when I saw this injured kitty" type of story. Remember, these people relate to emotions and feelings.

One might say, "I can remember the day I was watching T.V. and saw the starving child in Africa. His little dirty face staring hopelessly into the camera. My heart bled with sympathy. I instantly put myself in his place and felt sadness and hopelessness. I watched as he ate his one bowl of grits. As I listened to Sally Struthers, I realized that just 30 cents a day could change this child's life. So, I picked up the phone and adopted a child. I just had to... my heart drove me to express my compassion. Now, my heart flutters once a year when I get a letter from my adopted African boy, Muntabe."

The above scenario would be typical of a DE or E+ slant. Emotion sells to rightward-slanted writers. On the other hand, if your prospective lover is one of those straight–up–and–down logical thinkers, your approach will be completely different. You would want to relate to him–as the logical man. Therefore, illustrate how logically and prudently you make your decisions. Also, since he is not impulsive, you will have less of an opportunity to talk him into anything! So, relate to his rational mind, don't be an over-emotional drip! So, if you are trying to attract a logical man or woman, be logical. In the case of attracting a logical woman, perhaps a man could try explaining to her why it would be in her best interest to go out with him!

Slant Compatibility

Emotionality is one of the single most important handwriting traits. Therefore, the first thing you should notice about someone's handwriting is the slant. You need to know how expressive they are and how they handle their emotions. In a prospective mate's handwriting, you need to know how their emotional foundation will fit with your emotional foundation.

What kind of slant makes a better relationship? It depends. I recommend that you look for someone with a similar slant as your own. If you are the kind of person who is very expressive, outgoing, needs lots of affection, you liked to be touched frequently, you need to be told you are loved daily, etc., then you need to choose a partner that is similar in style because they will naturally be touchy, expressive, and affectionate. Find a CD, DE, or E+ writer.

I am not saying opposites cannot be happy together (ex: AB slant male & DE slant female). I have seen relationships work that have "opposite" emotional outlays, but they fail more often than succeed. Why? They fail because of different communication styles. They simply do not understand each other or cannot meet each other's needs. A woman with a similar emotional outlay automatically knows her partner's emotional styles, because they need the same type of affection. However, if opposites are together, this behavior must be learned. If you are with someone of an opposite slant, you must communicate (talk) openly, honestly, and frequently about your needs. Otherwise needs will go unmet.

> *"Opposites attract but usually don't stick!"*
> — *Bart A. Baggett*

We have internal programs which dictate the way we feel. We each have a program for expressing and receiving love. An AB writer's program is different than a DE writer's program. In a relationship, if you explain clearly what it takes for you to feel loved, and your partner explains to you what it takes for him to feel loved, you both can feel loved most of the time. It is a simple matter of awareness and communication style. Not to mention effort and follow-through.

If you are currently in a relationship with someone of a dramatically different slant, increase your communication about your needs and ask about his/her needs. I don't usually recommend a DE/E+ slant writer to become involved with an AB/FA writer, but it can work out–it takes maturity and open communication.

Depth of Feeling

Just as life is not two-dimensional, neither is handwriting. Although it looks like a snapshot of personality, it is actually a hologram. If you slide your finger across the back of some handwriting, you may find the pen has created a dent in the paper. This is the third dimension to handwriting. The amount of pressure exerted on the paper is "depth of feeling," sometimes called emotional intensity.

Emotional intensity refers to how deeply a person feels emotions and how long these emotions last. A light writer's emotions tend to pass quickly while a heavy writer harbors them inside for a long time. The harder the pen is pressed on the paper, the more intense any emotional experience will be. Have you ever dated someone who remembered an argument three weeks later? Was that person still irritated about something you said then? This person was probably a heavy writer. Are you the kind of person that can have a heated argument, then want to go to lunch with the person five minutes later because you forgot the argument already? If so, you are probably a light writer. As you can see, it is easier to get along with someone who has similar depth of emotions.

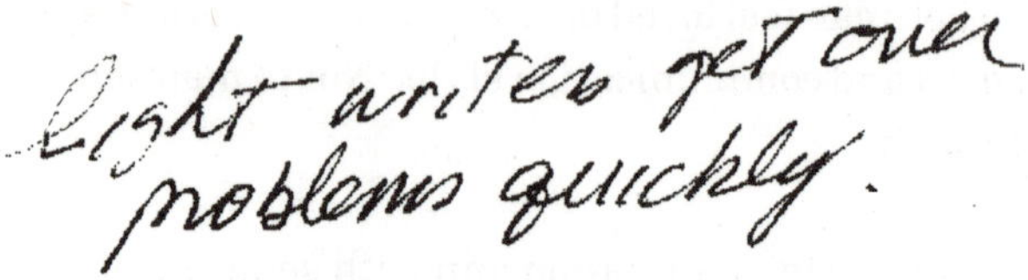

light writes get over problems quickly.

Figure 3.1: Light Writer

This pressure is average

Figure 3.2: Medium Writer

I press too hard on The paper !

Figure 3.3: Deep/Heavy Writer

Light Writer

This writer can endure a traumatic situation without being seriously affected, then or later. This writer may get steaming mad, but will have forgotten it by tomorrow. He will not understand why someone would still be angry or upset at yesterday's incident. Emotional experiences do not make much of a lasting impression on him. His feelings are not enduring or intense. Although he may be intense at the height of feelings, they burn out quickly and are gone. Although he may get extremely mad today, by tomorrow he will have forgotten the anger associated with the problem.

Medium Writer

This writer feels emotional situations for a moderate amount of time. If he is angry, he may forget his emotions after a while, but don't expect it to blow over in one day. This person has an average level of emotional intensity.

Heavy/Deep Writer

This writer has very deep and enduring feelings. Any emotional situation or feeling will stay with him for a long time. This writer may forgive, but will never forget. He has definite likes and dislikes. Entering a room where the color irritates him will make this writer nervous. If he notices a crooked picture frame, it bothers him. Heavy writers feel situations intensely.

Emotional Depth & Compatibility

When considering compatibility, it is essential to consider the "depth of feeling" or "depth of emotions." This is how deeply a person feels emotions and how long the feelings last. Do emotions stay a long time (people who press hard when they write) or do the emotions pass quickly (light writers)? To reiterate, the harder the pen is pressed on the paper, the more intense the person's emotional experience are felt and the longer they hold on to the those intense emotions.

We see problems in relationships when a deep-feeling person (heavy writer) is combined with a person who gets over emotions quickly (light writer). These people can go through the same situation and have completely different impressions of what happened. Many of the misunderstandings couples have relate to the emotional impact of event. An example may be that she supposedly doesn't care about him, since she has forgotten about the pain he went through last month, whereas he is still feeling it. Although they were equally moved at the time, she (light writer) has released the emotion associated with the event. He hasn't.

The heavy writer feels situations deeply and for a long time. He harbors emotions and remembers things. The light writer feels an emotion, expresses it, and gets over it. Women tend to be light writers more often than men. There are exceptions, but it seems women are more likely to express an emotion, and have it be done with. Men, on the other hand, tend to harbor their emotions and remember specific feelings for years to come.

The Three Zones
Another basic element of handwriting analysis is the three zones: the upper, middle, and lower. These zones are also called the philosophical, the mundane, and the physical zones. Please refer to Diagram 3.4.

The three zones correlate easily with the three areas of a person's life. The upper zone reveals the person's philosophical interest. These include religion, goals and plans, imagination, and other philosophical ideals.

The middle (mundane) zone reveals subject matter associated with living in the moment, today, now. In this zone, we find such traits as secretiveness, talkativeness, thinking processes, argumentativeness, and other traits relating to a person's daily environment and interaction among people.

The lower zone relates to a person's physical life. This includes travel, exercise, material items, and sex. The lower zone is the source of energy and drive. A loop of any kind, found anywhere in the writing, reveals imagination. Therefore, a huge loop in the lower zone signifies imagination in the physical realm. This can translate into exaggerated needs in an individual's physical life.

Two more important factors to know are the future and past zones. Any stroke ending to the left symbolizes a retreat to the past and/ or into one's self. A stroke ending to the right symbolizes an effort to go forward to the future and outward toward other people. It is considered healthier to express energy toward others and the future than living in the past, bottled up within oneself.

The intensity of any trait can be determined by the frequency of a stroke present in the handwriting. You can't judge a football team's season by just one play. Similarly, when analyzing handwriting, you must analyze enough strokes to get an average.

When in doubt about a specific stroke, ask yourself in which zone it is located and which direction it goes toward. This will give you a hint to its meaning. Remember that someone's personality is more than one individual trait. You must use the slant and emotionality factors as a foundation in order to stack the personality traits. This way, the entire person is revealed as more than the sum of his parts.

"Love is a spirit all compact of fire."
— William Shakespeare,
Two Gentlemen of Verona

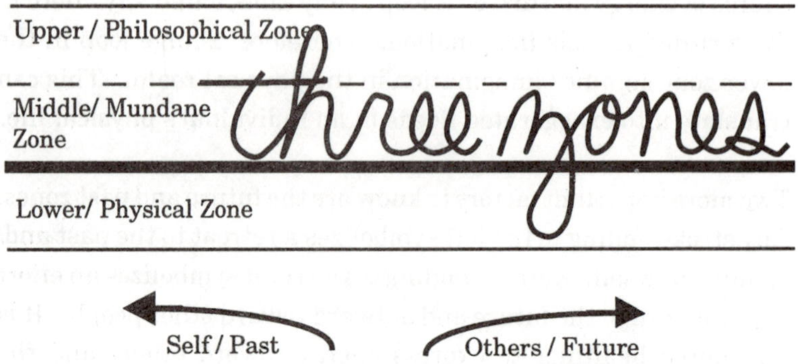

Figure 3.4: Three Zone Diagram

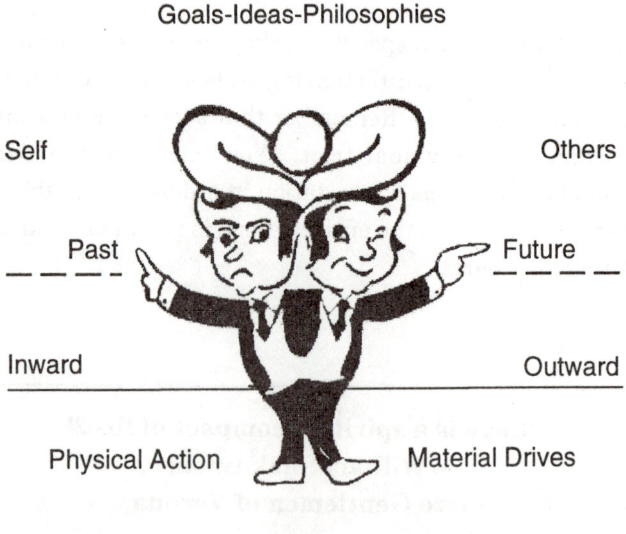

Goals-Ideas-Philosophies

Figure 3.5: Little Man Diagram

Emotional Responsiveness in Handwriting

The first step to understanding human nature through handwriting is understanding how a person responds to the environment. Emotions are perhaps the most influential aspect of all behavior. Emotions are the stuff of which the peaks and valleys of life are made: exhilaration, depression, feeling scared, lonely, jealous, or infatuated. Emotions are the starting point in this book, not only because of their power, but because they are the basis for relationships with other people. Emotions are connected with every aspect of human behavior.

As stated, the emotional responsiveness of a person is revealed by the slant of the handwriting. As a general rule, any stroke ending to the right side of the page symbolizes a movement toward other people or the future. Likewise, any stroke ending to the left symbolizes a tendency to withdraw into oneself or move into the past. With this point in mind, it is easy to understand why a writer who writes with a left-handed slant is much more shy than a writer who slants very heavily to the right side of the paper.

The emotional outlay of someone's writing can often be accurately estimated without using the following time-consuming procedure. However, it is strongly suggested you work through numerous samples using this scientific method until you are skilled enough to eyeball it. Slants can be deceiving. Since we are *only* measuring upstrokes, much of the downstrokes of handwriting give it an overall look of a certain slant. But, when measured, it can reveal a different emotional outlay.

The first step to determine if a person expresses her emotions at the drop of a hat or only after a natural disaster, is to find the baseline. The baseline a traditional school piece of paper gives you is rarely the *real* baseline. The baseline is the line between the initial upstroke and where the ending downstroke returns to start a new letter. You may have four different baseline strokes in a four letter word. If you don't measure each individual letter's baseline, you can't properly measure the angle of the upstroke coming from that baseline. So, find the starting point and then find the lowest point (where one letter becomes the next letter). Then, draw the baseline by connecting these two points.

Next, draw the upstroke by locating the highest point of the upstroke and then connecting it to the same place as the starting point you used for the baseline. If an upstroke is difficult to figure out, simply take the spot where the upstroke curves to an angle which is not rising. If it is really tricky, skip it and move to a different letter.

The final step is to evaluate the angle formed by the crossing lines. These two lines will meet to form an angle, what angle is it? Use the chart in Figure 3.8 to determine what the various angles represent. Position the gauge with the baselines on top of one another. Slide the gauge until the upstroke you drew fits nicely between two of the gauges upstrokes. If you can't tell, extend the upstroke line you drew out to the end of the gauge. This will usually clarify the slant. When a slant is clearly within a certain angle, mark the letter with that slant code (FA, AB, etc.) Do this same measurement for at least twenty upstrokes until a majority is revealed. Determine which slant is predominant. In most cases you will note the presence of several different slants in one writing. However, you will usually find a slant that falls predominantly into one category. If it doesn't, measure some more strokes. If the chart reveals two categories next to each other, don't worry about the variation. This writer falls between one or the other in responsiveness. If the writer displays a consistent and dramatic variability of slant you can deduce that this person has an unpredictable emotional outlay and fluctuates moods severely.

As you are learning, do this slant test many times for each writing until you become proficient at picking which letters to evaluate and even eyeing it properly. Chart 3.9 is a brief summary of the different categories your handwriting samples will reveal.

Determining Emotional Outlay:
STEPS AT A GLANCE
1• Find the starting point
2• Find the lowest point
3• **Draw the baseline by connecting these two points**
4• Find the lowest point (use the same point as you did for the base line)
5• Find the highest point of the upstroke
6• **Connect the two points with a line**
7• **Evaluate the angle formed by the crossing lines**

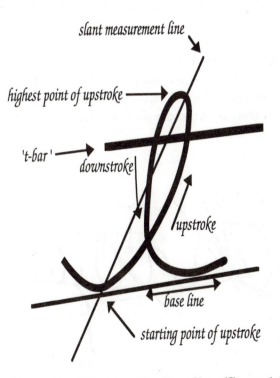

slant measurement line

highest point of upstroke

't-bar'
downstroke
upstroke

base line
starting point of upstroke

Figure 3.6: Finding the Baseline (Steps 1-3)

Figure 3.10 is a more visual description the personality types.

The emotional responsiveness of a person is perhaps the single most important trait in the handwriting. With this knowledge as a foundation, all the other traits can be added to it to create a comprehensive description of someone's dispositions and behavoir known as the personality. You should always ask how the emotional outlay will affect a specific trait. For example, an impulsive (E+) writer with the temper trait will react in an uncontrollable outburst of emotion quicker than an introvert (FA writer) would react with the same degree of temper trait. By the way, the experience of putting all the traits together, training, testing, and a certificate is the key differences between a professional analyst and a person armed with a Grapho-Deck only. Stacking the traits together takes the science to a whole new exciting level of depth and understanding.

Once in a while you will find someone who writes with one slant one day, and then another slant another day. My good friend Phyllis Mattingly, a world renowned handwriting analyst, described this trait as "A fast car with good brakes." In other words,

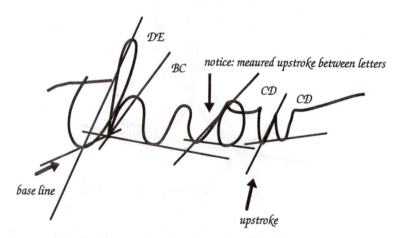

Figure 3.7: Measuring the Slant

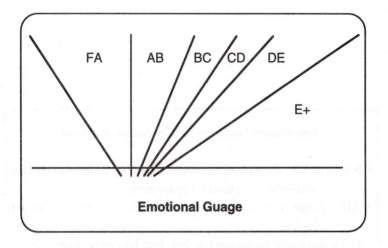

Figure 3. 8: Pocket Size Emotional Guage
(trace onto clear plastic to evaluate slants)

this person has developed the flexibility to be logical when need be, and is able to access his emotions when it is appropriate. Since these people don't always fall into one category or another, you must adjust your analysis depending on the environment. Most people with more than one slant simply write vertically when they are in the mood to be alone or study. Likewise, when they are in a social mode, their writing angles more to the right. Remember, the variation in slant is more than just a mood with these people. They process information and make decisions differently while in each emotional state of mind. Most would agree they can have two personalities depending on the situation. The only time for concern is if the writer has two or more opposite slants in the *same sentence* or sample of writing. That is more than a change in mood. It is an unpredictable swing in emotional expressiveness. This is two personalities which are out of control.

Now that you have an overview, each slant will be discussed in detail with examples for a full understanding of each important trait. For simplicity, masculine gender is used to define some of the following slants,but they apply equally to both genders.

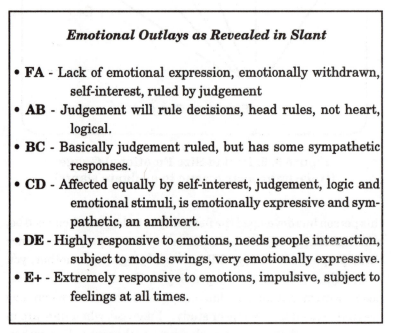

Emotional Outlays as Revealed in Slant

- **FA** - Lack of emotional expression, emotionally withdrawn, self-interest, ruled by judgement
- **AB** - Judgement will rule decisions, head rules, not heart, logical.
- **BC** - Basically judgement ruled, but has some sympathetic responses.
- **CD** - Affected equally by self-interest, judgement, logic and emotional stimuli, is emotionally expressive and sympathetic, an ambivert.
- **DE** - Highly responsive to emotions, needs people interaction, subject to moods swings, very emotionally expressive.
- **E+** - Extremely responsive to emotions, impulsive, subject to feelings at all times.

Chart 3.9: Types of Personality

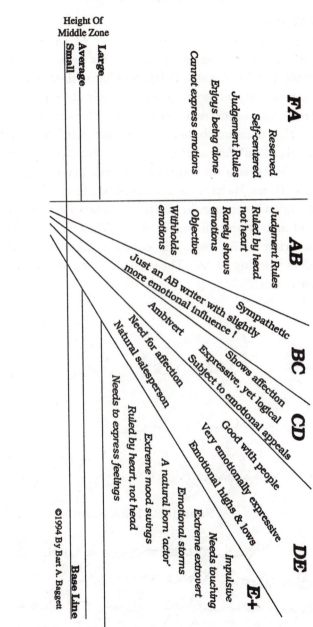

Figure 3.10: Detailed Emotional Gauge

FA Writer

The person who writes with an overall FA slant is emotionally repressed. It is an unusual slant. This person will be a social outcast with few friends. This writer has withdrawn into himself. He is reserved and shows his feelings only at times of great anger, extreme passion, or tremendous stress. This writer is an introvert. He makes decisions based on logic, therefore he is rarely impulsive. He doesn't find any need for expressing his emotions. In fact, he probably sees this emotional expression as an unnecessary waste of time. He has a hard time relating to an extreme extrovert, although it is common for him to be attracted to one. Many people do not understand this writer; it is difficult for them to know how this writer really feels. He enjoys being alone, and probably prefers working alone. These people often enjoy working with their hands.

Sample 3.11: FA Slant

Sample 3.12: Introverted Writer FA Slant

Introvert

In handwriting, introversion is signified by a predominantly leftward slant and/or small writing. The extent of how intro-verted a person really is depends on the extent of the other fears such as self-consciousness and lack of confidence. If the slant of the writing is left of the 90° angle, he is considered emotionally withdrawn. These people are not emotionally expressive. True introversion is the withdrawal into oneself. Therefore, people who write small may seem quiet and reserved, but may be as expressive as anyone else one-on- one if they have a DE slant. Look at the slant to determine emotional expressiveness. Like-wise, a person with a leftward slant who has really large hand-writing may seem social, but will rarely express emotions to others. The classic introvert has both small and leftward writing.

My friend John had a roommate named Nellie who was a classic introvert.   Nellie was severely withdrawn. She found safety in being alone. She was afraid of new people and especially fearful of expressing herself.   John told me that after two months of living together, she got mad enough to tell him since they moved in together, it had been bothering her that he left the toilet seat up. I thought to myself, "It took her two months to express *that*. How long will it take her to say something when John does something to really piss her off?" This example is typical of emotionally withdrawn people. They rarely express how they feel to others, until the last straw.   In fact, only two times will you really ever know how they feel: during moments of extreme anger or extreme passion (sex). I suppose during angry sex they will be twice as likely to speak their mind! Nellie had to be at the boiling point to express her feelings. Actually, the one time he really pissed her off, she wrote him a note because she couldn't express it verbally. Expressing emotions is difficult for the introvert.

Now, as a roommate, this girl was great. John could do stuff which would normally irritate most roommates and not hear about it for months. What a deal! He could have been stuck with some neurotic, hot tempered live-in that blew off the handle every time he left a dish unwashed. In this respect, he was lucky. On the other hand, she would walk around for two days brooding. She wouldn't talk to him until he would ask her what was wrong and practically beg her to tell him. It was like pulling teeth to develop a close friendship. He tried.

In a relationship, the introvert is important to understand. If you are an emotionally expressive person, the introvert might drive you nuts. They might drive you nuts anyway. In fact, if you are a man, any woman might drive you nuts. I can't speak from experience, but from what I hear, the reverse is also true.

I can't express how hurt I ... everything you have been s ... Normally, I would never ... I would just confront you ... hurt right now I'm afra ... crying and I don't want t ... Never in a million years ... anything negative. @ you ... other girl you were interested ... much @ you to sabbotage ... What do you tell your other

Sample 3.13: Nellie's handwriting

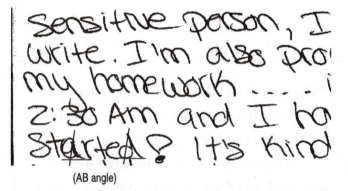

(AB angle)

Samples 3.14: AB Slant

AB Writer

The AB writer is more common than the FA writer. He is similar to the FA writer, but a bit more outgoing and socially integrated. This writer uses judgement to make decisions. He is ruled by his head, not his heart. He is a cool, collected person who's usually unexpressive emotionally. Some may see him as unemotional. He does have emotions but has no need to express them. He is withdrawn into himself and enjoys being alone.

The circumstances when this writer does express emotions include: extreme anger, extreme passion, and tremendous stress. He puts a mark in his mind when someone angers him. He keeps track of these marks and when he hits that last mark he will let you know you have gone too far. If he ever gets angry enough to blow his top, he won't be sorry about it later. He is ruled somewhat by self-interest. All his conclusions are made without outside emotional influence. He is objective and given to evaluating facts before taking action. He is very level-headed and will remain calm in an emergency situation. In a situation where most people might get hysterical, he responds with a calm, poised attitude.

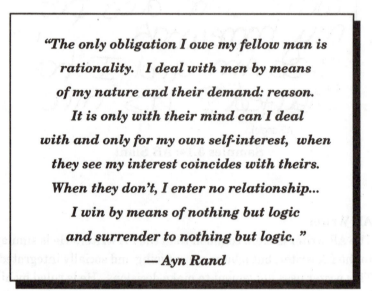

*"The only obligation I owe my fellow man is
rationality.　I deal with men by means
of my nature and their demand: reason.
It is only with their mind can I deal
with and only for my own self-interest,　when
they see my interest coincides with theirs.
When they don't, I enter no relationship...
I win by means of nothing but logic
and surrender to nothing but logic. "
— Ayn Rand*

Figure 3.15: Ayn Rand's signature

> *"Happiness is not to be achieved at the*
> *command of emotional whims...*
> *Happiness is possible only to a rational man. "*
> *— Ayn Rand*

This writer will work more efficiently if given space and time to be alone. He would rather not be constantly surrounded by people. In a relationship, he will show his love by the things he does rather than by the things he says. Saying, "I love you," is not a needed routine because he feels his mate should already know. The only exception to this is if he has logically concluded it is best for his mate to hear him express his love verbally.

This writer is not subject to emotional appeals of the heart. If someone is selling a product to him, she will need to present only the facts. She should present them from a standpoint of his sound judgement. He will not be taken in by an emotional story about someone else. He will meet emergencies without getting hysterical and he will always ask, "Is this best for me?"

One of the most well-known AB writers is author Ayn Rand, who pioneered her "objectivism philosophy" in her books *Atlas Shrugged* and *The Fountainhead*. The quotes shown here are from Atlas Shrugged. They nicely summarize her approach to life and its correlation with the basic philosophy of most AB writers.

BC Writer

This writer is basically ruled by judgement, but is slightly responsive emotionally and sympathetically. He is a slightly more emotional AB writer. He will be slightly responsive to appeals of the heart, but he won't be sold by them. One must appeal to his sense of logic and judgement, because it is how this writer makes decisions. To understand a BC writer, reread the AB writer and add another tablespoon of emotional expressiveness to it.

(BC angle)

Sample 3.16a: BC Slant

BC   BC   BC

(BC angle)

Sample 3.16b: BC Slant

CD Writer

This writer is moderately outgoing. His emotions are stirred by sympathy and heart-rending stories. He can be kind, friendly, affectionate, and considerate of others. He has the ability to put himself into the other person's shoes.

This writer will be somewhat moody, with some highs and lows. Sometimes he will be happy, the next day he might be sad. He has the unique ability to get along equally well with both: what psychology calls introverts and extroverts. This is because he is between the two extremes. Psychology calls this writer an ambivert. He can relate to introverts and extroverts. Although he can get along with people at the extremes, he will not relate to people who are too far out. He doesn't sway too far one way or the other, either

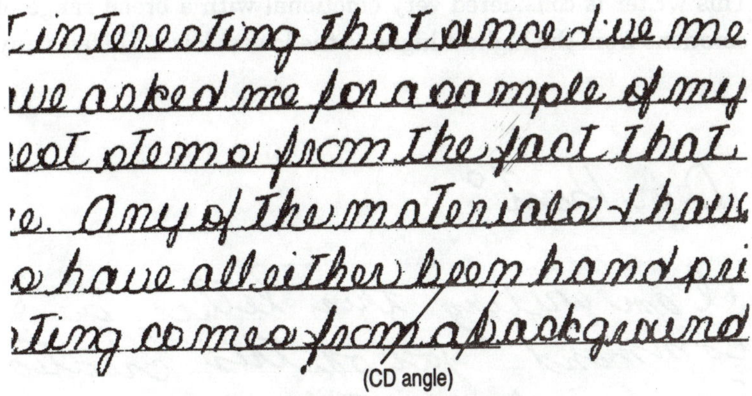

(CD angle)

Sample 3.17: CD Slant

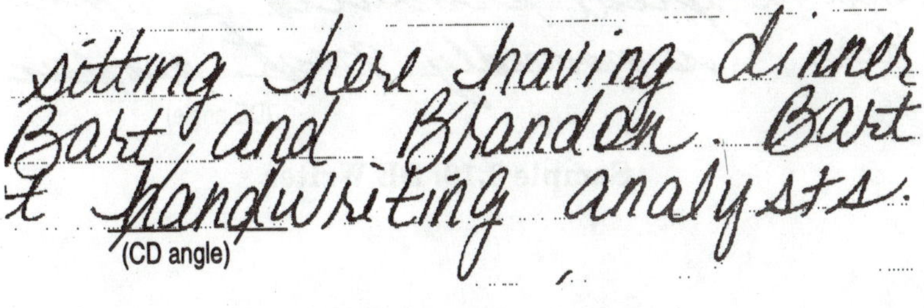

(CD angle)

Sample 3.18: CD Slant

too emotionally withdrawn or too emotionally unpredictable.

When convincing him to buy a product or an idea, a heart-rending story could mean a great deal to him. He puts himself in the same situation as the person in the story, yet he will not buy anything that seems overly impractical or illogical. This writer is an emotionally expressive person. He outwardly displays his emotions. He may even show traces of tears when hearing a sad story.

This writer tends to be middle-of-the-road politically as well as emotionally. He weighs both sides of an issue, sits on the fence, and then will decide when he finally has to. He doesn't relate to any far out ideas and usually won't go to the extreme on any issue.

DE Writer
This writer is considered very emotional with a broad range of emotions from the highest highs to the lowest lows. He feels any

Dear Bart:

I am writing this letter, as a
commend you on this creatio
napho - Dick. The difference be
and a great products is your:
hese supposedly great produc

(DE angle)

Sample 3.19: DE Writer

emotional situation very strongly. He'll flash to the very peaks of elation. Then, for some reason unknown to himself, he will burn out emotionally. These moods swings can be very disturbing to him and to others. Sometimes, he feels he can no longer produce anything. But, after given some time alone to recharge his emotional batteries, he will spring back into action.

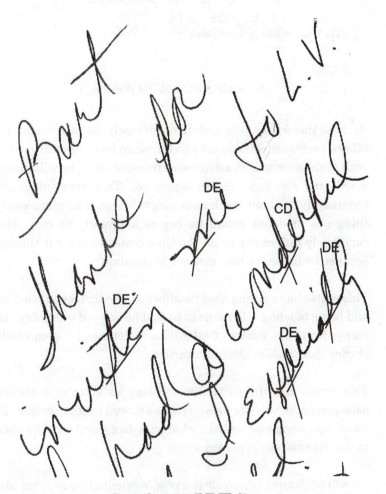

Sample 3.20: DE Writer

What happened to the guy
who used ~~the~~ dump drinks   E+
girls in drive-~~theatres~~. Oh, I   E+   E+   DE
~~Woots~~ ~~that~~ ~~plots~~ me.   DE   DE   E+

Sample 3.21: DE/ E+Writer

Because this writer feels situations intensely, he relates easily to others' problems. If he is not careful, when he comes into contact with someone who is in a depressed frame of mind, he will change moods and also begin to feel depressed. This writer often acts impulsively, without much forethought. Even if he plans everything out in detail before he begins a project, he may do it completely differently when the time comes to carry it through because he listens to his emotions at the time.

This writer has a strong need for affection. He thrives on touching and being touched. He needs to be told he is loved every day. He enjoys being the center of attention, sometimes he even retells stories that got him attention earlier.

This writer has the possibility of being an actor or a natural salesperson, simply because he relates so well to other people. He likes expressing how he feels, what he is doing, and what he plans to do. He is a people person.

He will work most efficiently in a people-oriented job as opposed to a job working alone or on an assembly line.

Sample 3.22: E+ Writer

E+ Writer

This is the writer with the farthest rightward slant you will find.
He is fully influenced by a tide of emotions. This writer reacts and
is influenced by his emotions at all times. He is very impulsive. He
can be quick to express anger or sorrow. Emotions will pour out
with terrific force. He will often say things he later regrets. This
writer could be subject to hysteria, especially during emergencies.

This writer is somewhat of an actor. Many times he hides his true
feelings. Sometimes he reveals less of himself than anyone else,
which is ironic because he needs to express himself. He protects
himself from being hurt by play acting. Many people will not
understand him. He becomes emotionally exhausted quickly. The
mood swings of this writer are wide and constantly changing. He
is on a constant emotional roller coaster, being happy and excited
one minute, and depressed the next.

He is affectionate. This is the natural romantic, if there is such a
thing. Since romance is emotion, not logic, the E+ writer has that
capacity. He often gives of himself. He will respond quickly to
praise. His need for attention makes him hard to ignore. His deep
emotional influence makes him vulnerable to tears when he hears
a sad story or when he needs a way of releasing tension.

This writer's biggest problem is probably being too subject to his

emotions. He forgets to be logical. His impulsive behavior sometimes gets him into trouble. This person is also often misunderstood because he is at the other extreme of the emotional spectrum.
This type of writer can be very emotionally draining to those
around him. He has two speeds: speeding or stopped.

In a relationship, this person will always refer to his feelings to
make decisions. If you are accustomed to predictable, stable,
logical relationships, the E+ writer may be too emotional for you.

Sample 3.23: E+ Writer

Chapter IV

Thinking Patterns & Intelligence

Are You Smart?

Intelligence is the capacity to learn, to reason, and to retain knowledge. The ability to be creative and the ability to be analytical are different forms of intelligence. The words smart and dumb are poor indicators of any real intellectual capacity, or lack thereof, in a person. However, when we were young, we were probably labeled smart or dumb in our minds and spent the rest of our schooling proving ourselves correct. Since, by our definition, intelligence is the *capacity* to learn, our formal level of education has little to do with how intelligent we are.

Psychologists do a tremendous disservice to young people by labeling them with an IQ score. Now, after decades of using this standardized intelligence test, IQ tests have been almost completely discredited as an accurate and predictable indicator of intelligence.

Obviously, "smart" people have different thinking processes from those we perceive as "dumb." The difference lies not in their brain capacity, but in how they think. The important issue is the method used to process and sort information; the education they possess has little to do with intelligence. Numerous research studies have found no correlation existing between good grades and financial success in life. It is a nice statistic to know because your childhood education was out of your control. However, you can still become successful (emotionally and financially) and can be just as intelligent as those with better educational opportunities.

Handwriting accurately reveals the various thinking patterns. No two people think exactly alike. However, there are enough similarities among certain types of thinking processes which can be grouped into specific thinking patterns. Some individuals may possess several types of thought processes. These people have a variety of thinking styles to choose from, depending on the circumstances. In general, they are the thinkers, the planners, and the achievers. Their versatility in the method of processing information assists them in adapting to the method most efficient at the time. For example, if a lady were painting a water color picture one weekend, she would require a slow, cumulative, and creative method of processing information. If she went to work on Monday as the director of a live talk show, she would be required to process information quickly, analyze incoming data instantly, and make rapid decisions. This woman has the best of both worlds in the way her mind works. Most people do not have this natural ability. In her handwriting, she would write her m's, n's , and h's in a variety of different styles. However, each style would be fluid and well formed. Therefore, we will look at the different styles separately. If you see handwriting that combines any of these, you know the writer has the versatility to use both styles of thinking.

We will discuss three basic groups of thinking patterns: Cumulative, Investigative, and Comprehensive. Then we will look at some variations of these three basic patterns. The thinking patterns are shown in the middle zone letters m, n, h, and even r. However, most of your information will come from the two lower case letters m and n. You will be looking at the way the upper humps are formed: curved, pointed, or retraced. You also will be looking at the way the downstrokes are formed: v-shape, looped, retraced, etc. In each of these strokes, you will be able to determine a different aspect of the person's method of thinking. Just observe the strokes of the letter to determine the pattern. As they say, different strokes for different folks!

I noticed something interesting when I was in school. During high school and college, both valedictorians of my class were cumulative thinkers. I knew both women fairly well. And, between you and me, they weren't the sharpest people I've ever met. In fact, they were average or below average in common sense. But they did master the skills of studying, memorizing, and testing in the American school system. Our school system is designed for the student to examine the material, memorize it, and then regurgitate it on a test. The process leaves the probing investigative student totally bored out of his mind, because he has to wait on the slowest student in class. In many cases, the child with the greatest natural ability to synthesize information and think creatively is stuck in a system designed for students to only achieve minimal requirements. You already know *intelligence has absolutely nothing to do with getting high grades in school.* Getting great grades involves such factors as motivation, attitude, interest, and self-discipline. The cases of learning difficulties are usually a matter of instructors teaching ineffective thinking and learning strategies. If teachers could present information in a style appropriate and conducive to each individual student's learning patterns, we wouldn't have so many delinquent students. Learn about your own thinking pattern and learn within that style. If you have a cumulative style, take one step at a time; on the other hand, if you are super-exploratory; jump into the middle and gather all of the facts as fast as you can in any particular order.

Cumulative Thinker

The slowest of the thinking patterns is the cumulative thinker. This is shown in the humps of the letters m and n . The more curved and round these letters are, the longer it takes for the writer to absorb information. However, once this person learns something, he tends to remember it much longer than the fast comprehensive thinkers.

To make a letter m, n, h, or r in a slow round gentle fashion the writer is ordinarily gentle and slow also. This person is a cumulative and creative thinker. She likes to have all the facts before making a decision. She thinks or creates much like a mason, stacking fact upon fact. Her thought pattern, the conclusion, will not be complete until the last fact is in place. This writer learns faster through demonstration than through written or verbal directions. She also learns easier through experiencing it herself, rather than by observing someone else doing it. Once she has learned new material and understood it, she won't forget it.

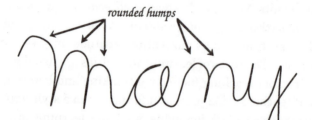

rounded humps

Figure 4.1: Cumulative Round Letters

More than half of your problem in other people. You have all. pick your wildest dreams.

Sample 4.2: Cumulative Writer

This is a methodical thinker, so she is able to build things and come up with new ideas based on previously-learned material. In an argument, she often loses to rapid–thinking people, but thirty minutes later she thinks about what she should have said. This reflects the *speed* of her thoughts, not the *quality* or *ability* to think intelligently.

She may think and work at a slower pace than other people. Therefore, she is better suited for a job that stresses consistency, repetition, and dependability in nature, where emphasis is not on speed. Many good artists have this type of mind. When an artist paints a portrait he has to put one layer of paint on top of another, waiting for the previous layer to dry. It is a slow, meticulous process that most fast thinkers do not have the patience to do. The same principle goes for many musicians. Learning to play an instrument requires slow, meticulous, cumulative practice. Once the basics are learned, he can build on it. Many musicians learn to play instruments and read music when they are young and think more cumulatively. They then develop the quicker thinking patterns as they grow older.

There isn't a "good" or "bad" thought process. However, you will probably feel more comfortable around people with thinking processes similar to your own. In a job situation, the job specifications will determine what type of thinking style is best suited for the job. Many teachers, assembly line workers, and artists have the round top letters. They also tend to be more gentle natured. Conversely, many of the most successful executives will have a majority of sharp pointed letters, rather than the round topped cumulative m's and n's because of their need to make instant decisions.

I went to school with a girl named Darcy. Darcy had the roundest, almost square, m's and n's, that I had ever seen. Many people thought Darcy was the biggest airhead in California. I understood the meaning of cumulative thinking when I tried to study with her. Because I have sharp angles on my m's and n's, I jumped right into the middle of the book to find the answer to the questions. She got flustered and told me she must start at page one and read each page until she came to the diagram which explained the answer. If she didn't start at the beginning, she would get confused. This is a great example of a cumulative thinker. Incidentally, she made excellent grades, but she studied much more and learned in a completely different style.   And yes, she was a bit of an airhead.

Investigative Thinker

The person with investigative handwriting characteristics thinks rapidly. She has a desire to satisfy her curiosity. She is able to grasp situations and new ideas without difficulty.

This writer can take ten good ideas and quickly formulate them into one idea which works. She often relies on the investigation of other people and doesn't take the time to dig deeply for herself. She is a quick thinker and will know rapidly if the information she has

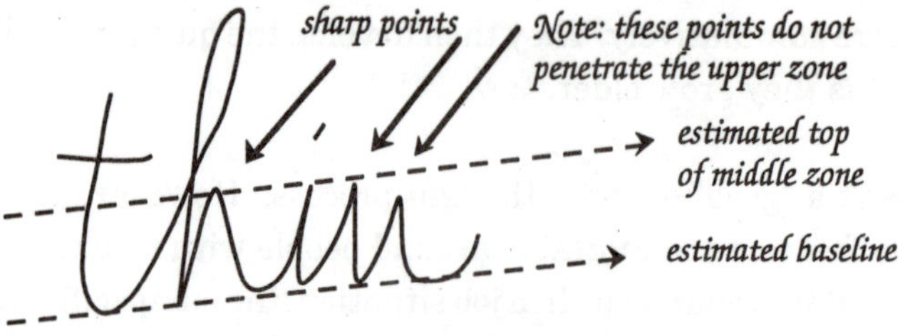

Figure 4.3: Curious Mind

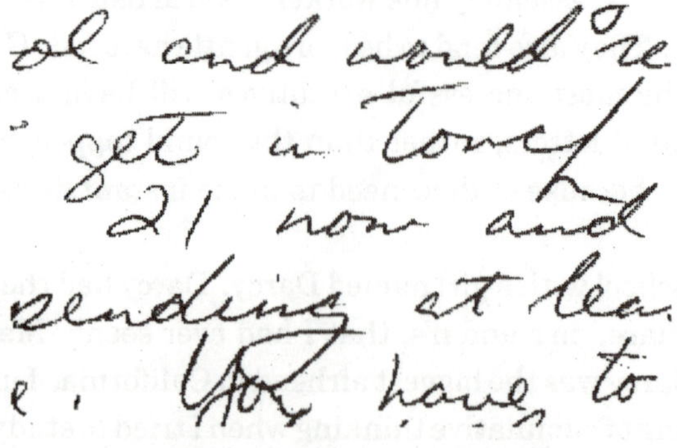

Sample 4.4: Curious Mind

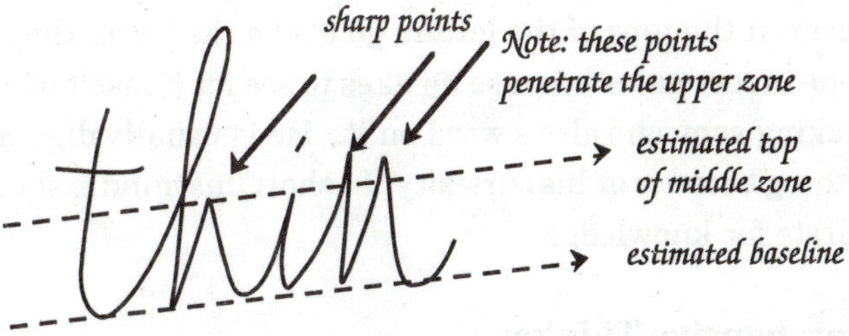

sharp points

Note: these points penetrate the upper zone

estimated top of middle zone

estimated baseline

Figure 4.5: Curious/Investigative Mind

been given can be used. Although she is often considered brilliant, her ideas are not usually her own. Rather, they are a synthesis of information she has received and processed. Her talent is to take someone else's ideas and research, then mentally evaluate their feasibility. This trait is common among executives because they do not have the time to get the facts themselves, relying instead on assistants. Again, this investigative nature is shown by sharp points on the top of the m's and n's.

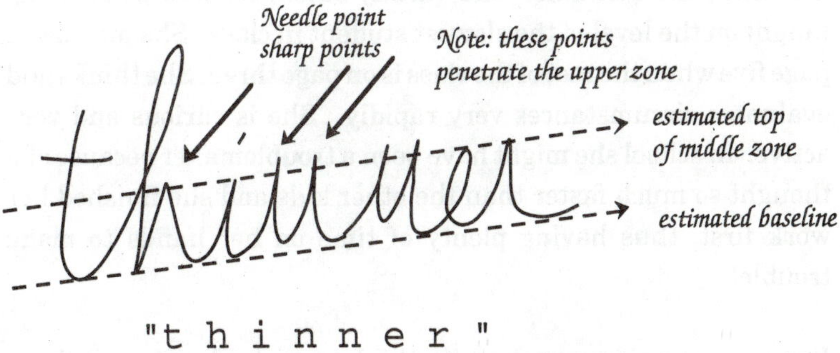

Needle point sharp points

Note: these points penetrate the upper zone

estimated top of middle zone

estimated baseline

"t h i n n e r "

Figure 4.6: Comprehensive Thinker

This person is a quick thinker whether these points go high or low. However, if the tops of the letters go above the top of the middle zone, he investigates because he likes to see for himself instead of just taking someone else's word on it. He is usually digging into something because of his curiosity. In short, his mind is sharp and he thirsts for knowledge.

Comprehensive Thinker

If you take the investigative trait one step farther, you get the comprehensive thinker. These people instantly size up situations, making instant decisions at a faster rate than even the investigative writer. Many people with this type of mind are geniuses, thus they may be seen as highly intelligent because they are 'street smart', as opposed to just 'book smart.'

This handwriting sample shows a comprehensive thinker. Many comprehensive thinkers write their m's, n's, h's and even r's with a sharp steeple point that is much sharper than the v-shape of the simply investigative. This is typical of most comprehensive thinkers.

The comprehensive thinker is often irritated by slow talkers or slow thinkers. When she drives a car, she gets irritated by slow drivers in the fast lane. She quickly becomes bored when being taught on the level of the slowest student in class. She may be on page five when the rest of the class is on page three. She thinks and evaluates circumstances very rapidly. She is curious and very active. In school she might have been a troublemaker because she thought so much faster than the other kids and she finished her work first, thus having plenty of time on her hands to make trouble!

It may seem as if comprehensive thinkers make decisions without even taking time to think. In reality, they analyze the facts so quickly it just seems this way. Comprehensive thinkers are usually analytical, too. These writers are natural geniuses. They

are Trying To Plan
time during That 5 wee
t will puts us in
, 3 Days. Let me Know

Anonymous

Mark Twain

Mark Twain

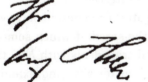

Adolf Hitler

My New ad — gettin
on The Democrats To Take
RAse Taxes — wow!

Anonymous

Figure 4.7.
Comprehensive Handwriting Samples

are very sharp, sometimes even too sharp for their own good.

In an argument, if they are sarcastic, they will always have a ready comeback. This writer will get bored easily and needs to be constantly learning new things.

In a relationship, people with similar thinking patterns tend to get along well. On the other hand, a very comprehensive thinking, aggressive, dominant man may seek out a cumulative, creative, gentle woman to complement his aggressive style by being a soft touch in his life. She will not be as sharp as he is, but he will not be as creative or gentle. Often, men and women that are comprehensive thinkers like to be around gentle cumulative thinkers to relax!

Analytical Thinker
This writing shows an analytical thinker. Analytical is a common trait shown on the bottom part of the letters m and n. It is a sharp "v" formation instead of a circle or a retraced line between the humps. Note: do not confuse investigative or comprehensive with analytical. The former deals with the *speed* at which someone processes information, the analytical trait deals with *how* they process information. The analytical writer sifts and examines facts. She interprets all facts by separating them, breaking them

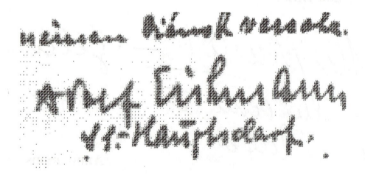

Figure 4.8: Analytical Writer

down, and organizing them from a critical point of view. This pattern of clarifying facts contributes to a strong reasoning ability. Her mind is constantly analyzing all situations she encounters. The more investigative and comprehensive someone is, the faster the analytical ability. Analytical describes the process as opposed to the speed of someone's thoughts. You will find both slow and quick thinkers that are analytical; both can be intelligent. The opposite of the analytical writing pattern is when they make loops at the baseline instead of v shapes. You will often find loops with cumulative thinkers and v shapes with investigative thinkers.

Messy Writing, Concentration, & Mental Focus
People often ask me,"What does it mean if my handwriting is really messy?" I often jokingly respond, "It means your handwriting is hard to read."

Handwriting analysis is the analysis of specific observable strokes in the handwriting which have been accurately categorized. Men's writing is often described as messy, unreadable, or small. A common description of women's writing includes such adjectives as flowery, big, and round. As an aspiring analyst, you should immediately attempt to break down these vague descriptions into specific strokes. It is unwise to try to analyze handwriting by having someone describe it to you, without actually seeing it. You must look closely and carefully at each individual stroke. Otherwise, you will make yourself and handwriting analysis look bad. I often take questions on radio talk shows where this happens. Callers want an instant perfect personality profile of a prospective lover simply by telling me, "He writes real messy!" The only way to be accurate is to ask specific questions about the writing designed to tell me the individual strokes. I focus on one or two traits. However, it is not possible for me to see the whole picture without seeing the writing. Attempt to avoid these situations.

Messiness does not have a specific meaning, but there is a specific meaning to the size of the letters. The overall size of the writing indicates how much energy can be concentrated on one thing at a time. The person who is able to direct his thoughts intensely upon one idea, a particular object, or an individual is said to have the ability to concentrate. The smaller the overall writing is, the greater ability to focus and concentrate the writer possesses.

If you compare very small writing (Figure 4.10) to large writing (Figure 4.9), the difference in mental focus becomes obvious. The larger writing is scattered. Many people who lack an intense ability to concentrate have the type of mind which darts in different directions constantly (shown by needle-pointed m's and n's with large writing and often a variable slant (not pictured). You should also notice the i-dot is not close to the stem. This signifies a *lack* of attention to detail. Another indicator of a scattered person is the lower loops running into the writing below. This signifies too many projects going on at once. This person is not necessarily smarter than the person who writes tiny; however, the concise writer would be more suited to work in a field such as bookkeeping while the big writer would be more suited to a profession that requires less concentration of thought, such as politics.

The size of the handwriting (the concentration ability) will be the first thing to fluctuate with the mood of the writer. Personally, when I am running out the door to a party, my writing is very large, slants uphill (optimism), and has a distinct right-ward slant (outgoing). When I sit down to balance my checkbook, my writing is small, precise, and much more vertically slanted. These are specific indicators that reflect the mood I am in at the time of the writing. Most of the other traits do *not* change, regardless of the mood or the circumstance. If your handwriting seems to change dramatically, notice the situation you are in at the time. If it is just a mood, don't worry. If you have a chemical imbalance in your body or exhibit dual personality tendencies, worry.

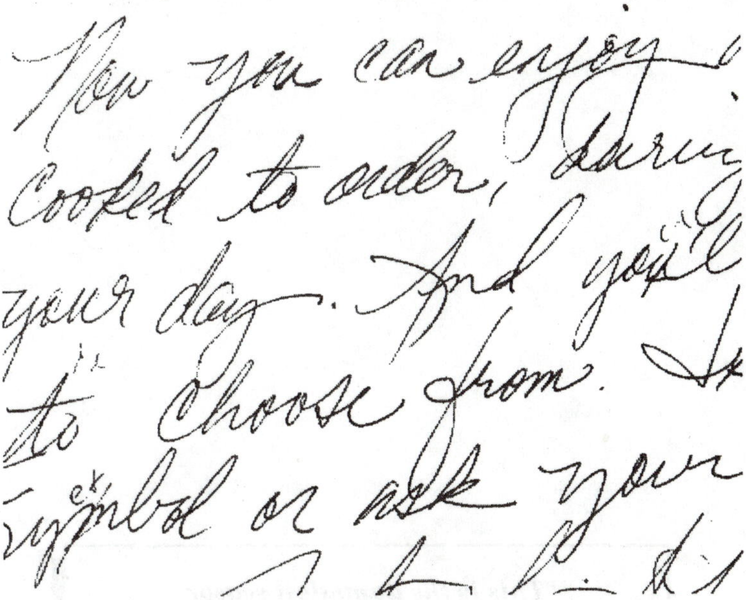

Figure 4.9: Scattered / Unfocused (actual size)

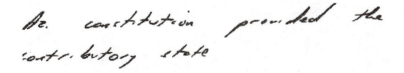

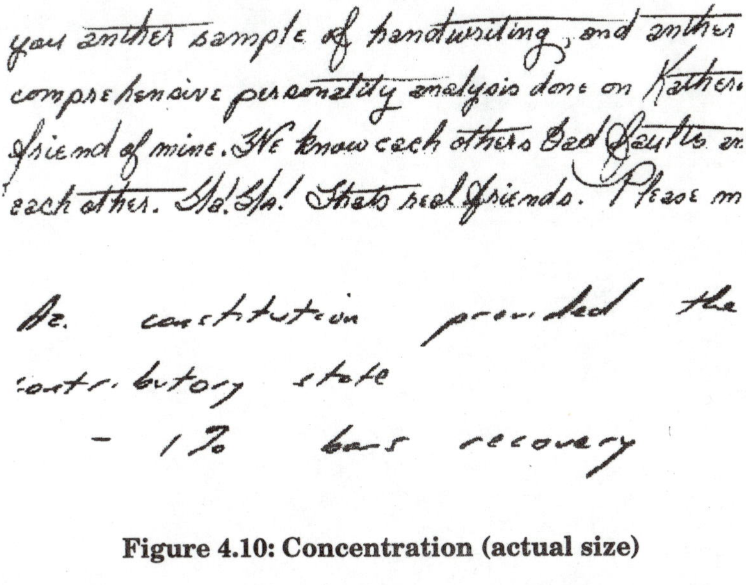

Figure 4.10: Concentration (actual size)

> *"This is the damndest season*
> *I have ever seen: The Durham Bulls*
> *can't lose and I can't get laid."*
> *— Susan Sarandon*

Chapter V

Dating Strategies

Meeting People Using Handwriting

If one of your major problems is meeting men or women, you will gain a lot from this section. I didn't start learning handwriting analysis in order to pick up women, but it helps. In fact, I once had a woman pick me up using it. I say "picking up" a bit loosely. I mean to meet a stranger and start a relationship on any level. To meet someone new, all you have to do is ask your prospect for his or her handwriting. I have found this approach is often the only way you can begin a good conversation with people who may be otherwise too busy to visit, such as waiters, waitresses, cashiers, receptionists, etc. They will take the time to talk about themselves. You can be as direct or indirect as you feel appropriate. You can say something like the following:

"Have you ever had your handwriting analyzed?"
"No."
"Write something for me and I'll tell you about yourself."

Or, if you prefer, you can elaborate a little more:
"Do you write or do you print?"
"I do both, why?"

"I just read a book that claims that by looking at someone's handwriting you can know a lot about his personality. Have you ever had your handwriting analyzed? Will you write a few sentences and sign your name? Let's see how well it really works."

It is that simple.

Why do most women who I approach write for me? Because we are going to talk about her favorite person, herself! If she says no, which she has every right to do, she is uptight, waiting on her boyfriend, or simply doesn't want to talk to me. For me, history proves it is usually the latter. If that happens to you, you are better off not wasting your time. Don't worry, it won't happen often.

The same scenario works with women meeting men. In fact, it may work even better, because all guys would love to be approached by a woman, even though it's often perceived as taboo. But if you just want to have a little fun by analyzing handwriting, then it's OK! Also, guys love to talk about themselves. For women, I want to emphasize the importance of screening out the bad apples right there on the spot. It gives you an opportunity to talk informally for a while and gain insight into his personality. Seriously, the scumbags and jerks are really insecure, overcompensating cowards. When you begin to talk about his personality from an intelligent standpoint, he will either drop the macho act and join you in an intelligent, pleasant conversation, or he'll run away, tail between his legs like the scared little boy that is hiding under all that macho bull. If a man says he doesn't write cursive, ask him how he learned to write in third grade or didn't he make it that far in school? Anyone can remember how to write cursive. It is like remembering to ride a bicycle. So, ask for a cursive sample. The sample may seem choppy and unfluid if they really haven't written cursive in years, but it still reveals the personality accurately.

By starting a conversation in this way, you've accomplished the following:

1. You broke the ice. You struck up a conversation, which is the most difficult part for most people.

2. You had a conversation about something important, personality. You spent a few minutes analyzing how he or she reacts to you. This provided the opportunity to move on to a deeper level of rapport which wouldn't have happened with the typical line, "Come here often?".

3. You gained insight into the true personality. Is he overly sensitive (big looped d's)? Does he have large sex drives (big lower loops)? Does he have major resentment or anger at women (needs a challenge), etc.? (Refer to the trait dictionary for more traits and where to find them in the handwriting.)

4. You lead the conversation and you have the choice of whether to pursue it or not. You're in control. If you don't like what you've found, you say, "Thanks! It was fun analyzing your writing. It was nice meeting you. Bye!" Otherwise, you continue the conversation looking for things in common. You now have the opportunity of starting a wonderful relationship.

Now is good a time to review some basic guidelines for approaching strangers. I know many of you don't need this advice, but for those of you who do, let's discuss it. If you must go to bars, go. Realize there are much better places to meet people, like sports clubs, associations*, charities, malls, and even grocery stores. In these environments, it isn't obvious you are out searching for a prospective date! The best place to meet strangers is a location where a friendship could develop without the presupposition that a *romance* or a *good time* is your primary motive.

One association I highly recommend is Toastmasters International. You will learn to overcome shyness, speak clearly and calmly in public, and meet new and interesting people. Call your local Chamber of Commerce for the local club information.

Approaching Strangers

One of the biggest problems singles have is approaching strangers. They feel as if they are walking into a lion's den. My perception of meeting new people is that it is fun, exciting, and challenging. I like to see how fast I can turn a complete stranger into a friend. Before you can have the opportunity to turn on any of your charm, you must take an essential step—make eye contact. A person's eyes are the window to his soul.

If everyone received an obvious invitation to come over and talk to a stranger, would it be difficult? No, it would be easy. It would be like showing up to a party with your invitation in hand, you belong there. Good eye contact is the invitation of the single's life. Before you approach anyone, you simply look for some positive eye contact that says "I noticed you," or "I approve,"or "I might be interested in getting to know you better." The most obvious invitation is positive eye contact supported by a smile. The easiest way to receive that invitation is *give positive eye contact and give a smile.* Sometimes, you won't get a smile in return; that is good because you know he or she isn't interested and you don't have to waste your time. Eye contact establishes if there's interest or not. If you read the signs correctly, you won't approach people who aren't interested. This saves you time and protects your ego. *Rejection should only hurt your feelings if someone knows you well enough to reject the real you.* Otherwise, rejection just means they are declining an opportunity to get to know the real you based on many superficial factors out of your control. The best way to increase your chances of opening a conversation is to look for and get that non-verbal invitation: eye contact. What do you do then?

You are now ready to initiate conversation because you have an invitation. But, before you walk over, use a simple visualization technique to remove any fear of rejection. Pretend you are in the front row of a movie theater. Look at the screen and see and hear a black and white film of yourself approaching the stranger. See and hear a kind, open, and personable response. Envision the person inviting your screen character to sit down and visit. See this vividly before you walk over. Once you roll this movie successfully through once or twice, simply put yourself into the scene. Roll the short film once again. But this time, *see the action from your own eyes in full living color.* Feel yourself receiving positive feedback. Imagine getting the result. Remember, if you envision yourself getting negative feedback, you cripple yourself. If you envision success, you will receive success. Now, walk over to meet.

Then, simply use the best pick up line ever: "Hi!"

You smile.

You wait for a response. Read all the non-verbal and verbal clues. Does the person want to have a conversation? Did he turn toward you? Did he smile? Did she lean forward? Did he invite you to sit down? Did she make prolonged positive eye contact with you, again? If you get positive feedback, talk about whatever you want. If you get negative feedback, leave.

Not every person will be interested in you. When an approach doesn't lead where you expected it to, don't take it personally. Don't wear your ego on your sleeve. She may not want to talk to you because you were wearing a shirt that reminds her of her ex-boyfriend. She may just be having a bad day. I have noticed a newlywed sitting alone is notoriously cold to strangers. It seems her world revolves around the ring on her finger. Most I have met rarely have the confidence to make eye contact or be too nice to a stranger. It's too bad, because there are a lot of nice people out there who just want new friends, not a new lover. Don't worry about rejection, they are rejecting an offer, not you.

If meeting people and creating chemistry are of specific interest to you, order the latest Bart Baggett catalog. It includes articles, hard to find tapes, courses, and seminars. Call 1-800-398-2278.

Overcoming Shyness

There are many various ways to change your behavior in the presence of new people. If you consider yourself shy, self-conscious, or insecure, if you have ever had second thoughts about approaching a stranger, the following mental exercise is especially for you. It is based on the science of neuro-linguistic programming and will provide a process for fast, permanent change.

The Laid-Back Pattern

This simple pattern was created by relationship counselor Ross Jeffries. Whenever you are in a situation in which you used to feel self-conscious, immediately think about a time when you felt completely powerful. Do it now. It is important for you to imagine a situation in which you felt totally confident of the outcome you were looking for as you approach the project. It could be a sports event, a test in school, or the most obvious: a time when you saw someone you liked and knew he/she would like you. As you think about that time now, notice how you feel. Notice how your body posture is. Notice your breathing patterns. Notice what you are saying to yourself inside your head. Are you saying, "Go for it, do it now, I am going to be successful?" It is imperative you fully associate yourself into a state of knowing you will succeed and feel totally confident in that past situation.

As you see that totally confident you in your mind's eye, begin to make that image bigger. See the image of you in your best clothes, most powerful posture, and with the most confident look on your face. As you feel more confident, allow that picture in your head to grow even bigger. You now see a giant you that is *unstoppable*. When you have that giant picture of you clearly in your mind's eye, come back to the situation in which you used to feel self-conscious.

Think for a minute about your internal time line. A time line is an imaginary line in your mind which represents your lifespan in the past, now , and in the future. Many people represent their time lines differently. There is no right or wrong way. Do you access things in your past from the left side of your mind or your right? Perhaps you see the past as behind you and the future as a straight line in front of you. I see my past on my left side, my future extends way out to the right. Whichever side of your brain you use to access past images, make a note of it. The next time you are ready to approach a stranger, use this knowledge in the following mental exercise. Practice in often, so it will be easy to do quickly.

See the person you want to approach. Fully associate the giant you in your mind's eye. When you totally feel like the giant you, multiply the giant image by 100 times going off into the past of your time line. Have you ever stood between two mirrors? The reflections seemed to go on forever? Use the image and place all one hundred of those giant images right behind the shoulder of the person you want to meet. This is the most important part: *Lean the image of yourself back 30 degrees*. Did you notice how relaxed you feel when you lean back. You don't seem as anxious. Do it now, lean back all the giant images behind the person you are about to approach. You feel laid-back and relaxed.

Before you walk over and say, "Hi," do one more thing. Just above the other shoulder you can envision your most appealing outcome. If kissing motivates you, envision that person kissing you with all the passion of a Harlequin novel. If having sex motivates you, image yourself naked as a jaybird having wild sex with the person. Take this new and motivating image and place it just above the shoulder of the person you are about to go talk to on the future side of your time line. As you see both the images of you as a confident giant totally laid back on one side and your possible result on the other, *you will feel so empowered that a successful encounter is guaranteed. Take action.* Go say, "Hi." Use the laid-back pattern on yourself whenever you have second thoughts about approaching a stranger. The results will amaze you.

Flirting Successfully

Flirting is an integral part of meeting new people. You can meet people all day long in a business context, but never end up with a date. Both men and women should be aware of the importance of flirting. So far, we have discussed various methods of approaching prospects as well as the attitude you must carry. But when it comes to flirting, men and women must behave differently. Males must undersell themselves, while female flirts must oversell themselves. Neither should ever be obnoxious. Because men have traditionally had the role of approaching and initiating contact, men are more sensitive to rejection. Therefore, women must make it clear they are interested. A male must not be as obvious. Remember the Economics of Love principle discussed earlier.

Male Flirting Techniques

- Keep her curious and challenged–
  Make her wonder if you really like her.
  Make her work for it!
- Be protective-like a big brother–
  But not jealous. This makes her feel safe.
- Focus on the woman and tune out the world–
  This shows her she is important, not just a toy.
- Have good manners–
  Nothing turns a woman off more than a loud belch!
- Project confidence, ease, and stability.
- Reveal <u>something</u> about yourself–
  This shows inner strength,confidence, and the
  capacity for intimacy.
- Seem dependable and honest–
  There are enough flakes.
- Talk about important issues–
  Not mundane things. Avoid superficial B.S.
- Use a soft and gentle tone of voice.
  Not an anxious or nervous tone.

Figure 5.1: Male Flirting Techniques

Men who get the most from flirting tend not to advertise their strengths. They create a curiosity about themselves. Part of the magic formula for a male flirt is not to appear as if he is flirting. I have listed specific qualities of a successful male flirt. Some of the Flirting techniques listed here were adapted from Joyce Jillson's book *The Fine Art Of Flirting.*

As you know, patience and a low-key flirting technique are the criteria for the successful male flirt, exactly the opposite is true for women. Women must be repetitious with their flirting gestures because men fear rejection so much. Men need four or five reassuring signals that you are flirting–an invitation of a sort. These signals should be short and sweet. You don't want to be easy,

---

A Successful Female Flirt

• Appear successful–
   But don't compete with a man.
• Be discreet–
   Men like to think women keep secrets.
• Maintain a neat, clean appearance–
   Unless you want to attract pond scum.
• Make slow catlike movements–
   This is subconsciously very feminine and sexy.
• Make prolonged eye contact with a slight devious smile–
   This makes him wonder what you are thinking.
• Primp–
   This shows your femininity.
• She never offends a man's sense of pride or masculinity–
   Men have sensitive egos; never upstage his manliness!
• Walk with self-confidence–
   But don't be cocky.
• Maintain poise and composure–
   It shows class, and you will look good to his friends.

Figure 5.2: Female Flirting Techniques

just make it obvious you are flirting. Successful female flirts tend to make bold yet quick gestures, whereas men must be subtle or else be perceived as too aggressive.

Women can be bold, but must back off completely. The best flirt I have ever seen walked up to me, flirted for a few seconds, and then disappeared. She unexpectedly reappeared, gave me total attention, and then vanished. The obvious flirtation gave me permission to talk with her, but her walking away made me curious if she was just flirting or if she was really interested. This is the key for a female flirt. Over-exaggerate the flirtatious signal, but don't hold it for very long. The secret is quick but bold flirtations. Give a generous space between the flirting signals (at least 3-5 minutes). This is so the guy wonders if it was his imagination or if you were really flirting, otherwise a woman appears too bold.

Once you begin a conversation, realize both of you have ulterior motives beside simply visiting. You are actually interviewing to determine if the person is the kind of person you like. And, like it or not, they are doing the same to you. Two important things you can do after making the initial contact are: 1) develop rapport, and 2) investigate their personality.

> *"Love's greatest miracle is the curing of coquetry."*
> — *Francois, Duc De La Rochefoucauld, 1613*

Special Supplement for the Confused Man
If you are a man, you must realize very few women are cruising around looking for sex; they don't need to. It isn't that women are not interested in a physical relationship—they are. They enjoy sex, sure, but they want it only in a certain context. The context usually involves *sincere* mutual appreciation and trust.

Be aware of your first impressions on women. They are smarter than many guys give them credit for. In fact, women don't mind letting those macho–jerk types think they're not aware of what's going on. Don't be surprised if you buy her drinks all night and then she slips out the back door! You deserved it! The fact is, if you are thinking about getting a woman into bed, you are a fool if you think she doesn't realize it. Women can smell insincerity a block away! Don't be a sleaze. Don't be after a one night stand. If you are thinking about sex, women can sense it. This attitude usually doesn't work and makes you look stupid. Besides, is cheap sex really what you want?

Have you ever noticed women really dig guys that don't even try? I have. I thought it wasn't fair. It's not that the men didn't try, but they didn't seem to need a woman that night! These men are laid back, patient, and confident they deserve a good woman. They have confidence that they will get what they want. You can approach as many women as you want, but change your mindset from getting laid to getting to know her. Then you will have success at both, if that is what you want. First impressions are important. If you use the handwriting to break the ice, the first impression is you want to get to know her mind, not just her body.

If you are a woman, be easy on the guys. Not all men are con artists! Some guys are really sincere, but are just unaware of the image they are projecting. Be direct, but kind, with this type. You have every right to say that you are not interested. In fact, it is encouraged. There is no reason to lead a guy on when you feel from the start he's not good enough to kiss the soles of your shoes. Many guys are very insecure and getting harshly rejected will not only bruise their ego, but it makes them resent all women.

> **"Sex: the thing that takes up the least amount of time and causes the most amount of trouble."**
> — *John Barrymore*

Talking to Strangers – The Conversation

After you have made a successful approach, you have to take it in for a landing. The initial conversation sets the tone to taxi home or abort the mission. As mentioned, I recommend talking about handwriting rather early in the conversation. If you choose to turn the conversation to handwriting, tell the person what their writing reveals, ask if it is true, sit back and listen. After you have seen so much about a person in five minutes, you will be surprised how much more they tell you if you ask the right questions. This is when you make the transition from "parlor game" to "I'm seriously interested in who you are."

Don't make the mistake of getting so interested in analyzing the writing that you bullet straight through, never allowing a conversation to develop. This has happened to me. I give her an incredibly accurate analysis, I like what I see in her writing, I look up after I'm all done and what does she say? She says "Thank you, that was fun"...and walks off. But it was my fault because I was thinking about impressing her with my knowledge instead of developing rapport.

Don't make the same mistake. As you look at each trait, get her involved in looking at the writing and/or elaborating on what it reveals. By the time you've discussed a few of the major personality traits, you both know a lot about each other.

Your job when first meeting a new person is to intrigue him or her enough to spark curiosity about you. That's it. If it is appropriate to exchange phone numbers to get that opportunity to satisfy the curiosity, do so.

Men always ask me what the handwriting reveals about sex drives. Since it is such a popular topic, I will explain that it is possible to find out about a person's sex life, if that is your interest. By casually mentioning the way the lower loops are shaped, you can reveal what it means with regard to someone's relationships and sex drives (see sex drives chapter). Don't force the issue. But if you get a smile and some positive non-verbal response simply pace the response and lead with another question, giving them a chance to elaborate. This is the part of the conversation where you find out if he/she has a girlfriend or boyfriend. (And if so... find out if he/she is happy or not!)

As you analyze this person's writing, you are seeing a side of him not everyone sees. You are developing deep levels of rapport, instantly. You must respect that. You must genuinely be interested in the person. Handwriting reveals deep, dark issues. I once made a waitress start crying hysterically because I mentioned an issue with her father who happened to have recently passed away. Be sure you are diplomatic.

Don't ever use the information you discover against someone. Do not disclose what you learned to others and don't embarrass anyone. Remember, you are trying to be a friend. You are dealing with delicate emotions and feelings. The more diplomatic, sensitive, and genuine you can be while analyzing writing, the more they will assume you will be that way as a friend, and maybe a lover. It shows a real lack of integrity to use such personal information found in handwriting to hurt someone, so use this powerful tool with integrity.

Romance vs. Manipulation
I was recently at the filming of the T.V. talk show "The Montel Williams Show." The topic of the show that day was starting relationships. They had a hypnotist who claimed he could use forms of hypnosis to speed up the process of getting a girl sexually attracted to him. Another panel member explained some techniques for making a man fall in love with you. What she did was study some of the subconscious reasons that men and women felt chemistry. She then explained the reasons so the women could create a situation where the man would feel those desired emotions. I was shocked at the audience's reaction. Some were

offended by the concept of creating romance by hypnosis, awareness, or any conscious effort. They insisted on holding to the belief
that you had to fall in love ignorant of what was really happening.

Ask yourself to honestly look at the first stages of a new relationship. Do you dress up, wear cologne, drive a certain car, go to
candle-light dinners, walk on a moonlit beach? I do. Am I
artificially inducing the environment? Yes! And it works. It's
called *romance*. Yet, if I slowly touch a woman's hand in a certain
manner, with the knowledge that she will be sexually aroused,
some people call that manipulation. I don't agree. Knowledge is
often like a car: you can use it to successfully take you where you
need to go, or you can swerve off the road and hurt someone. With
knowledge comes *responsibility*. The knowledge in this book, and
the Creating Chemistry chapter upcoming, is intended to be used
to assist you in finding and embarking on a successful relationship, not to manipulate and hurt people.

Meeting the Lover of Your Dreams

Let's take a look at the fine art of courting. First, the oh-so-complex
meeting stage. My advice is to just do it. Focus on the outcome you
want, not the outcome you fear. You can meet people just about
anywhere you go, if you are aware of how to do it. Take notice of
people's first impressions of you. Do you look rebellious, slovenly,
conservative, cocky, goofy, unhealthy, or mean? Most people make
quick judgements, then spend the next few weeks trying to prove
their first impression was accurate.

You need to be aware of your first impression. If you are not
successful with the image you are projecting; change it. Men don't
need to spend hundreds of dollars on GQ high fashion. No one
wears those clothes in the real world anyway. If you do, you are
obviously trying too hard. Here is the final word on fashion. Go
to a place where you see women you would like to date. Look at the
way the guys are dressed and who they are with. Model success.
Look around you. If the guys with all the beautiful women are

Basis for a lasting relationship.

dressing a certain way, take notice. You should dress in a similar fashion as these "babe magnets." If you are wearing thongs and plaid shirts when the cool guys are wearing cowboy boots and Levis, change clothes. If you look like a dork, you will attract more dorks. The clothes aren't important, nor is your face. The important thing is your attitude, and clothes are a reflection of that attitude. It is as easy as that. Women should use the same modeling techniques. Find a woman you respect and model her dress and attitude. Do as she does and you will get similar results.

Have you ever noticed that some of the most heinous guys are with beautiful women? Why? The first thing you must realize and accept as truth is, men do not have to be attractive physically to be attractive to gorgeous women. For women, it is a little different. Men place a woman's appearance high on the scale of important factors. But, from the woman's view, physical looks are less important because men can make it up in charm, success, confidence, power, money, style, humor, or any other unique characteristic.

Whatever the reason, looks seem to be more important to men.

If you don't believe me, take Billy Joel and his beautiful wife Christi Brinkley as an example. Billy looks about as average as my local mechanic. But Christi is sweet, rich, successful, drop-dead beautiful, and in love with Billy. I happen to love Billy Joel's music and have always respected him. I respect him even more now that he's married to her. He knows he deserves the best in this life, and can have it. His talent and attitude is his key to success, not his looks. Use this principle to your advantage.

People view you about the same way you view yourself. If your self-esteem is high, people perceive you as better looking. Crazy but true. The famous plastic surgeon Maxwell Maltz wrote a book entitled *Pyscho–Cybernetics*. In it, he documents numerous cases of men and women having plastic surgery which made their faces and bodies beautiful according to today's society. Yet, after the changes were made, the patient's life didn't change. What's more, the clients who saw themselves as unattractive before the surgery still saw themselves as unattractive afterwards. Their new features didn't change their perception of themselves.

Our internal self-representations create the image we project to others. Therefore, whether you think others find you attractive or unattractive, if you *begin now to see yourself as very attractive*, then others will view you that way, too. In reality, the color of your skin and the shape of your bones only affect someone's first impression. Personality can make an average person beautiful or a beautiful person heinous!

"Personality can make an average person beautiful or a beautiful person heinous!"
— Bart A. Baggett

Offering Something of Value

A woman wants a new relationship (i.e., a man) to bring something better to her life. If you seem boring, mundane, average, or scared... what can you bring into her life, but more problems. The corporate world refers to this special quality in business ventures as the Unique Selling Position (USP). The theory applies not only to marketing razors and widgets but to marketing yourself as well.

What makes you unique? You need to offer something different than everyone else is offering. If you are a man, you must realize women are looking for more than a chance to have sex. The fact is, they deserve more. I know this is a fact because I constantly talk to women about it. One example comes to mind. There was a cute cocktail waitress I had met at a jazz club by analyzing her handwriting. (I did just what I say in this book, asked her for her handwriting and told her about herself.) She was fascinated. As the night went on, she kept ignoring her other customers to talk to me.

The band eventually stopped playing and it was time for me to leave. I had a choice: Do I get her phone number right then, or do I come back another day? As I recalled the stinger in her handwriting, I decided to wait. (The stinger is the "needs a challenge" stroke.) So when she wasn't looking, I snuck out. This sent a clear message that I didn't *need* her and I wasn't desperate. I returned six days later and at the door she practically threw herself at me. She then slipped her phone number to me the minute I sat down. I was with another woman, too! The point of this story is to realize why she was so interested in me. When we were on our first date, she said, "I meet guys all night long with nothing but bullshit to say to me. 99.9% of these guys just want to screw me. You were different, you had something to offer." This is the paradox about courting a good-looking woman who is exposed to hundreds of sexually frustrated men a week. Men need to set themselves apart. Women are not interested in meeting another hard-up loser.

I once said to a male client who was experiencing a sexual deficit, "Sometimes in order to have sex with a woman, you have to make her think you don't want to." This quote is an example of the "Economics of Love" theory. Supply and demand. The harder you are to get, the more women will pay attention. Remember, if a woman is attractive, she can get sex any day of the week. She doesn't need you to offer her that. Offer a woman something most other guys don't: sincerity, respect, and a challenge.

What Is Your USP?

What is the most desirable quality in your personality? What is your *Unique Selling Position?*

Part of the answer is *attitude..* Some men want to get a woman to give in and *let him have sex with her.* These guys see sex as a goal they win by manipulating a woman. Just like in a sports game, they score only after hard work, aggressive behavior, and overcoming resistance. This whole perspective implies the woman doesn't want to participate. Personally, I don't find it gratifying to manipulate a woman into doing something she wouldn't normally do. I do find it gratifying when, through my own personality, communication skills, and charm, she is so attracted to me that she wants to be *with* me. In fact, it is a real nice feeling.

If a man must have a goal, it should be to get a woman to *want* to have sex with him, instead of to *let* him have sex with her. The entire perception that one is giving the other anything is a faulty mind set. A sexual encounter is a shared one in which both willingly participate. If your perception is not that way, I suggest you reframe it immediately.

When you make sex the issue, you are playing a game– a game you can't both win. Your goal is to establish rapport and be interpersonally attractive. As you become more selective, your prospects will sense that, thus increasing your USP.

The Challenge Game

"I want a challenge," cries the lonely girl after dumping yet another loser. The element of having a challenge is important to many people in a relationship. You've heard the saying that good girls want bad boys. Well, it usually seems this way. Perhaps the ideal guy would be a tough, long-haired guy in a leather jacket and boots who drives a motorcycle, sends flowers for no reason and calls when he says he will. If he exists, he's taken.

When you are courting, the single most self-defeating move you can make is to throw yourself on the person you like. I don't just mean physically. I've known men whose first words out of their mouths after meeting a woman are, "You are so beautiful, I'm in love with you." And they proceed to smother the poor woman from the first sentence. And if you do it physically, that's even worse. I've personally had several women verify this notion. One had a date with a good-looking guy she was very attracted to. But, the guy attacked her before the appetizers arrived. "He touched me as if I was his own petting toy," she said, adding, "I thought I liked him before he mauled me. Now, he's never going to get it. Never."

Most men know this is bad strategy, if not just stupid. But few understand the reasons why. The reason is known as the "Give me a challenge or give me death" syndrome. This society has a big dose of it. If everyone in the world had diamonds growing from their trees, the value of diamonds wouldn't be very much. The same supply and demand economic theory applies to the value of a person's affection. If he gives it away so easily, it can't be worth very much. Any woman can get some slimeball in a bar to grope at her and put his hands all over her for the night. The same holds

> *"The more selective a person is,*
> *the more selection that person has."*
> *— Bart A. Baggett*

true for a woman. When a woman acts easy–sleazy, she turns away the quality men.

I subscribe to a procedure which has always worked. When you get a person's phone number for the first time, don't call right away. Wait a couple of days before you call. This time delay will increase the curiosity about you. It will make her wonder if you are still interested. Then, when you call, it is a surprise. After all, every other Aqua Velva called her before she woke up the next morning begging her for a date.

What if she isn't home and you get her answering machine? What do you do? Hang up. *Never leave a message on an answering machine if you haven't had a date yet.* If you leave a message, the ball is in her court. You want to keep the ball in your court. You call every day until you catch her at home, then act like it is the first time you called. Nothing can be worse for a woman to come home and find three (pathetic and lonely) messages from the same guy she doesn't even know on her machine. It decreases the man's worth because his supply has increased without a responding request for demand. I've seen this happen with both men and women. There is another reason this theory works. She can't <u>not</u> call you back if you don't leave a message. This will help you keep your confidence. After you have gone out on a date and established whether or not you might have something going, then you can leave a message. But don't leave more than one without getting a return phone call. The moment you sound desperate, she will find a guy who isn't. Don't let a little thing like an answering machine make you appear weak.

Selective Reinforcement

A good relationship is sometimes like a slot machine in Las Vegas. One partner isn't sure when the other is going to pay off with a compliment or other positive feedback. Have you ever wondered why millions of people a year put money into a machine, pull a handle, and watch three wheels spin around?

The answer lies in one of the oldest psychological experiments. Years ago, they put a rooster in a cage with a lever. Each time he pecked the lever, he would get a piece of food. Once it became a habit, they selectively gave the rooster food. Sometimes when he pecked the lever, he got food. Other times when he pecked the lever, he got nothing. Much like a slot machine. A funny thing happened, the rooster kept pecking the lever. It seems that the chance of receiving the treat is more motivating than a consistent response.

In a relationship, this behavior rings a bell. Most women who admit to dating jerks invariably say, "He's a jerk, but not always. Sometimes he is nice." On the other hand, the nice guys are always nice. We can learn something from the rooster and the multi-billion dollar slot machine business. You should reinforce the behavior you want, but do it *selectively*. This way, the person will consistently do the behavior hoping for the reward. It works in Vegas, it can work on your next date.

> *"The course of true love never did run smooth."*
> *— William Shakespeare,*
> *A Midsummer Night's Dream*

> *"The happiest conversation is that of which*
> *nothing is distinctly remembered,*
> *but a general effect of pleasing impression."*
> *— Samual Johnson*

Chapter VI

Creating Chemistry

Developing Rapport

What is it that makes two people have chemistry and other people have no spark? The answer lies in non-verbal communication. Research states over 80% of all communication is non-verbal. Most people spend the time getting to know someone by just using their voices to compare brain content. This is not what makes chemistry. Let's face it, the great romances of history were not based on intellectual stimuli. In fact, the proverbial sweeping her off her feet is more often done with a sultry glance than a loquacious dialogue. So, instead of studying <u>what</u> you are saying, let's look at <u>how</u> you are saying it.

Have you ever gone dancing and ended up falling in lust on the dance floor? I have. What happens on a dance floor is a fast- paced version of what happens when two people connect over time. The beat of the music paces both of you so your bodies display the same movement, rhythm, and even breathing patterns. When this happens, you may find yourself thinking, "He sure is a good dancer!" You think he is a good dancer because he is doing just what you are doing. At the end of the song, or two songs, your body language implies that you two go together like peanut butter and jelly. If you stop to ask your mind why, you couldn't explain it. It's just... chemistry.

Chemistry Is Rapport
What is rapport? Rapport is the ability to enter someone else's world and make them feel you understand them.

Overall, who is attractive to you? What kind of people do you enjoy spending time with? Is it someone who disagrees with you on everything, has totally different beliefs and values, and who dislikes doing the things you love to do? Of course not. We want to be with people who are like us and yet unique. We want to be with people whom we share a common bond. There is some truth to the phrase, "opposites attract." The elements of difference add excitement, but without a foundation of commonality, the attraction soon fades.

So how do we create this special state of mind called rapport? In simple terms, we create rapport by experiencing things that we have in common. Most people think this is best done through words. You can use words to discuss common friends, common experiences, or similar beliefs. Discussing the fact that you went to the same college and had the same teacher only scratches the surface of true rapport. You have communicated through words some common elements. Why isn't it enough?

Studies have proven that only 7 percent of what is *communicated* between people is transmitted through words. Thirty eight percent of communication comes through the *tone* of voice. Remember your Mom calling your name in *that* tone of voice—you knew you were in trouble. Didn't you? No other words were needed. Fifty five percent of communication, the largest part, is transmitted through physiology, meaning body language: facial expressions, gestures, and other non-verbal body movements. Did your dad have a certain "You're in deep trouble now" look? His mouth tensed up and his eyes cut through you like knives. He didn't have to say a word, but you knew you were grounded for life. UCLA researchers revealed words are the least-utilized means of communication. Below is the breakdown of how we really communicate.

Transmission of Human Communication	
7%	Words (What we say)
38%	Tonality (How we say it)
55%	Physiology (Body Language)

Why Some Get It, And Some Don't

If we try to develop rapport just by using words and the content of our conversation, we are using only 7 percent of our capacity to communicate. That makes us look pretty ignorant when you remember scientists already say we use less than 10% of our brain capacity! It makes me feel a little more competent since I am aware of how to communicate using the other 93%. However, the scientists never told me how to gain access to the other 90% of my brain! Don't despair, the following section will show you how to gain access to the lost 93% of your communication style. As far as your brain... that's up to you.

The vast majority of communication or impressions of people are a result of the things you unconsciously notice. You have the ability to communicate with someone's subconscious mind without their even knowing it. The following pages explain a very powerful technique to get rapport with almost anyone, even difficult people. While words work on the conscious mind, pacing, matching and mirroring tonality and physiology works on the unconscious mind. When done properly, their brain will be thinking "Hey, this person is just like me. He must be okay!" Once this happens, there is a bond—rapport.

"Love is the merest look, the lightest touch, The thought almost too subtle to recall, When love is deepest, words may be too much." — Kathi Coolidge

Matching to Develop Rapport

Sometimes you will be in situations where you think you want to meet someone, but all the prospects seem cold as a fish. What do you do then? This happened to me recently in a New York City bar named The Whisky. It is a really trendy hip bar where all the waitresses wear one-piece velvet kitty suits. When I asked the waitress what she called her outfit, she responded bitterly, "Obscene!" I was sitting with my friend Paul looking at the sights. Our waitress was friendly, but was wearing a wedding ring. It wasn't a small wedding ring, it was huge. She was very married. We jokingly say, "The bigger the rock, the bigger the commitment." This woman was *very* married.

This bar seemed to be a hang out for the young socially hip crowd of New York. Since I was a visitor, I didn't know anyone and no one seemed interested in knowing me. We tried to make eye contact with the people around us, but nothing sparked. After the traditional approaches, we decided to resort to the old standard — analyzing handwriting. Our waitress and the hostess were both leaning against the couch next to our table ignoring our attempts to gain eye contact. Paul leaned toward her, tapped her on the shoulder and asked her for a sample of her handwriting. She asked the usual questions with a bitter attitude, as if we were just trying to pick her up. (Which as true!) It was a short conversation, and she went back to the bar. About ten minutes later, she was back hanging out with her friends, ignoring us. Paul decided there weren't any good prospects in this bar, so he left to make a phone call. I told him I would meet him in the lobby of our hotel, which was next door, in a few minutes. After he had gone, I tried to start a conversation again. Both her and her friend acted like it was a chore to turn their necks around to acknowledge my presence. I figured I wasn't making any new friends that night.

After I finished my drink, I got up and headed for the door. Just as I was leaving, the hostess stopped me. She said, "You're not leaving are you? You said you would analyze my handwriting." I looked at her peculiarly. She was still cold, but wanted a free analysis. I said, in the same tonality she had spoken to me,"Why should I analyze your handwriting? Both you and your friend have been total bitches to us all evening. I'm one of the best handwriting analysts in the country. I offered to analyze yours for free, and you took 15 minutes to rudely acknowledge my presence. I don't think so. Go buy my book!" Then I turned to walk away. She grabbed my arm and moved around in front of my path.

I stopped and looked at her again. Her body was open and facing toward me. She smiled with an innocence. She even put a look of sympathy on her face as she said, "I'm sorry I was rude. I really want you to do my handwriting. I'm new in town and they told me being a bitch was the only way to keep guys from hitting on me. Please." And she handed me the napkin with her handwriting.

Again, I copied her tonality and attitude, "OK, since you asked so nicely. By the way, what's your name?" Her name was Vicky, and she was from South Carolina. Since I used to live in Texas, I could relate to the shock of the New York attitude compared to the typical Southerner's. We talked and I analyzed her handwriting. She told me she hadn't dated since she moved to the city and didn't want to. However, she said she wanted to see me the next time I visited New York. As she was writing down her phone number my buddy Paul walked back into the bar. He looked at her, looked at me, looked at the phone number, and the look on his face said, "Why are you talking to that bitch?" His perception changed as she extended her hand to introduce herself.

Paul was surprised I had developed rapport after such a cold first encounter. After I explained to him what I did, he understood completely. After all, he is an expert in rapport skills, too. I simply mirrored her attitude; I was just as bitchy as she was. Once I did this, we had rapport. She felt as if I was just like her. After we met on that level, she dropped the mean exterior. Vicky was a sweet woman and I'm glad I was smart enough to be rude to her!

"I Feel As Though I've Known You For Years."

Every human has hundreds of conscious and unconscious communication patterns. One of the problems in human communication is that we tend to operate in our own patterns instead of the other person's patterns. It is evident in poor performance in sales, dating, and relationships. When we become aware of others' patterns and we match or mirror those patterns, it is called pacing. When you pace someone, you get into rhythm with the person on as many levels as possible: getting into an ebb and flow of how the person thinks, acts, and processes data. By pacing someone's patterns, powerful rapport can be developed. When you are mirroring a person in such a way that you are talking the way he or she talks, sitting the way he or she is sitting, moving in the general patterns he or she is moving, breathing in the same general rhythms, and appearing to share the same values, you are pacing and thus establishing rapport.

You don't have to mirror everything about another person to get rapport. But if you could, do you know what happens? People will absolutely adore you. They will feel they've known you for years. They will feel as though you are their best friend, someone who totally understands them, someone with whom they share a deep common bond. But you don't have to mirror everything about a person to create rapport. Just the tone of voice and similar facial expressions, for example, are usually enough to build rapport with most people.

Animal Magnetism?

Before understanding rapport theory, many years ago, people thought a person either had charm or didn't, as if it was based on some sort of animal magnetism or mystical hypnotic ability. The great lovers were thought to possess this power. It wasn't magnetism. It was (and is) the ability of conscious and unconscious pacing of behavior patterns. People who are skilled at building rapport pace unconsciously. Studies have shown there is a difference between people who are highly successful in influencing and those who are not successful in influencing others. The people who are less successful tend to establish only a small amount of rapport before they move into their influence strategies: sales pitch, come-on, passes, etc. Conversely, successful influencers are people who develop a very strong rapport based on several levels <u>before</u> using any particular influence strategy. This does not mean they spend an excessive amount of time establishing rapport; it is possible to build strong rapport on many levels in only several minutes. It is simply a matter of pacing effectively on a number of levels. N.L.P labels a variety of pacing techniques: Emotional Pacing, Tone and Tempo Pacing, Language Pacing, and Pacing Physiology. The way I got rapport with Vicky the hostess in the last example was by using Emotional Pacing and Tone and Tempo Pacing. The essence of developing rapport is being flexible in your behavior to match their behavior. You will often have to adjust and change your approach with each of the responses you get. Remember, rapport is above all a ferocious commitment to be flexible. If what you are doing isn't getting the results you want, change your approach. You only truly fail when you give up. Each time you try something and it doesn't work, you just learned another way to get a specific response. Change your approach until you get the desired response. Rapport requires flexibility.

How I Gained Rapport with a Harley-Riding Cowboy

I remember a business negotiation where this came in very handy. When I first developed the Grapho-Deck, I needed a manufacturer. Because the Grapho-Deck is sixty different cards with different handwriting/personality traits on each card, I thought a playing card manufacturer could handle the job. I visited a card manufacturing plant outside Forth Worth, Texas, one rainy winter afternoon. Terry was the sales representative assigned to me. Terry was about 6 feet tall, two hundred fifty pounds, bearded, and pure cowboy. I had worn a suit, tie, and my penny loafers. Above Terry's desk was a Polaroid picture of his Harley-Davidson motorcycle and his ex-wife sporting a leather bra and two tattoos. I could see we were very different, but Terry didn't have to know that.

I immediately took off my tie and jacket and put on my best "good–ole–boy Texas accent." By the time we toured the factory he had given me a good idea of the price my Grapho-Decks would cost. However, I wasn't through. We decided to go to lunch at a local Mexican restaurant. I ordered the same thing as he did and totally mirrored the guy in every detail. Every time he took a sip, I took a sip. We talked about Harley-Davidsons and drank beer.

When he leaned back, I leaned back. When his voice went soft, mine went soft. Toward the end of the meal, he stopped in mid-sentence and said, "Man, it seems like I've known you for yours. Some people are like business acquaintances. I feel like you're a real friend." After he said that, I knew it was just a matter of time until he gave me the best price in town on my Grapho-Decks. In fact, not only did I get a great price, I left with two posters and 15 decks of cards for my friends. This stuff works like magic.

> *"When the eyes say one thing and the tongue another, a practiced man relies on the first."*
> *— Ralph Waldo Emerson*

How to Make Someone Really Dislike You

Have you ever met someone who rubs you the wrong way but you can't put your finger on why? I've heard women refer to men as having a certain sleaze factor. When I asked them exactly what elements added up to this sleaze factor, they rarely had a specific answer. They said, "It's just an overall feeling of sleaziness. It wasn't what he said, it was the way he said it." What happens in this situation is the guy is mis-matching the women. He is doing everything *not* to gain rapport, non-verbally. Perhaps he touches her shoulder when she doesn't want to be touched, therefore totally violating her space. He may even talk really fast when she talks really slow. There are a million ways to mismatch someone to create a feeling of discomfort. I suggest you learn to avoid all of them.

I remember a situation in which describes a classic case of *not* developing rapport. It was during my college days back in Malibu. One night I was sitting alone in the library reading the newspaper. An acquaintance of mine came over to talk to me. He was an old teammate of mine when I played collegiate lacrosse. He was obviously disturbed about something, but not angry. He stood in front of me looking down. I sat there calmly with the paper in my hand and said, "Sure, tell me what's on your mind." The gist of his complaint was that he had heard I had said something bad about his fraternity. As he was explaining the story, his physiology changed. He began breathing very fast and his face turned red. He began talking faster, really getting involved in the story. As he was getting extremely emotionally involved in his anger about what I had supposedly said, I mismatched him. In other words, I did everything completely opposite. Each time he raised his voice, I lowered mine. My body stayed rigidly straight. In fact, I sat like a stone sculpture as he talked himself into a rage. I did everything opposite, I even told him the situation was of little importance to me, when he obviously felt it was the end of the world. *It is important to ackowledge someone's emotional state.* In fact, I can't think of one thing I did or said which would have developed rapport!

Learn from my mistakes, don't ever mismatch an angry person! The story ends by him becoming so infuriated, he began pushing his finger in my chest. By that time, it was too late to develop rapport. When I pushed his hand out of the way, he got more physical–we wrestled to the ground. We made a big scene in the library and eventually got pulled off each other. Neither one of us got hurt in the fight. Regardless, it should never have happened. Before the incident, we considered each other friends. He wasn't a bully and I wasn't quick-tempered. The only reason a small discussion inflated to a fist-fight was that we completely mismatched each other!

If I had known the essence of developing rapport at that time, I would have matched his body language, voice tone, and attitude. First, I would have stood up. Standing above someone gives a false sense of superiority. If I had stood up, we would have been equal to begin the discussion and his anger wouldn't have been supported by a false feeling of power. The second mistake I made was letting him do all the talking. I should have become just as excited and told him how awful this situation was. As he got excited, I should have gotten excited, moved my arms and said, "I can see why you're so angry. I'm angry too. That really would piss me off." By matching and mirroring his physiology I could have developed rapport. Although the rapport was an angry state, he would have perceived that I felt just like he did. Then, I could have used more advanced rapport skills to lead him away from the angry state into a calmer state. This is called pacing and then leading, which can only be achieved by first attaining a solid state of rapport. In this case, my lack of understanding the non-verbal communication patterns caused an argument, a fight, and the loss of a friend.

They Will Only Notice How Much They Like You

If you think the act of pacing or mirroring is obvious, you're wrong. People usually don't have a clue you are mirroring their physiology. I remember during a seminar when this point was driven home. We were discussing how you can talk with someone's tone and tempo to develop rapport. The audience believed the person you were mirroring would think you were making fun of them. A man from New York stood up and said in his typical fast-paced New York accent "Ain't no way you kued tak to me that way, an I not know wa you were doin!" I responded with the same fast tempo accent. "You may be right, man. I was in NuYawk just last week. A lady asked me if I had a quota foe do meeta and I told her to piss off. She didn't notice how I said it." The entire audience laughed hysterically and the guy from New York sat there with a dumb look on his face. Then, a man in a cowboy hat raised his hand and asked sincerely in a slow Southern drawl, "Yer tell'n meee, he didn't even know you was makin fun of 'em?" I said in the same accent, slow pace and tonality, "Yer ab-soooo-lutely right,sir. He didn't haf the faww-giest I-dear." The cowboy looked at me a bit confused as the entire audience laughed hysterically. It was obvious to onlookers what I was doing, but not to the people I was mirroring. You don't have to go to that extreme; I was making a point. But realize using your rapport skills effectively, you are communicating positive feelings directly to someone's unconscious mind. By using your voice effectively, you can pace without mimicking, but match as closely as possible the tone and tempo of the person you are talking with, and greatly enhance rapport.

You Now Know How To Create Chemistry
This chapter has briefly outlined part of the neuro-analysis technology about creating chemistry*. Chemistry is actually the romantic word for sexual rapport. It is wonderful feeling connected to another person in a deep state of mutual attraction. These simple rapport building techniques can help you gain access to this pleasurable state whenever and with whoever you choose. Using these chemistry building skills and handwriting analysis, you will be able to create that magical state called chemistry between yourself and anyone you choose.

The subject of creating chemistry and falling in love is an ongoing field of research for me. The sophisticated techniques of NLP and Time-Line can create dramatic and lasting states of attraction almost instantly. Although I do not have room to explore these concepts thoroughly in this book, I do offer special reports, articles, audio tapes, video tapes, and seminars that show you exactly how to create sexual chemistry with anyone you choose. If you find yourself wondering what else there is to learn about this topic, please call for my Special Report and current catalog of new books, tapes, and products. Call 1-800-398-2278.

"Fear always springs from ignorance."
— Ralph Waldo Emerson

Chapter VII

Fears & Insecurities

People spend a great deal of time worrying about things that never happen. Many people worry about what other people think of them. Some are concerned that their loved one will leave. Others feel threatened at the first sign of change. In life, we tend to be motivated in two ways. The first is to move toward something which is pleasurable. The second is to move away from something which is painful. Think about every decision you make every day. Did you get out of bed this morning because you were completely passionate to start another day? Or, did you get out of bed because your boss causes you great pain if you are late? These are two different motivational strategies. Think about which one is stronger in your life in various situations. The answer will give you the key to motivate yourself into action you previously wouldn't have done. For example, many people fear being rejected so much that they let the opportunity to meet someone new pass them by. If pain is the primary motivational factor in this situation, simply ask yourself how much pain you will have the rest of your life if you remain alone and let this wonderful person pass by. If you actually see yourself being alone the rest of your life, you will be faced with a choice of being alone, massive pain, and the possibility of being rejected, minor pain. Given those choices, your mind will choose less pain and you will take action to meet that person. Handwriting reveals many of people's fears and insecurities. Some major ones include self-consciousness, sensitivity to criticism, jealousy, stubbornness, and a fear of failure/change.

The Fear of Ridicule

Remember asking someone to dance? If it made you nervous, you felt the fear of rejection. If rejection scares you, what does acceptance do to you? Many people seek acceptance so much they fail to realize that rejection is a stepping stone on the way to massive acceptance. Most great ideas have never been accepted without first being rejected. The German philosopher Arthur Schopenhauer stated, all truth goes through three stages. First, it is ridiculed. Second, it is violently opposed. Finally, it is accepted as self-evident.

I know this is true because I have been through all three stages with the entire concept of understanding someone's personality from handwriting. People used to ridicule the concept. Then they stopped criticizing it, but opposed the use of it. Now, people pay me to teach them how to do it. Next time you feel self-conscious, realize it is the first step to being accepted.

The self-conscious person fears ridicule, therefore she is careful not to place herself in a position to receive any ridicule. She wonders what people will think if she acts in a certain manner. When encountering a new group of people, she may stay on the sidelines until she has the people categorized, or she may behave in a positive, attention-getting manner to assure herself that people will think good thoughts about her. It will always take time for her to warm up to others, and only then will she be herself. This is a major fear which inhibits behavior in both men and women.

In handwriting, the humps that slant downward signify diplomacy. If the humps slant uphill, an over-awareness of self or self-consciousness is revealed. The person whose 'm' and 'n' humps slant uphill often feels self-conscious.

In the sales profession, this self-consciousness is called "call reluctance." This person takes the word "no" as a personal criticism. Therefore, there is an internal struggle when performing this type of work. Although this person may be a great salesperson, she still feels insecurity. She will perform better if someone else is with her because the fear of ridicule from her peers is far greater than the fear of ridicule from her clients. Many times this type of person becomes a sales trainer, because when she is training, she doesn't have to put herself in a position of being told "no" as often as the salespeople do. This sales example can be applied to meeting new people to date as well. Have you ever felt self-conscious? Do you have a fear of being rejected?

One interesting note about being self-conscious is the person may not be sensitive to criticism (have a loop in the d stem), she just may fear the possibility of receiving ridicule. It is a classic example of Winston Churchill's famous quote, "The only thing we have to fear is fear itself." Self-consciousness is a preoccupation with being observed, no matter the result of the judgment.

As far as relationships are concerned, the self-conscious person may be hesitant to approach a stranger to start a relationship. But once he or she is involved in a relationship, the trait becomes less important. However, if your partner is self-conscious, you must recognize this fear and be prepared for some very insecure moments. Self-conscious people are overly concerned with what other people think, including you. This fear inhibits people from attempting their goals, dreams, and desires.

The Desire For Approval

The desire for approval is a primary motivating factor for achievement. I remember in junior high, it was really important to wear Izod shirts, loafers, and a Members Only jacket. I also played football just to be cool, and wore my jersey on game days. It seems kind of silly, considering I rarely played and I was so skinny my hip pads kept sliding down off my 98lb frame! I'm not sure now whom I was supposed to be impressing. But those things sure seemed important at the time.

If you look carefully, you see grown men and women act in the very same way that I did when I was in junior high. Now, I think I was being silly for wanting to wear an Izod when I was 12. I finally gave up that stupid game when the polo shirt became the in thing and it was twice as expensive. I just couldn't keep up. Adults play a much more expensive game. I know a top real estate broker who only buys his ties from one store in Carmel, California. Since he lives in Southern California, he must make a special trip to buy ties. He wears them because they are exclusive and expensive. He said he drives a BMW because "Poor people can't." He read somewhere that the typical achiever personality owns an expensive four-wheel drive Jeep Cherokee, but never gets it dirty. So he went out, bought one, and never gets it dirty. He thinks all achievers have a fear of being average. In reality, he has a deep seeded need for approval. He perceives not being wealthy as grounds for ridicule and criticism. To set himself apart and prove his success, he must decorate his life with labels. Does this sound like a 42-year-old man with the same fears as a 12-year-old boy? It is, but the cost of playing the game is quite different.

So, his goal is to be an achiever; someone in the top 10% income bracket, someone who has made it. Unfortunately, his definition of being an achiever is what brand of cars and ties he owns. In my opinion, genuine achievers purchase specific products because they are the best quality and the most comfortable. Because of this person's *over awareness of self*, he is more concerned with appearing to be successful than achieving success. This was his spur to achievement. Whatever the spur, he was financially successful by most people's terms. If he didn't care what they thought, he wouldn't have worked so hard to earn the money to buy the high-priced toys.

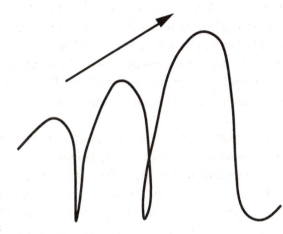

Figure 7.1: Self-Consciousness

Figure 7.2: Sensitive to Criticism

In his real estate business, true to form, he has graduated into a management position. He spends time training others to sell. One of the underlying factors in this decision is his *call reluctance*. He would rather not be put in a position to be rejected. But, true to definition, if he goes with a salesperson to show him the ropes, he will perform well. He is more concerned about his salespeople not liking him than the prospect not buying from him.

Another important aspect of being sensitive to criticism is the ability to be sensitive to what others are feeling. Much of this sensitivity is imagined, but, regardless of reality, the sensitive person compensates to make the other person approve of him. This creates tremendous rapport in a sales situation. Most of the top salesmen I have ever analyzed have a certain amount of sensitivity to criticism. Why? Sales is a people business. A good salesperson must be aware and sensitive to what the prospect is feeling in order to sell him the product. Most people buy on a feeling. People who are sensitive to what others feel and think about them and are emotionally expressive are better salespeople. Consequently, great leaders tend to have some sensitivity to criticism in order to know what behavior makes people like them better. People rarely follow a leader they do not like or respect.

How Being Sensitive to Criticism Can Work for You
A thank-you note means the world to people. My grandmother loaned me more than five thousand dollars while I was in college, but the rest of the family could never get a dime from her. Why? I always made it a point to let her know that I cared. I would always express my appreciation for a lunch or a $25 Christmas check. I also called her for *no special occasion*. I didn't do these things to get a loan, I did them because I knew she liked them. I've seen her handwriting. She also has a desire for attention. I probably feel the same amount of love for her as the other grandchildren do. But because I express it more often, she pays special attention to me. Small acts like this show you do care. And believing someone cares about us sometimes makes this world livable. If you are involved

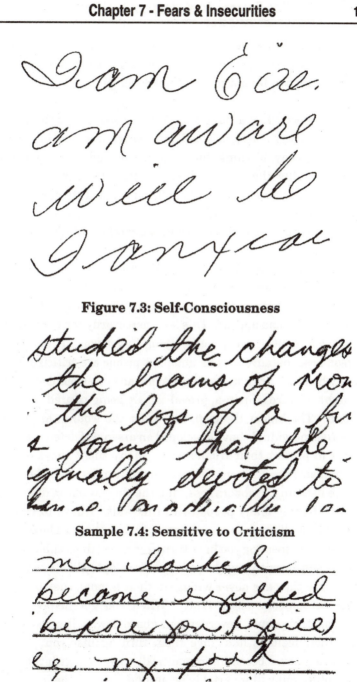

Figure 7.3: Self-Consciousness

Sample 7.4: Sensitive to Criticism

Figure 7.5: Girl From El Paso: Notice "d loops"

in a relationship with a sensitive person, *be aware of everything you say*. Sensitive people pick up on every negative or positive emotion. Be careful not to hurt their feelings.

When someone has a huge loop in the lower case d, he is very sensitive to personal criticism. The sensitive areas will include his hair, face, body, clothing, financial status, and even his family. Also, the taller the d stem, the more pride the person takes in himself. Therefore, if you had a tall, very open d stem, you would have someone that goes to great lengths to look good and impress people. This person is obsessed with what others think about him.

You may know people who are very sensitive to criticism, but don't admit it. These are probably the same people who never take the blame for anything in their lives. When this fear gets too large, traces of paranoia appear. This isn't necessarily the clinical kind where you believe everyone is trying to get you. It means the person is so insecure that he imagines people are criticizing him even when they are not. It is like having an open wound and every thought or word of non-approval is salt being poured into that wound. The bigger the loop, the wider the wound. Most over-sensitive individuals have developed an arsenal of defense mechanisms to protect their fragile egos. Many times these defense mechanisms are sarcasm, distrust, secretiveness, dishonesty, selective listening, stubbornness, and the obvious one of displacing blame. I know many people with this trait. I have to walk on eggshells at all times to avoid hurting their feelings. The moment they begin suspecting you have turned on them, the trouble begins. Note: someone with huge loops in the d's is highly likely to turn on you. Since they are never wrong (in their minds), they believe it must be someone else's fault. When you get involved with oversensitive people, never let your guard down. It is too easy to hurt their feelings and have them turn against you. I don't recommend ever becoming romantically involved with this type. But in life, you will invariably be around many of them.

In case you got the impression that large-looped d's are always bad, that's not the case at all. In fact, they can work to your advantage on frequent occasions. Because these people care so much about you approving of them, they continually do things to assist you in thinking good things about them. For example, I once dated a beautiful young girl from El Paso, Texas. Her personality was average in many respects; however, she was extra sensitive to criticism. Every time I told her how pretty she looked or even called her "mi amore´," she would melt. I made her feel good, which made me feel good. So, if you are with someone sensitive to criticism, that means they are also susceptible to sincere compliments. Give them what they need — approval. When you fill others' needs, they will give generously to fill your needs.

I have found that the best salesmen in the world have loops in their letter d. It helps to have a certain degree of sensitivity to know what your client is thinking. Sensitivity is not a bad trait in small quantities. What if your date has big d's and you stare admiringly

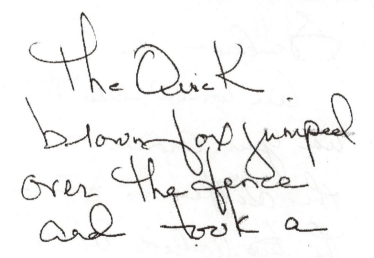

Sample 7.6: Oversensitive to Criticism
Notice the extra large d loops.

into his eyes? When you compliment his eyes, he will melt with joy. Or he may be wondering if you are noticing that his eyes are too close together! The writing shown in sample 7.6 and 7.7 are samples of almost paranoid people.

Oversensitiveness can be a problem. Many people spend too much time feeling pain about what others think. If the loop in the 'd' is huge, it is a real problem. Be careful. All the people I have ever known with an inflated looped 'd' have felt betrayed at one point or another without just cause. When they feel betrayed, watch out for their defense mechanisms!

If these loops are inflated to a disproportionate size, you know the fear of criticism is unreasonable. Huge flat topped looped d's which do not return to the baseline signify this fear is approaching a level of paranoia. These troubled individuals will imagine others are criticizing them. Many of them allowed their fears to sever the relationship completely. Invariably, you will be the victim of their feelings of mistrust at one time or another.

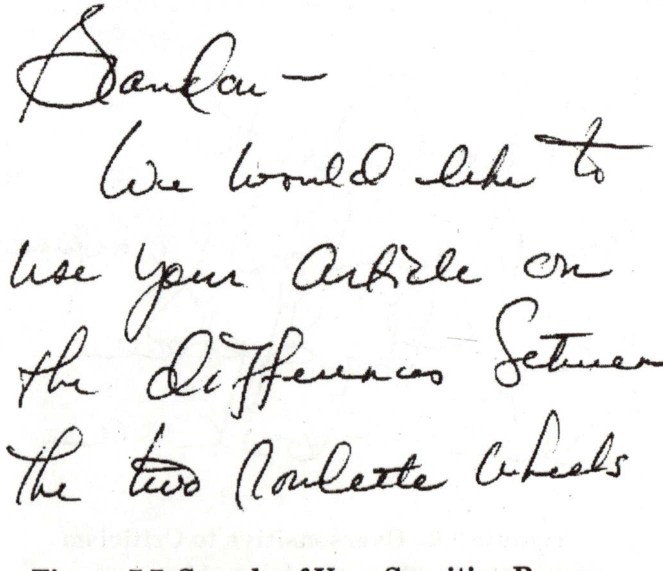
Sandra –
We would like to
use your article on
the differences between
the two Roulette wheels

Figure 7.7: Sample of Very Sensitive Person. Notice the d-loop.

A truly paranoid person often has built up so many defenses, they might tell you, "I don't care what others think." Their defenses are so strong they may actually not feel the pain of their open wounds anymore. If they have a huge looped d and say they don't care what others think...*you know they are really in a lot of pain.* If you choose to get into a relationship with a paranoid person, realize that he is subject to unreasonable fears. It can be a challenging situation. I have found that when having a close friendship or relationship with a borderline paranoid person, as shown in handwriting, he will eventually feel you have turned against him and he will turn on you. If you have experienced this, go look at the ex's old handwriting. Don't be surprised to find extra large looped d's.

Realize that anyone with a DE or E+ slant will naturally relate to others' emotions, therefore can be sensitive to others' feelings. So, even if this DE/E+ writer has no loop in the d stem, he may still behave with compassion and sensitivity. The sensitiveness in the letter d only relates to the pain he feels when he perceives or actually gets criticized on a personal level. Don't confuse being sensitive in the romantic sense to having a fear of criticism.

Since a person who is sensitive to criticism cares what you think, let them know you approve. Give frequent compliments. Since they are searching for approval, let her know you like what she is wearing. If you give sincere compliments to these oversensitive people, you will have them eating out of the palm of your hand because you are supplying what they need the most: approval.

The traits of self-consciousness and sensitivity to criticism are sometimes confused. Although many people who have one also have the other, remember they are different traits and have separate meanings. Self-consciousness is a fear of what others might think, a fear of ridicule, a fear of rejection. Self-conscious people sit on the sidelines around strangers until the fear of rejection subsides. On the other hand, sensitivity to criticism is the pain one feels when criticism is actually received. Self-conscious people fear the future, what might happen. People who are sensitive to criticism feel pain when it is happening. Therefore, you could have someone who fears rejection, feels very self-conscious and actually feels no pain if they do get criticized. Likewise, you could have someone who goes full speed into a situation and only slows down when criticism is really received. These are two of the most important fears in the human psyche. It is important that you learn to recognize them in yourself and others if you are going to master your relationships.

Dale Carnegie wrote a book called *How to Win Friends and Influence People.* I highly recommend it to anyone who wants to learn the fundamentals of winning friends and influencing people. It is a classic. It is one way to improve your relationships with other people. Now, with the aid of handwriting to know people's needs and desires, we can determine to what extent we need to compliment, listen, or lead.

Low Self-Image

Low self-image or low self-esteem is the most damaging single personality trait anyone can possess. It creates unhappiness, dissatisfaction, and spawns a multitude of related problems for the person and those around him. Someone's self-esteem is the weighted average of how much value he feels he possesses.

Self image creates many problems such as a lack of motivation in children. For example, Dwayne said to his sister when she invited him to leave home and live with her, "I'll talk to you about needing a place to live... if it becomes an issue." He has such a low self-image, the only time he does anything is when his back is pressed against the wall. He has no initiative, drive, sexual imagination (y loop) or enthusiasm (t-bar). When he was kicked out of his house, he slept in his car for two days, moved in with friends and then came home when he couldn't pay the rent. He has no goals because he doesn't feel comfortable committing to them. And typically, he doesn't invision anything in the future. In his case, he always prints, has no lower zone strokes, few upper zone strokes and is a light writer. He has no self-direction and no passion for life. Because his self-image is so low, he will never leave a bad situation until it is intolerable, hence the statement "when it becomes an issue." And, this almost goes without saying, Dwayne will never be able to plan to improve his situation from a good one to a great one. He doesn't have the vision or confidence to feel he deserves it.

Therefore, if you become involved with someone who has a truly *low* self image, you will have trouble. She will look to you for her own strength. She consistently achieves less than she is capable of accomplishing. Self-image is what you feel when you think about yourself. Don't confuse it with vanity. I have seen many people who think they are really good looking, and maybe they are, but their self-image is very low. However, they don't believe they deserve the attention their looks bring them. In fact, seven out of ten beautiful women I know do not have high self-images. Self-image has nothing to do with looks. *Self-image is the weighted average of the level of approval you give yourself during various situations.*

Many people display a high level of confidence in certain situations, yet have a low self-image. I know many basketball players who are totally confident each time they get on the court. They know they can perform well in that context. However, in the rest of their lives — relationships, financial, educational, etc. — they feel completely inadequate. Therefore, their self-esteem is low. Self-esteem is a result of a weighted average of all the feelings of worth in each situation throughout life.

> *"Self-image is the weighted average of the level of approval you give yourself during various situations." — Bart A. Baggett*

Do you know someone like this? Personally? When you don't have internal beliefs that you can achieve, you won't plan very far ahead. You won't set high goals, and you resist change. Any time you see a low self-image, you are in for a struggle. Many people with low self-images will bend over backwards just to keep you around. Realize that these people work from a perspective of *not losing* what they have rather than focusing on what they could gain. On the other hand, a person with good self-esteem works from the internal perspective of *moving toward* what they want. They are confident that whatever they have is secure and if something were to happen they could simply gain it all back.

When searching for the ideal relationship, avoid people with low self-esteem. A medium self-esteem is tolerable, but a high self-image is ideal. But remember, a person with a high self-esteem will not stay in a bad situation and will not tolerate being mistreated. If you tend to control, manipulate, and mistreat your lover, you won't get away with it if you have a mate with a high self-esteem. They will not tolerate this kind of treatment. A person with this much internal strength knows what she deserves and expects it. If you don't deliver, she will leave. A low self-image person will stay in a lousy situation for a long time for one of two reasons: 1) she is afraid leaving will bring worse conditions; 2) she believes bad treatment is what she deserves. When a person's self-image becomes higher, all aspects of life change for the better. People leave bad relationships while attracting new healthy ones to replace them. If you have low self-esteem, take actions to change it now. There are many ways to improve this important element of your personality. You should investigate all the ways which interest you. However, the easiest way is by changing the way you cross your letter t. Although it sounds too simple to work, I have received dozens of letters from clients who have done just that: changed their writing. Apparently, the daily reinforcement of knowing they were raising their self image combined with the powerful neurological effect of changing the muscular tension in their hand created impressive results.

I often suggest changing certain aspects of handwriting to those clients who really want to change. One client of mine, Haden Basante, described himself before I worked with him as "a complete loser, a wallflower, an introverted idiot." After using the Grapho-Deck, listening to my tapes, and changing his handwriting, Haden reported to me that his personality had been transformed. He could easily meet new people anywhere and had total confidence with strangers and friends. In a letter to me he stated handwriting was the only tool in all the self-help books he had ever read which would inspire you and give you the tools to work with making change fast, simple, and easy.

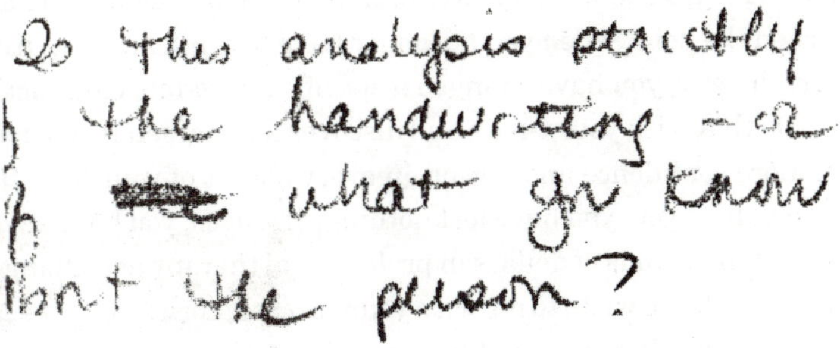

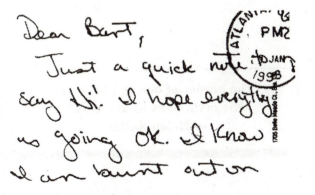

Figure 7.8: Original handwriting

Figure 7.9: Handwriting after client raised t-bar.

Another example of how handwriting changed a life is my good friend Christian Chrane. Now, seven years after I suggested she raise her t-bar, she now says that was the turning point in her life. Ever since she made the decision to change, her confidence and self-respect have been an asset to her, not a problem. She went on to get a respectable degree from Texas A&M and own a 70-acre ostrich ranch in Texas. I would say that is a dramatic turnaround from an insecure high school girl who didn't have the confidence to leave a boyfriend she didn't like!

I am not suggesting that the simple act of raising your t-bar will change your life. I do believe it is one tool which will significantly impact your level of self-esteem. If you are serious about changing your life, you will give it a thirty-day trial run. My experience has shown it takes about thirty days to change a habit. Once you have reached the point when you no longer have to think about writing a certain way, you have changed a specific neuro-muscular activity. Do that with your t-bars and discover for yourself if you don't feel more confidence and power in every aspect of your life. If it doesn't affect you, you have lost nothing; if it does, you have saved yourself thousands of dollars in professional therapy and changed your life. Please write to me with your success stories. It gives me great pleasure to hear about how you changed your life using one of my suggesstions. You've got nothing to lose, except a low self-esteem.

> **"The heresy of one age becomes the orthodoxy of the next."**
> **— Helen Keller**

Stubbornness

Stubbornness is a defense mechanism. It develops from the subconscious fear of being wrong. Stubborn people must be right all the time. Once they make up their minds, they don't want to be confused with the facts. You can lead a stubborn person, but you can't push him. The best way to deal with this person when you encounter their stubbornness is to immediately back off and try a new approach; an approach in which he thinks it is his idea. The stubborn person will do something if it is his idea. Don't ever make him look wrong.

Stubbornness is found in the t or d stem which is separated to form an immovable-looking brace. The t can actually look more like an Indian tepee than the letter t. This brace analogy is appropriate because a brace is sturdy and immovable, just like a stubborn person. They rarely admit they are wrong. It is a trait common among children, teenagers, and other insecure people. Many bosses are known for it. Ha!

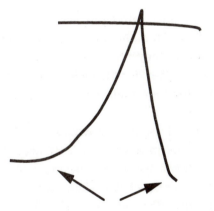

Figure 7.10: Stubbornness: notice the brace in the stem.

Self-Deceit

Self–deceit is one element of the communication letter o. If you reread the pathological liar section, your understanding of this trait will be enhanced.

It is found in a loop on the left side of the lower case o. Self-deceit means that the person is not aware, on a conscious level, of what he is hiding from. It reminds me of the ostrich who sticks its head under the sand to hide from its fears. There is something unpleasant in his life right now which he is not ready to face.

Invariably, each time I analyze someone's handwriting who has the self-deceit loop, they disagree with parts of my analysis. They say, "I'm not like that at all." Meanwhile their friends are behind them nodding their heads off because they know I am right! Each time I analyze writing on a T.V. or radio show, I avoid analyzing handwriting that contains self-deceit because these people make me look bad. Although I am completely accurate in my analysis, they rarely admit it. They don't know themselves, therefore can't agree. When you see it, know they won't always agree with what you tell them about their personality. But you know the truth.

I have noticed people with self-deceit have a certain element of insincerity about them. This is because they actually are deceiving themselves about who they are, therefore you may feel they present a false image. They don't truly know themselves because they are afraid of what they might find.

To illustrate this trait, I use the following story. There once was a happily married wife in a small rich suburb. She had two children, a four-bedroom house, a pool, and a Mercedes in the driveway. She spent her time being a housewife who liked to play golf at the country club. She had a good life. Then, one afternoon she got a phone call from a worried friend. The caller told her that her husband was just seen going into a motel room with his secretary. Her husband must be having an affair. Thinking quickly, the happy housewife tells the caller it must have been a mistake because her husband has been home all day. Now, what does she do? She decides to deceive herself about the truth. Otherwise, she feels she must leave her husband, get a divorce, and raise the children on her own. This is not a pleasant option. Because she wants desperately to keep her life intact, she tells herself it must be a mistake. She lies to herself to avoid the pain. Soon after that phone call she noticed a small loop develop in the left side of her o.

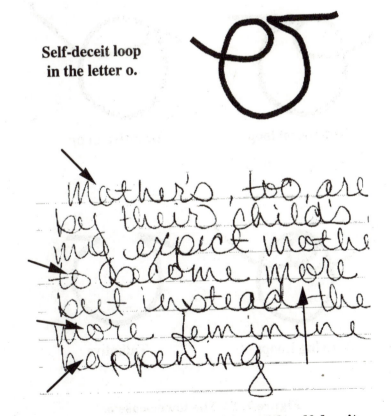

Self-deceit loop in the letter o.

Figure 7.11: Sample of writing with self-deceit.

To fully understand why self-deceit reveals itself in the letter o, you must understand the other traits revealed by this small but very significant letter. A loop on the right side reveals a secretiveness toward others, while two loops reveal a person who keeps secrets from others and himself. In other words, he lies. The fourth way listed below is to make an o without closing the top. This open topped o reveals an open talkative person. For a complete description of all the traits an o has to offer, see the trait dictionary in the appendix.

Self-Deceit loop

Secretive Loop

Lying Loops

Talkative

Figure 7. 12: The lower-case o.

Using Fear for Motivation

A person's fears are one of the most important aspects to understand. People are generally motivated by either fear or desire. They move toward things they desire and away from things they fear. Therefore, knowing what someone fears can give you the knowledge you need to motivate him in the direction of your choice.

On the other hand, you can use someone's desires to motivate. The next chapter discusses drives. These drives are the desire to move toward something: sex, travel, change, etc. When you want to influence someone (into loving you), understanding the fears and drives will help you supply what is needed.

> *"All lovers swear more performance
> than they are able."*
> — *William Shakespeare*

Chapter VIII

Sex Drives

The sex drives are shown in handwriting in the lower zone letters' loops; the y's and g's. People often want to know what trait can signify a huge sex drive. The longer the lower loops, the bigger the physical drives. Because any exaggerated desire stems from an equally exaggerated imagination, those people with huge sex drives also have a tendency to blow everything else out of proportion. In the case of women, these are the type that break a nail and think the world is coming to an end. You know the type. They also tell you the same story of getting a speeding ticket for a week, until a new and better tragedy comes along. On the bright side, they may make great storytellers, but if you are trying to form a relationship, it could be trouble. For starters, if she exaggerates everything, her insecure feelings will also be blown out of proportion. If you forget to say "I love you" one day, it means you don't love her anymore. If you look at another woman, in her mind, you might be having an affair. I'm not suggesting that this scenario is typical of every woman with large lower loops. But what is typical is that every fear and/or desire is multiplied inside her mind. I have a simple formula for those who tend to over-exaggerate. I just take the square root of the problem to find the core of the issue. This usually reveals a real version of the truth.

My grandmother has this tendency. Now, I can't honestly say I know anything about her sex life. It is my policy not to discuss sex with anyone past the age of Social Security. One story comes to mind. She once planned a trip to California to visit me. She worried six months in advance about how I was going to pick her up from the airport. She only worried about the rental car for three months in advance. On the positive side, if I send her a nice thank you card, she embellishes it so much that everyone she talks to thinks I'm a saint. If you think you want a person with great insatiable physical (sex) drives, ask yourself if you really want the rest of the package.

The big imagination goes along with the width of the loop. The depth of the loop is actually the sex drive. You can imagine that if you have both big and long, you have a real firecracker. Some men think, "Well, I'd like a woman that wants sex at least four times a day. So, I'll find one with real long loops that are blown up like a balloon." Be careful. Most men couldn't handle it! If you're the type of guy who likes to lift weights 12 ounces at a time and your best form of exercise is watching football on Sunday, you're in trouble. A woman with a strong physical drive needs the physical activity. She needs change and variety. She likes sex in different positions and often. If you can't handle it, don't get involved. Remember, when football season rolls around and you would rather watch the game with the guys than play touch with her, she'll go somewhere else to satisfy her needs. This doesn't mean she *will* have an affair; but frustrations will find an outlet. If your mate suddenly takes up jogging ten miles a day and is planning to run the Boston marathon, you're not meeting her needs.

On the other hand, if you are the type of person who is looking for sport sex regardless of the rest of the personality, a large lower loop might be just what you want. Don't be surprised when she exaggerates the facts about your encounter to her friends. And don't think you're the only one!

Do Big Loops Always Signify A Nymphomaniac?

Big loops always signifies a big imagination regarding sex. What is a nymphomaniac anyway? In any case, just because a woman has a big sexual imagination does not mean she is easy. She may really enjoy sex and need it frequently. She may think about sex often. Whether she is easy or not depends on her self-esteem, values, and opportunities. Most people with big loops are very sexual. *I always look at the y-loop to spot the possible nympho.* However, I've known women with very big y's that expressed this huge imagination and physical drive in avenues other than sex.

Two cases which come to mind were very attractive women in their early twenties. One ran cross country track for Stanford University and the other was training for the Olympics in synchronized swimming. Both exercise at least two hours per day. So the drives are present and the outlet is physical, but it isn't sexual. Those are the only two examples I have come across in all the years I have been analyzing handwriting in which I couldn't directly see a relationship between the size of the lower loops to an embellished physical imagination regarding sex. Good luck with your research!

Tumultuous Lori

One real life example which helped me realize the power of the lower loop was Lori. We met one night outside a Dallas nightclub. She was surrounded by ten high school age boys. She was being a tease, lifting her shirt half way up, almost showing her breast. I made some sarcastic comment about being cruel to the kids. She liked my sharp tongue and we had breakfast at Denny's that night. Lori was a topless dancer and was very proud of her new breasts. After all she paid good money for them, why not show them off? Later that night, she ripped off her shirt and showed me her new breasts. I hadn't even asked to see them. Although nothing sexual happened, I know something could have if I had chosen to respond to her passes. She did stay the night. She said she didn't want to go home because she was in a fight with her live-in boyfriend.

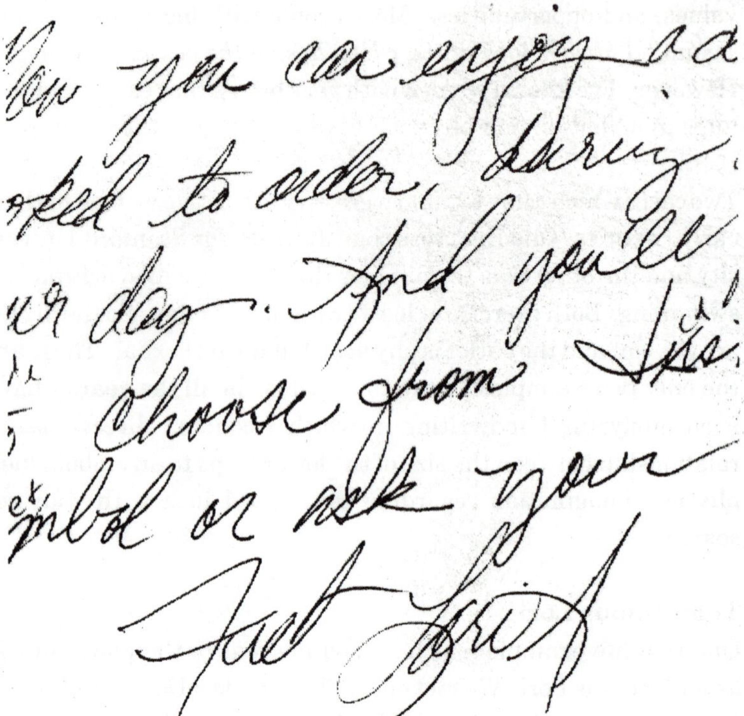

Figure 8.1: Tumultuous Lori's Handwriting.
Notice: big lower loops (sex drives) ,
high ending strokes (need for attention),
and hard and heavy right hand slant (impulsiveness).

Notice in her handwriting the strong desire for attention. I liked Lori, but she was on the wild side. She described herself as "tumultuous." We became good friends, but I didn't hit on her. I was satisfied as just friends and this made her want me more. She told me everything about herself. She even told me she used to have sex and/or masturbate eight times a day. That is a big sex drive! She also described herself as co-dependent. In other words, a part of her needed a man at all times. Her desire for attention and her strong sex drive made her very fun to be around. She had a very creative imagination and was very spontaneous. I remember one time in bumper- to-bumper traffic, she took off her pants and stood up with her head out the sunroof. She liked to attempt to get a reaction out of me. Later in the relationship, she did.

The Male Sex Drive
Although handwriting does not reveal gender, we all know that men and women are different. Women often ask me if the sexual overtones I frequently see in female handwriting applies to men as well. The fact is they do apply. However, because of the difference in gender roles, the resulting behavior is often varied. Most gender differences are generalizations. Both you and I realize there are always exceptions to these sociological generalizations. However, they are useful to understand and you will benefit from hearing them.

First, you need to understand the longer the lower zone letter extends, the stronger the physical drive. This drive is an energy drive. It is often transmuted into travel, exercise, sports, etc. However, in a man's writing the width of the loop relates more to the concept of *trust* and *intimacy*, rather than sexual imagination. The sad truth is, in general, men will have sex with women whether they have a strong sex drive or not. Some guys see sex as just something to do. In many a man's mind, having sex is not necessarily associated with the relationship/commitment realm of his life. This is why many men can have sex with no emotional attachment. On the other hand, most women get emotionally attached to men with whom they share sexual experiences. Or rather, women only share sexual experiences with men to whom they are emotionally attached. This difference is fundamental in understanding the role of sex in a relationship.

In handwriting, you can't necessarily tell if a man is easy by the size of his y, g, or j-loop. Therefore the loop will simply tell whether or not he needs sex bad enough to hunt for it! Since the length of the lower loops are energy, you can predict the amount of drive he possesses. This drive is very important in his career. The longer the lower zone descenders are, the more driven a man will be toward success. The bigger the loops, the more imagination. The correlation is high between sex and a physical imagination. As men get older, they tend to transmute that drive into career-oriented activities, while older women tend to keep that drive in the physical and romantic realm. (Of course, entrepreneurial women have the same traits as entrepreneurial men: long descenders, high t-bars, enthusiasm, and a tendency for independence.) The lower zone letters signify the same thing in men's and women's handwriting. However, gender generalities can be helpful. Your interpretation of the outcome of these desires should be considered along with the general tendencies and differences of each gender.

One generality about men is that many have a fear of intimacy. Women complain that men don't express their emotions or are afraid of commitment. There is truth to this generalization. When men were little boys, they were encouraged to be masculine. Don't cry. Don't whine. Don't hold other boys' hands. Little boys are programmed to be very different than little girls. Little girls were given permission to cry, to be weak, to be vulnerable, to hold hands, to express their emotions. These programs help mold a little girl into a feminine woman.

In handwriting, one can see these tendencies reveal themselves in a man's handwriting. Many men press very hard onto the paper. This intensity of emotion is like a sponge. It absorbs but doesn't express. Likewise, many men adopt printing instead of cursive handwriting. Cursive reveals the subconscious mind easier than printing. If a man needs barriers or has a fear of intimacy, he might choose to print as yet one more barrier to the outside world. When studying intimacy, always evaluate the lower loops. Although men who only print may be good mates, the signs will not be as easy to read.

The reason I mention these tendencies in each gender is because they are such frequently-asked questions. The answers about printing, cursive, and depth of feeling are generalities. I hope you can use them to understand the two genders. However, evaluate each person separately. No general tendency applies to all people.

Exaggeration
Another important point about people's huge lower loops is that these people have two speeds: full speed and stop. Because their imagination makes everything bigger than life, they blow everything out of proportion. I had a girlfriend with these huge lower loops. What I noticed more than the quality of the sex was the pain and anxiety she created over the smallest of incidents. To get perspective on any story she told me I simply took her story and divided it by three. (I could have used the square root formula, but I needed a calculator!) This simple formula brought any situation into the realm of reality. So, when she had a reason to be angry, I divided the cause by three and solved the problem. To be honest, I enjoyed her big y's when it had to do with sex, but not when it had to do with her jealousy and insecurities.

I do my best not to make judgement calls on morality choices. Yet the simple plain truth is: there are men and women who really just want to have a one-night sexual encounter. As you know by now, that is not what this book is about. If you want to target those men and women using the knowledge in this book, go ahead. The reason I say go ahead is if the traits in a person's handwriting reveal that they will behave in a certain manner, then they will find a person to fulfill those desires, whether it is you or someone else. I hope that you will use the knowledge in this book to evaluate your own needs and search for the person who fulfills most of them in a healthy, mutually-satisfying way.

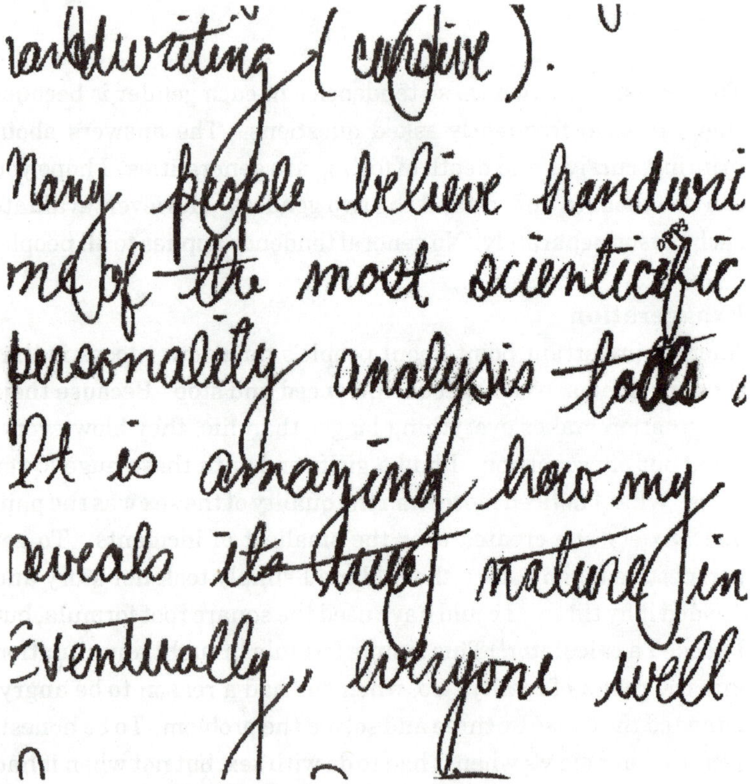

handwriting (cursive).

Many people believe handwri
me of the most scienticific
personalety analysis tolls ,
It is amazing how my
reveals its true nature in
Eventually, everyone will

Figure 8.2: Sample of Huge Sex Drives and a Big imagination. Notice large lower loops.

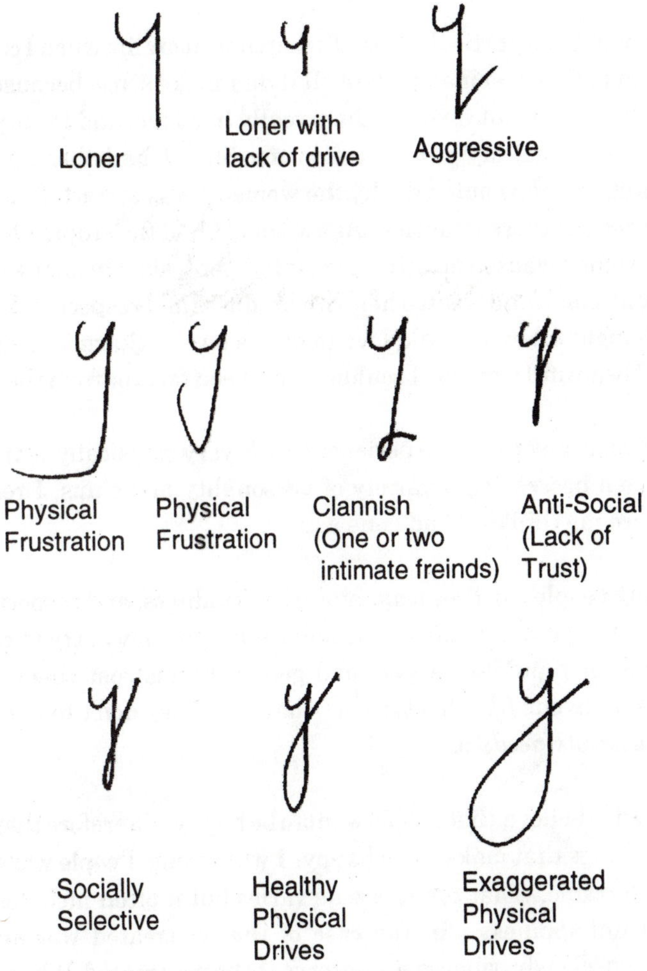

Loner

Loner with
lack of drive

Aggressive

Physical
Frustration

Physical
Frustration

Clannish
(One or two
intimate freinds)

Anti-Social
(Lack of
Trust)

Socially
Selective

Healthy
Physical
Drives

Exaggerated
Physical
Drives

Figure 8.3: The meanings of the lower loops.

The Attraction Factor

People are attracted to people who satisfy their needs. This is not always what they say they want, or even what is good for them. That was a bitter pill for me to swallow because it took me many misunderstood rejections to learn this lesson.

I remember a particularly confusing time in my life when I couldn't seem to find a woman to date. It didn't make sense because I felt really good about myself, others really liked me, and I was just as successful as any other time in my life. I had these positive qualities and wondered why the women I was attracted to didn't appreciate those qualities. At the time, I had the stupid idea that all women wanted an attractive, intelligent, sincere man who was a gentleman and treated her with kindness and respect. Likewise, I thought all men would love to date a sweet, charming, sincere, and beautiful woman. I couldn't have been farther from the truth.

Through a series of experiences with very physically attractive women possessing a variety of personality make-ups, I realized where my thinking had gone astray.

Many people say they *want* sincerity, kindness, and respect. But what they really *need* is someone to put them down, try to control them, manipulate , argue, and generally mistreat them. Why would anyone *like* this type of behavior? They don't like it, their personality *needs* it.

I used to believe that people want to be happy. Therefore they seek out things that make them happy. I was wrong. People want to be comfortable. That comfort zone varies but it often includes pain and unhappiness. In the case of the mistreated woman, she subconsciously believes she deserves to be mistreated. When a nice guy treats her with respect, she gets bored and finds someone who will treat her with the same respect she has for herself.

How many people do you know who constantly seek out the same type of partner as the last one? Many women seek out the rough-guy type who hurts them over and over. They get the same guy with a different name, every time. What this taught me was that these women were attracted to those guys who fit their profile. Hence, when I didn't fall into their predetermined profile, I didn't feel rejected. I just didn't fit their needs.

I used to overlook the shy, quiet, gentle girls who might have made terrific girlfriends. Instead, I ended up with the spunky sarcastic tornado women who blew into my life and blew out. That is not what I thought I wanted. I thought I wanted a steady relationship. But, in reality, it fit my lifestyle at the time. Subconsciously, I needed the excitement, challenge, and fun-loving spirit more than I needed the stability a calm relationship would bring. You should be aware of what you or a potential partner really needs. The following true story is a perfect illustration of how a person's subconscious needs reveal themselves into reality while completely ignoring what is good for her.

Danielle: The Sad Sexy Self-Destructing Slut

Many years ago, I attended a handwriting analysis conference in San Angelo, Texas. There, I learned quite a bit about people and their handwriting. But the most valuable lesson came not from a lecture, but from a cocktail waitress named Danielle. Experience was my best teacher at that conference.

After a day of lectures and discussions, I found myself in the hotel lounge. I was dancing and drinking with four women, who happened to make up the executive board of this particular organization. They were all very competent handwriting analysts as well as fun people. (By the way, I have found when you spend your free time with people who are already accomplished, your chances of becoming more successful increase dramatically.) I thought if I could spend my evening with anyone, why not with the leaders? As I was the youngest person at the conference, I kept my eyes open for an attractive woman who was closer to my age. Although I

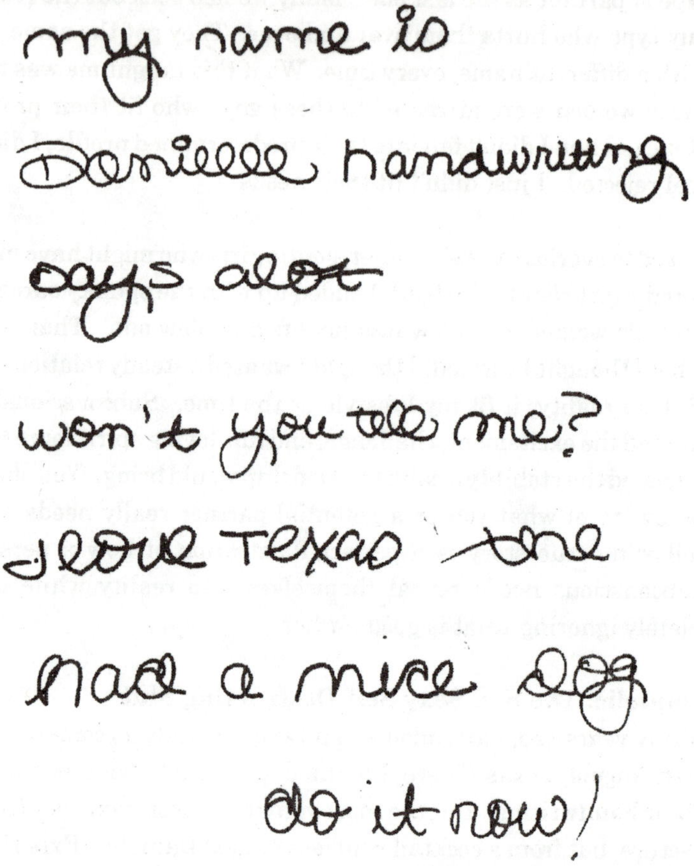

my name is

Danielle, handwriting

says alot

won't you tell me?

I love Texas the

had a nice dog

do it now!

Figure 8.4: Re-creation of Danielle's handwriting.

Danielle's Handwriting Summary	
Trait Name	**Handwriting Stroke**
Lives for the Moment	No upper zone loops
Low Self-Image	Very low t-bar
Self-Castigation	Sharp backward t-bar
Large Sex Drives	Oversized lower loops
Needs a Challenge	Hook–like stinger in a,o,and c.
Failure Complex	Down-turned y

really enjoyed dancing and visiting with these older women, I was looking for something a little different. Shall we say... a romantic evening.

The most likely candidate was the waitress. She was drop-dead beautiful, long blond hair, and had a body like a model. She had everything in the right place. Although I learned from her personality, her good looks certainly made the lesson more enjoyable.

To make a long story shorter, I asked her for a sample of handwriting on a napkin. She complied just like most people do when you make that offer. Unfortunately, I never made it home with the napkin. Therefore, the handwriting sample shown here is my best rendition of what I remember it looked liked. I analyzed her handwriting and then my analyst friend analyzed her writing also. Danielle sat in bewilderment as her life unfolded in less time than it takes to down a drink.

Danielle was quite a character. The first thing I noticed in her handwriting was that she had *no upper loops*. No upper loops signifies a lack of a stable morality or ethics. I jokingly call this type of person a sociopath. This means that whatever feels good at the moment, she does. It is a nice trait to find if you like one-night stands. However, I would never date or depend on someone like that. She had an imagination twice the size of reality (huge lower loops) and a failure complex so bad she could screw up a one-man funeral.

Danielle also possessed an anger directed at all men (stingers), a desire for attention (high ending strokes), and basically a logical, self-centered, emotional outlay (AB writer). Linda saw that she had an eating disorder in her handwriting. Danielle was amazed because it was absolutely true. Judging by her thin, lean body, she could have had a serious eating disorder, but from a man's perspective, it looked all right to me! (Doesn't this kind of male insensitivity just make you want to purge?)

Linda saw something I didn't: potential. Although Danielle had some big round m's and n's she also had just as many steeple pointed ones (fast thinking patterns and not depicted in sample writing). It surprised me she was such a quick thinker. Linda told her of her unlimited potential and that her lack of self-esteem was always holding her back. When she said this, I saw a sense of happiness and joy in Danielle's eyes that was magical. "You mean I'm not stupid? I can be successful some day, I am smart?" It saddened me to see a person with such a good mind to be stuck with such a low self-confidence level about her intelligence. As the story unfolded, her father had frequently told her she was stupid and incompetent. Like most impressionable children, she believed what people said. Words are very powerful things.

Danielle, like many people with low self-esteem, dwelt on the bad points. The reason I didn't mention her potential is because the handwriting only reveals what the personality is at the time of the handwriting sample. The future is not mine to predict. It is the sole responsibility of the individual. Besides, people with no upper loops have difficulty visualizing the future. They are stuck in today, the moment. At the time Danielle wrote for me, I didn't perceive her as having any of the fundamental personality traits to achieve any substantial success. She had a good mind, but too many self–sabotaging traits to achieve lasting success. Of course, I didn't tell her this, as it was my opinion and wouldn't have been a benefit to her.

On the other hand, everyone has their own destiny or potential in their own hands. If Danielle changed she might achieve something. Since I'm not into fortune telling, I don't talk about what will or could be when I analyze handwriting. I do, however, point out the positive traits and encourage the client to accentuate the positive and eliminate the negative. But, from the writing, I could tell this woman was pretty screwed up. I was right. In Danielle's case, I saw certain traits which told me she had the cards stacked against her in achieving any level of success or happiness. It would take dramatic, drastic changes for her to overcome her problems. Although she had some really messed-up subconscious personality traits, she was congenial, friendly, funny, and cute. The handwriting reveals the best and worst of a person at the deepest level. Danielle was quite fun and personable on the surface. I really liked being with her, although my logic reminded me that her real personality was not what I was searching for. But I wasn't going to marry her. And... it was all for research. I hope you appreciate the sacrifices I made to write this book!

Back to the story. After ignoring her other customers for about fifteen minutes because she preferred to talk to us, she went back to serving drinks. She took every opportunity to come by and talk. Around closing time we started talking about my travel plans after the weekend. Coincidentally, she was going the same direction as I was in order to spend time in her hometown. So, I invited her to ride with me to Lubbock and I'd take her home on Monday. At first, she thought I was kidding. "Are you serious?" she asked insecurely. I could drive five hours alone or spend it with a knock–out blonde, of course I was serious. I asked her to meet me after she got off work and she agreed. What she didn't know is that I had not renewed my hotel room for that night, so I needed a place to stay. I thought with so many women at the conference why should I spend thirty dollars for a cold hotel bed when I was sure I could find a more comfortable bed for free. I did.

After we left the bar, we walked around the park for a little while. We held hands and she invited me to stay at her place that night. When we got to her apartment, she went to tell her roommate she was home. She then asked me the most incredible question. Danielle said, "You know, it seems like I've known you all my life but I forgot to ask you what your name was... what is it?" I stuttered, "Bart... Bart Baggett." I tried to hide my immense feeling of accomplishment by getting such tremendous rapport with a woman that she invited me into her home and agreed to spend two days traveling with me without even knowing my name.

This is just another testimony to the power of handwriting analysis and simple rapport development skills. People get so wrapped up in talking about themselves, they drop all those little social traditions, like handshakes, asking your name, and even the proverbial phrase, "Not on the first date."

Since I am a decent guy, I offered to sleep on the couch and she insisted that I sleep in her bed and she would sleep on the couch. I reluctantly agreed. I said goodnight and slept like a rock. Yes, I actually slept. The next morning when I went out the front door to get some clothes from my car she woke up abruptly, still half asleep, and said, "You're leaving. You're leaving me. Aren't you?" I was shaken at the honest pain in her eyes. It was obvious she must have been through a massive amount of betrayal and emotional pain. I went over to the couch and put my arms around her. "No, I'm not leaving you. I am just going to the car for a second." I could see she had some major problems she needed to work through. I knew my background as a therapist could help her, but it wouldn't be easy. I was glad she trusted me, because that is the first step. I made her bed and thanked her for the hospitality. I went to the conference for two morning classes then returned to pick up Danielle for a trip I would never forget.

As I mentioned, I slept at her place, I didn't sleep with her. By her handwriting, I knew she was insecure, sexual, and probably sexually easy. But, it is important that we use the knowledge handwriting reveals to help people, not take advantage of them. Guys should never throw themselves on a woman. In this case, she probably would not have put up any resistance. Anyway, most women prefer men who play hard to get. The only time you need to be sexually forward is to establish whether you are just friends or possibly more. Since I had already kissed her the night before in the park, that part of the relationship was established. It was romantic. Now, the fun part started, I just sat and waited until she chased me down and caught me. I knew she would do this for two key reasons I saw in her handwriting: the stingers and the lives for the moment traits.

She had big stingers in her handwriting. (See Figure 8.5) This trait tells me she needs a challenge. The harder a man is to get, the more she wants him. The trait itself goes much deeper into the subconscious. It has to do with an internal anger toward the opposite sex. This resentment or anger is released by capturing or controlling the man for a short period of time. The bedroom is often the only place a woman can control a man. Most women know that a man is most easily lead astray by his penis.

Figure 8.5: Stinger

This challenge aspect runs deep in our society. It is common for a person to want someone a little challenging. However, this trait denoted by the stinger signifies that the person has a deep subconscious desire for a constant challenge to satisfy this anger. It is a deep emotional issue which leads to constant challenges, conflicts, and often problems. If you see a woman or a man with it in their handwriting, don't ever become their sole possession. Always keep that element of "you have to chase me if you want me, because I don't need you." The stinger trait applies equally to both genders.

In Danielle's case, playing hard to get was the perfect strategy. Even without seeing her handwriting I knew it was. As pretty as she was, how many guys got near her bedroom and didn't try to sleep with her? Not many. If they didn't, they must have either been gay or knew exactly how to handle this type of woman. I'll give you a hint... I'm not gay.

The second reason I knew she would become involved with me quickly is because she had the live-for-the-moment code of ethics.

Her ethics depended on which side of the bed she woke up on. In other words, her ethics were random. This is signified by hand-writing with no upper loops. Later in the trip with Danielle, she outlined her sense of morality. In a nutshell, she said, "I only sleep with guys that I like." Didn't I say sociopaths lack their own sense of morality? You will often hear them talk morality, but it came from someone else's search. It is just lip service. They change morality with the wind.

It took the five-hour trip to really get to know the girl behind the handwriting. In the handwriting, I saw a huge imagination, a very low self-image, a lack of morality, and a self-castigating complex. (Self-castigation is a t-bar being crossed to the left, toward self with a sharp point). As we talked, her stories painted the sketch I had in mind. As I heard her life story, I realized she attracted people that would actually punish her. Her last boyfriend actually beat her on a regular basis. She always put herself in situations to be punished. It was very sad.

She stayed with her ex for two reasons. First, she thought she deserved the punishment. That backward t-bar says the subcon-scious needs to be punished to release some of the guilt. In fact, this trait was such a part of her that the only type of books she read were true crime novels —books which tell the stories of serial killers and rapists. Yes, she filled her mind with garbage that confirmed all the misery she felt in her own life. (Sick, isn't it?) The mind is a very powerful computer. *Your life will be an exact reflection of how you program your mind.* Her mind turned into reality many of the terrible situations that she read about in those books. The second reason she stayed with a woman–beater is that her self esteem was very low. She didn't have the courage to leave

> *"Your life will be an exact reflection of how you program your mind."*
> — *Bart A. Baggett*

the bastard. She had no faith in her own abilities to make it on her own. To make matters worse, she had financially supported him. Why would anyone get in a relationship like that? The answer is within a person's *needs*, not *wants*. I think she finally left him when he got arrested for selling and using drugs. But she went directly into another miserable relationship. Her self-esteem was so low, the only time she felt desired was when she was in bed with a man. Of course, we all know that a woman has even lower self-esteem following sex than before sex in these circumstances. This is an example of how a woman with low self-esteem abuses sex much like a person abuses drugs. The temporary high one gets is always offset by the down feeling after the drug wears off.

In Danielle's case, her imagination was so active (huge lower loops), each sexual experience was tremendous. It was like comparing cocaine to coffee. Her imagination amplified every sexual experience to a bigger and better experience. To be blunt, she had incredible orgasms. But this imagination has it's draw-backs. The feeling is so grand, she needs sex more often than the average person. She constantly thinks about it. When she gets it, she wants it in different positions and places. This exaggeration tendency also goes beyond sex. Every *emotion or fear* is exaggerated. Therefore, when she felt scared, she was terrified. When she broke a nail, call 911!

I'm the type of guy who helps little birds with broken wings. I could tell she was scared and really wanted to feel loved. I felt like a boy who had picked up a hurt puppy and was bringing it home to Mom. Her past experiences explained many of her problems. She had many significant emotional experiences that caused her pain. Her dad had molested and raped her. She had been raped as an adult as well. In fact, we were driving through Lubbock, Texas, and we passed a specific motel. She unemotionally pointed it out to me as the place she was raped. This really didn't surprise me. It did surprise me when she pointed out two more motels and mentioned they had remodeled them since the last time she had stayed there.

How many nineteen-year-old women know what the motels are like in a Bible-thumping town like Lubbock, Texas? I realized she had been using sex for many years to survive. She even knew the names of the strip clubs in the town. I didn't know Lubbock had any strip clubs! She said she just served drinks, but never danced. But I wondered. Not all women with big lower loops, no ethics, and a low self-esteems are this sleazy, but it's a good indicator that they are sexually promiscuous.

Note: A guy with big lower loops and a low self esteem can be just as much of a "slut." However, in American society those guys are called studs. It just doesn't seem fair.

Remember, it was the combination of many traits that made Danielle so unique. Her behavior was a result of the combination of her sociopathic behavior, low self-esteem, strong sex drives, anger toward men, and her self-castigating behavior. Each trait is like a chemical. When you mix them together, you often get a combustible reaction. Danielle was very combustible.

I suppose you want to know what happened in Lubbock? Well, I had the option of spending the night with her on very sexual terms or take her home. I chose to take her home. I was close enough to know my presuppositions and opinions were very accurate. But, after the motel comment... I was a little nervous to jump into the sack with her! I'll do a lot in the name of research, but risk death by disease? I don't think so. Learn from my experiences. Avoid getting involved with people that have a combustible combination of personality traits like Danielle's.

The next chapter is all about combustible personalities. Now that you know how to spot a certain sex drive, ask yourself what else you get with it? I found out personally that there is more to a great partner than a good sex drive. In fact, I have made more than my fair share of dating blunders. It is time to dig more into my tumultuous past and reveal some of my past mistakes.

Chapter IX

Dating Blunders

Have you looked back on a certain person that you used to date and asked yourself "What was I thinking?" If you have ever wondered what you ever saw in that once-upon-a-time special person, you understand what I mean by the phrase *dating blunders*. Those are the dates that you wish had never happened. Those are the three months you spent getting to know him only to find out you hate the person you worked so hard to get to know! We have all had experiences we wish had never happened.

In the stories I will relate, there were specific personality quirks that I believe caused the date to become a blunder. Some of these particular personality traits I have seen repeatedly in people with major problems in relationships. It is these traits I jokingly call Hell Traits. I derived the phrase Hell Traits from a certain phenomenon among college fraternities called Hell Week. Hell Week was one week out of the semester in which the members of the fraternity would create pain, discomfort, embarrassment, and overall hell for the young men being initiated. Often, as I was in the middle of a terrible breakup or heartache I wondered if going through Hell Week wouldn't be easier than dealing with this person. Therefore, each time I see a trait in a person that has *very bad* memories I refer to it as a Hell Trait.

Each of the two following stories relates a few of my Hell Traits to real life experiences. As you go through life, you may formulate a slightly different list of Hell Traits than my own. However, I have had certain experiences that have created this memorable list. The next chapter discusses all the Hell Traits in detail. Each trait, in a specific person, brought just a glimpse of hell into my life. Luckily, I got out unscathed, but much wiser. If you find a person with two or more Hell Traits... run, don't walk, to the nearest exit! Only in my worst nightmare have I seen one person with all of them. Uh! Oh!

A Date from Hell — Sheila

Have you ever had a date from hell? I have had more than my share of these dates. In some cases it was more than just one date! Some were the relationships from hell. To give you an example of one of those dates, here is the story about my date with Sheila. Sheila's personality involved four Hell Traits to learn about: dual personality, low self-esteem, a failure y, and self-castigation.

Dual Personality

Sheila and I met one Thursday night at a movie theater. As we talked, I noticed her conservative style of clothing. She came across as a sweet country girl and even told me she liked to cook and sew. She said she had a teddy bear quilt and hand-painted country plates on her bedroom wall. She has a cute southern accent and an innocent smile. This first encounter painted an image of a woman who would make a sweet girlfriend. So I asked her out .

When I went to pick her up, I was surprised to actually find pink teddy bears on her quilt and country style plates on her wall. I thought to myself, "my first impression must have been accurate." Before we left, some interesting things surfaced despite her cute accent. Although she does enjoy being on the ranch in central Texas, she has a saucy side that supersedes most city girls' wild side. To my surprise, Sheila had busted out the black pumps, black nylon hose and a leather mini-skirt. It was then that I questioned her proclaimed "country girl" image.

She told me she used to live alone in College Station, Texas. There, she had her day friends and her night friends. Does that imply a split personality? She then explained about her Arabian boyfriend who owns a few Los Angeles nightclubs and used to fly her out to L.A. for weeks at a time. When in L.A., she got chauffeured in limousines and wore the latest Rodeo Drive fashions while partying until dawn. She admitted she liked the high life, but some part inside her yearned for a nice life in the country raising animals. In other words, she was two parts struggling to combine themselves into one person. I thought to myself, "You can't judge a book by its cover." And at least I was right about that.

I soon decided her "bad girl" personality was too much for me. She was a very attractive woman, but something was different from the girl I met in the movie theater the day before. I could handle the leather mini-skirt and the hose, but she was wearing this earring that I couldn't accept. It was a nice earring, the problem was that it was in her nose! Since we met, she had gotten her nose pierced and was wearing a diamond earring on her left nostril! (This happened a few years before it was normal to pierce random body parts.) It really destroyed that country girl image I found so attractive. So much fire from this little southern belle.

We left her house and drove to the restaurant. We actually had a pleasant time at dinner and then had a few drinks at the bar. I couldn't help but keep asking questions trying to understand the incredible dichotomy in her personality. I thought the date was going to end without any major situations arising. Then Sheila suggested we swing by a party that was on our way home. I knew a few of the guys at the party so I felt comfortable. It was a pretty mellow get together. None-the-less, Sheila was being very affectionate toward me. She began holding my hand and then put her arms around me. I thought nothing of it because I only knew a few people at the party. I suppose everyone has dated a woman with a ring in her nose at one time or another. She got up to go to the restroom and when she returned she insisted that we leave the party immediately. When we got into the car I asked, "why the abrupt departure?" She then explained that the guy who owned the house was coming home any minute. I said, "So?" She went on to explain that she went on a few dates with him last week and he thought she was his new girlfriend. I said "You took me into a party where all of his friends thought I was moving in on his girlfriend? Thanks!" Needless to say, I was not happy to have been just minutes away from being the victim of a jealous boyfriend's rage.

Although I could have ended the date, my curiosity was piqued. What made this girl tick? When we returned to her house, she made some coffee and we talked for about an hour. It was at this point that I finally got the opportunity to look at her handwriting. Then, it all became clear. By the way, I now always look at the handwriting *before* the first date.

The first thing I noticed as she pulled out old samples of writing was that there were two different slants of writing in the samples. I asked her if the same person wrote all of them. She said, "Yes." I know sometimes the slant and size of writing changes slightly with moods, but this was a different can of worms.

One sample of writing told the whole story. The first two sentences were a solid AB slant. That of course, signifies the withdrawn, self-concerned, logical emotional outlay. Then, the next few sentences measured extremely heavy rightward DE and E+ slanted hand-writing. That, of course, implied an emotionally expressive, impulsive, outgoing emotional outlay. This was trouble. I was on a date with a woman with two different personalities.

As her writing changed, she actually became this new person with all the corresponding emotional reaction patterns. Now, just because writing changes slants with moods, it doesn't make that person a multiple. It is common for the slant or size of the handwriting to fluctuate slightly with mood. However, it is not common to have one sentence consistently measure AB while the second paragraph measures an E+ slant. In a case like this, the person has developed two separate neuro/psychological profiles to deal with two separate environmental situations. This sometimes develops to compensate for a confusing environment as a child, such as receiving mixed messages from two separate parents. The child needs to act one way to gain approval from one parent, and act another way to gain approval from the other one.

Regarding my hell date with Sheila, I should have run away after the nose-ring thing. But, after finding out she had taken professional massage classes, I decided we could be friends. Seriously, as we talked over coffee, she revealed many things about her life that made the hell traits in her handwriting come alive with tangible meanings.

Self-Castigation

Sheila shared with me some of her dating history. I thought I made a blunder having one date with her. However, I looked like a saint compared to the blunders she had in her past. As she told me about her past, she broke down and cried. She complained that most of her past relationships had ended with her in the hospital. She had a list of injuries: two broken wrists, one arm, and both ankles in the past two years. "It seems," she said solemnly, "I always go out with assholes." (I tried not to take that comment personally, since it was only our first date.) I was confused by this abusive pattern. Since I make an effort to avoid pain, it seems logical to me to stop dating people who are physically abusive. But remember, our subconscious desires dictate our actions. She had self-castigation (a desire to punish herself) and a need for a challenge (this is the primary trait that signifies a woman is attracted to asshole type men.)

People who have the self-castigation trait often feel guilt. The only way to remove that guilt is to force some sort of punishment on themselves. It is often, but not always, in the form of physical abuse by a mate she has chosen. In Sheila's case, she chose men that actually beat her. As a result of the beating, her guilt went away. Her conscience was clear. As an added bonus, she received loving sympathy from those around her. Wanting sympathy for failing is a classic example of a failure y, which is another hell trait she possessed.

I suppose it would have been most valuable to get access to her ex-boyfriend's handwriting to deduce a profile of the type of guy that would actually physically abuse someone. Although I didn't get a sample in this particular case, I will give you a typical trait scenario that indicates a high probability that the writer will resort to violence. Watch out for the following traits when combined with each other: low self-esteem, temper, sarcasm, heavy writing, aggression, and DE and E+ slant. A combination of all these will guarantee an aggressive, unpredictable, emotional person. (See the Trait Dictionary in Appendix A for location of these traits in the handwriting.)

Low Self-Esteem

She had very low self-esteem (very low t-bar). Hence, she would stay in a bad situation much too long. She frequently thought that she deserved this bad treatment. Also, she feared that if she left him, her life would become worse. Low self-esteem combined with the self-castigation easily explains the constant physical abuse, and her compliance. She went on to say, "My worst fear is to sleep alone." She's always had a roommate, or more realistically, a lover since she was fifteen. She would rather give herself to a stranger than face the night alone. I felt pity for her. I could only imagine how little respect she must have for herself after sleeping around every night, all those years. Because she never has had much faith in herself alone, much of the positive feelings about herself came from the approval of others. Therefore, one avenue of feeling loved was to seek sexual approval and pleasure from men.

Modern psychology has a name for this tendency: co-dependency. It is a constant need to be involved with someone and put his needs before your own. It is more often discussed in reference to women. However, because of the complexity of co-dependency, I cannot outline a specific handwriting style that defines it. There are too many variations. However, some clues to co-dependency can be seen in the low t-bar (self-esteem) and in the large lower loops (tendency to exaggerate physical needs).

The Failure Complex

The last and most serious red flag revealed by her handwriting was her failure complex. She had that infamous downturned y which always leads to screwing up whatever she feels might bring success. It is basically a fear of being successful. In a relationship, a person with a failure complex expects sympathy each time things don't work out as planned. Sheila and I would not have been compatible on that issue. When people fail, I don't play that game called sympathy very well. I tend to give rewards and positive reinforcement for success. That's my program. Her program was to give up and get sympathy from everyone. For example, when she got too stressed, she took the first plane home to Texas for a weekend with her parents. Her dad and mom would comfort her and console her on how hard life must be. This happened about once a month.

Most people with failure complexes have tragedies that are always inconvenient and unpredictable. As an example, Sheila had a tragedy at a most inconvenient time. My car was in the repair shop during part of our short friendship. I needed a ride to a local college in Los Angeles for a course on handwriting analysis. She promised to take me a week ahead of time. The day before the course, she called to confirm. Yet, when five o'clock came, I waited and waited. She didn't show up, didn't call, thus I had no ride. I was a little nervous because I had to attend the class, since I was the teacher. Luckily, I found a friend to loan me his car. This was my first lecture on the problems of a failure y in a relationship!

Sheila's Handwriting High Points:

Dual Personalities	Distinctly separate slants (in the same sentence)
Low Self -Image	Low t-bars
Self-Castigation	Sharp pointed leftward t-bars
Failure Complex	Downturned y
Needs a Challenge	Stinger-like hooks in a,c,or d
Large Sex Drives	Large lower loops
Lying Loops*	Small double loops in the letter o

*Not mentioned in story, but in handwriting and important to understand the entire personality.

Stinger
(Needs a Challenge)

Different Slant
(Dual Personality)

Backwards t-bar
(Self-castigation)

High ending stroke
(Need for attention)

Large lower loops
(Sex drives)

Double Loop in "o"
(Lying loops)

Downturned "y"
(Failure Complex)

Low t-bar
(Low self-image)

Sample 9.1: Sheila's writing with Hell Traits.

The next day, I found out what tragedy had happened that caused her to be such a flake. She had gotten so stressed the day before, she left at 3 AM to travel to her vacation house in Laguna Beach. She didn't tell anyone that she was leaving, she just "couldn't handle it anymore." After she received a dozen consolation phone calls from her friends, she came home. This pattern of running away is common among failure-driven people. When they get too close to a successful venture, they break, they run, and have an excuse not to cross the finish line. She broke, she ran, and I almost walked!

The Whole Package

Now, let's put all these traits together to establish a profile of the kind of man she needs. (If there is such a man, God help him.) She has low self-esteem, a desire to be punished, two personalities, and a failure complex. What kind of man does she need? A good therapist. The things she doesn't need are a little less obvious. She doesn't need a man who is passive and kind. She doesn't need someone who likes her too much, because she doesn't like herself. That wouldn't seem realistic to her. Our minds create a reality that is congruent with our subconscious images. She needs someone to punish her when she is bad, which, in her mind, is most of the time. Since failing is bad, he should punish her and console her when she fails, tough job. I also don't see any one man dealing successfully with both personalities. I see her skipping through life never being happy because her programs dictate behaviors that conflict with the conventional definition of happiness. I would venture to say the best she could ever expect in life is contentment, not happiness. (Contentment probably includes tragedy, problems, and pain.) But she might find satisfaction if she keeps seeking out guys who give her what she needs. I am glad to say I'm not anything like the type of guy she needed.

I got the privilege of watching Sheila prove the accuracy of my handwriting analysis over the next year. After I blew her off, she immediately hooked up with the most chauvinistic and abusive woman-hater I knew: Theo. In fact, almost everyone who knew Theo thought he was the biggest jerk in town. I knew she would be very content with this relationship. She would go to his house and spend the night, he would get what he wanted (sex), and she would get what she needed (mistreatment and someone to hold). He would treat her like dirt and she would like it. He wouldn't call her, and she liked him more. He was just as much trouble as she. I suppose it takes one to know one.

What did I learn from my date with Sheila? Always look at the handwriting before the first date. I have learned my lesson. By the way, Sheila's personality can be better understood if you look at each trait separately and stack them together in your mind. The handwriting sample isn't very clear, but it is the best I could locate. Focus your attention on the most relevant personality traits, the Hell Traits. Sheila had many other interesting handwriting strokes that space doesn't allow me to evaluate. I hope that you will never see this particular combination of traits in real life, but I am confident you will see each trait individually. I merely want to point out the separate handwriting traits that build a problem-case like Sheila. Therefore, the most important of Sheila's Hell Traits are highlighted. Look out for them! When you see them in a prospect, do as the knight did when he saw the Killer Rabbit in *Monty Python And The Holy Grail,* "Run away, run away!"

The point of this story is to investigate what a person needs. If you are a person who supplies those needs, hang on. If you are not that person, let go. Don't try to give people what you think is good for them; they will spit it back in your face. What is best for someone does not often coincide with what they need. Show them clearly and honestly what you have to offer. If you match their needs, then you have a relationship to pursue! Many will be like Sheila (screwed up). Your only option is take your losses and walk away. There is no good reason to stay in a relationship that doesn't support your needs.

You are destined for unhappiness when you try to be what another person wants, not realizing what their subconscious mind needs. I am thankful I can see what people require, at a subconscious level, from their handwriting. I don't waste time and emotional energy on people who will never appreciate me. I encourage you to do the same.

Profile of a Nymphomaniac — Marsha

I have made many blunders in my choices of women to date. Of course, I learn from each one. The next lesson I learned was from a dancer named Marsha. The major mistake was letting my emotions get involved before looking at her handwriting. The second mistake was not running away once I saw her writing. As Paul Harvey might proclaim, here is the rest of the story. It is a classic example of not heeding one's own advice. I saw all the street signs that told me the bridge ahead was out, yet I ignored the signs and took an unexpected swim.

When I was still in college, I participated in as many school events as possible. One of the things I did besides academia was a song and dance contest among the organizations on campus. Since we always performed as partners with the sorority known for the most beautiful and coolest women, I wouldn't miss the opportunity to spend two weeks with co-eds in dance tights! It wasn't uncommon to party after practice until five or six in the morning with the ladies. So, on this occasion I did. In the process I got real close with a girl in our group, Marsha. I really liked Marsha the first time I met her. She was cute, funny, outspoken, sarcastic, dirty-minded, and spontaneous—all the qualities you look for in a comedienne! So, as the night progressed, we laughed our way into each other's hearts. The next night, after practice, we continued getting to know each other. This time, the late night party took place at my house on Corral Beach. About eight of us were in the little house partying, so Marsha and I snuck out to the beach where the waves and full moon were mesmerizing. A walk on a moonlit beach is a good way to spontaneously inspire someone to become romantic!

We sat and watched the moonlight glimmer off the rolling waves. It wasn't five minutes before she rolled me on my back and began kissing me. I like *that* kind of aggression in a woman. Besides, it removes all curiosity as to whether or not she likes me! So, we kissed on the beach for awhile until we were interrupted by the party. My friend Craig, who always enjoyed his beer, decided to lay down in the middle of Pacific Coast Highway and wait for speeding cars to come within spitting distance before he would move out of the way! The girls screamed with fear and Craig and I laughed at the excitement. No harm done. After we got him off the pavement and back into the house, we called it a night. In fact, that night, I fell asleep between Marsha and her roommate on my queen-size bed. Although we just slept, I can say with pride that they were both wearing a pair of my boxer shorts. If I couldn't get into their shorts, at least they got into mine! Ha!

That was the start of a wonderful relationship, I thought. I did certain things absolutely perfectly. One, I didn't try to get her in bed the first time I had the chance. It was obvious we liked each other, we were holding hands before the beach scene. Even so, I waited until she made the first move. Being patient and passive may not always be an effective strategy, but for Marsha it was the correct one. After I saw her handwriting, I knew I was correct because she had stingers. If you recall, stingers signify that she needs a challenge in a relationship (see trait dictionary). Therefore, when you see stingers in a sample, you know they like to chase. Don't throw yourself at her or him.

You can be kind, just don't ever become "easy." Always make him work to keep your attention. If he ever, just for a moment, thinks that he has got you in his web (has control), he will begin to take advantage of you. He may eventually leave you for another challenge. This, of course, applies equally to women with stingers.

To get back to the story, Marsha had this trait in an intense way. Therefore, I played it smoothly by showing interest, but not showing a strong emotional attachment whether we went out or not. I invited her over "to study" on a Saturday night. Sure! She's no dummy, we both knew we wanted more than a study session. So, after she finished her homework I started in on the old back rub technique. If you ever get a chance to rub someone's back to the classical music of Tchaikovsky... do it! We were sitting up on the bed with the candle light dancing to the music. Eventually, the pressure of my hands became synchronized with the rhythm of the music. It wasn't long until she was so "touched" by the music she turned over and... well... I won't go into any more detail. But, let's just say it was an experience that verified all the large lower loops theories in handwriting!

This part of the story brings up the next facet of her handwriting: huge lower loops. Since the lower zone is physical imagination, any loop in that area relates to her body: exercise, travel, or sex. The larger the loop the larger the imagination. In Marsha's case, she had tremendous lower loops that went into the writing below it (too many irons in the fire). So, the large loops mean huge insatiable sex drives that can only be satisfied by a variety of people and/or different positions. She may not be having sex with all of them, but she will be thinking about it. The reason I felt she needed sex with many different partners is a combination of the desire for a challenge trait and the insatiable sex drive. That trait kept her moving from one challenge to another, constantly trying to satisfy her insatiable sexual desires with constant variety.

One final note in this profile of the proverbial *nymphomaniac* is the self-image (the height of the t-bar). Marsha does not have a high self-image or high goals. Her t-bar is not always low, like many, but it is by no stretch of the imagination consistently high. This indicates much of the sense of approval she feels is derived from other people. This tendency would have been multiplied if she had big loops in her d's, but she didn't. You and I know that promiscuous sex does not raise self-esteem. However, much like drugs, it is a quick high that temporarily eliminates the pain and then drags the esteem lower.

Back to the story. In this particular relationship I opened myself up to the misjudgments of the heart. I started to really like her. I actually believed the pillow talk when she said, "I've never felt this way before about anyone." I'm older and wiser now. It took me awhile to understand if she did it with me *that* quickly, she had done it before *that* quickly, and will do it again just as quick. I used to be cocky and thought I was special if a woman gave her body to me on the first date. It isn't always my ability to create instant chemistry! She might make it a habit. But, what I should have trusted was what the handwriting revealed, which I chose to ignore.

I told myself, "I know she's got big y's. She told me she used to sleep around, but now she's got it under control." Also, I ignored the fact that I knew she needed a challenge and I let my guard down. After the Saturday night study session, I didn't hide excitement and affection toward her. In other words, I let her know I liked her too soon. As I asked around at school about her reputation I realized the big y theory was accurate. If rumors are to be believed, she had slept with three of my own fraternity brothers in the past year, as well as numerous other guys. What I thought was something special, she thought was just another weekend fling. One time, she had sex in the bathroom during a party! It happened because she told my friend Karl that he was over-sexed. He responded by taking off her clothes and doing her in the bathtub. I guess she was right! Furthermore, at this time, she was engaged to another man. She was easy. In fact, our entire affair took place a few days after she broke off her engagement. Are you convinced yet that big y's mean a big sex drive, imagination, and variety (like on the bathroom floor)? In fact, all my experiences support the big 'y' theory.

But the final mistake I made, besides not running away after the sight of her handwriting, was not paying attention to the different

Marsha's Handwriting High Points

Dual Personality   Distinct separate slants
(in the same sentence)

Low Self-Image   Low t-bars

Sarcasm   Pointed t-bars

Needs A Challenge   Stinger like hooks in a,c,or d

Large Sex Drive   Large lower loops

Confusion of Interests   Long lower loops into the
writing below

Desire For Attention   High ending strokes

Distinct slant variation
(Dual Personality)

Long & Large lower loops
(Sex drives & Variety)

FA Slant

DE Slant

Change in military practices effec
economy + govt.
Hoplete phalanx
tyrant - leader the put together a
peasant farmers and a merchant
sponsored public works
Power corrupt - became tyranic
Tyrany was, in consistent, wrt
of community. But he generally
freek development a great deal.
More people were in a posistior
what was going on. Tyrany involv
Tyrany broke the monopoly th
had developed.

Low t-bar
(Low self-image)

Stingers
(Needs a challenge)

Sample 9.2: Marsha's Handwriting

slants in her writing. To reiterate, the backward and forward slants revealed a dual personality. I should have expected her to revert to a different person, but I had already become emotionally attached to her nice personality. Don't let this happen to you. If you see major problems with a person, run away. Don't take a chance of falling in love with the good parts only to have your heart torn apart by the bad parts. Pay attention to what you are reading. Be aware and learn from my mistakes. Be aware of the risks if you choose to get involved with a dual personality-nymphomaniac!

What happened the following week, after that great backrub, was a total personality switch. She became the Ice Queen of Malibu. She was cold, distant, and aloof. She acted like nothing had ever happened and I was just another acquaintance. "Hi, how ya doing, gotta go, see ya around." Now, I got the chance to feel how women feel when men sleep with them and then turn around and ignore them. It's not a pleasant feeling. As time passed, I realized that the personality which interacted with me on Saturday night really was intensely attracted to me *that night*. Anything could have triggered the personality switch, and the new personality didn't know me the way the other personality knew me. So, I guess I could wait until the good personality came back. Alas, don't forget, the game was about conquering a challenge as much as it was to temporarily build her self-esteem.

The problem was that I let my heart take total control of the way I felt. I actually wanted more of her. That's not bad in itself. However, by the handwriting, I should have seen the pattern of getting involved then withdrawing into herself until time for another challenge came around. I saw this pattern in action just two weeks later when we were all out again. She chose another fraternity brother, instead of me, to spend the night with! Although it hurt to be rejected, I should've counted my blessings for getting out of such a head-case's life. However, I found out, once my emotions become involved, my logic sometimes goes on vacation.

So, take my experience as a warning to you. I got involved with a
fun, cute, sexual dynamo that blew my mind and then blew me off.
I got hurt. If I could turn back the clock, I would have just run away
without ever getting involved with Marsha. Hindsight is 20/20. In
the next chapter, I will reveal what may become the most important information you will ever discover...

> *"Many a man has fallen with a girl in light*
> *so dim he would not have chosen a suit by it."*
> *— Maurice Chevalier*

Chapter X

Hell Traits

This section details those personality characteristics I highly recommend avoiding! People with too many of these traits can make your life a living hell. Be forewarned, if someone's handwriting reveals these traits, this person is trouble. Of course, the degree of trouble depends on the intensity and frequency of the trait in the handwriting. Please double check your analysis before you scream "Psycho!" and run for the door. But, back up a few feet the first time you see any one of the traits in this chapter. Unfortunately, you may find you have a few Hell Traits in your own personality. A personality clash could arise because the Hell Traits in your own personality don't mix well with the Hell Traits in someone else's. Once you begin looking at people's handwriting on a regular basis, you will realize just how many people in your own life have some Hell Traits. Hell Traits are like deadly chemicals, in very small quantities we can deal with it, but taken in big doses, we can't survive. The best way to avoid pesticides is to eat all-natural food prepared without chemicals. Likewise, the best way to deal with someone's Hell Traits is to avoid people with Hell Traits.

Hell Trait #1
Dual Personality

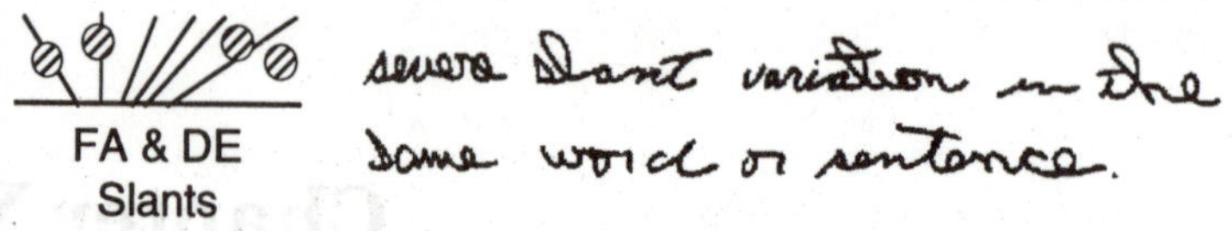

FA & DE Slants	*severe Slant variation in the same word or sentence.*

Figure 10.1: Dual Personality

Dual personality is shown in handwriting by an obvious slant variation, leftward to rightward, in the same sentence. This person has trouble making emotional decisions because of the varied emotional influences. When a stressful situation arises, she withdraws into herself, into her introverted personality. There is a fundamental duality within the psyche that creates unpredictable emotional responses. Some people call this person just moody, but, it goes deeper than just mood swings. The actual biological synaptic responses in the brain function in two different distinct patterns, depending on the circumstance. As you can imagine, having two separate biological responses to the same situation can create quite an unpredictable relationship. It does.

This is not quite the same as the famous Sybil character with more than eight separate personalities. If you were to see an actual Sybil's handwriting, you would find more than eight distinctly separate handwriting styles. In fact, you would probably think they were all written by different people. My label of the "Dual Personality" is a more practical way of describing someone with access to both ends of the spectrum of emotional responsiveness (FA/AB to DE/E+). Since most people consistently use primarily one emotional outlay, I consider the variable slant writer unusual and unpredictable.

Dating a dual personality has its advantages and its disadvantages. Usually, the nice personality is especially extra sweet. She is kind, generous, fun loving, and entertaining. That is the personality you see on the good days. That is the personality you fall in love with. Then... whamo! The other personality comes out. This personality is usually a real bitch/bastard. The ones I have known have had these two dispositions: sweetheart vs. total bitch. I suppose a man's dispositions would be: gentleman vs. asshole. Believe me, you don't want to be around when the bitch or asshole comes out!

Remember the story of Marsha? One day she would be very affectionate and loving toward me, then the next day she wouldn't speak to me and wouldn't tell me why. This is typical of a dual personality. When in her other personality she displayed all the characteristics of a pissed-off introvert (FA writer). She harbored her emotions and dwelled on them within her own mind.

Sample 10.2: Dual Personality. Notice the two distinct slants within the same sentence.

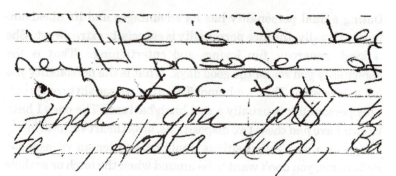

Sample 10.3: Two distinctly separate slants.

As stated earlier, these people are very hard to deal with. I have to admit that this particular girl was extremely fun to be around, when she was in her sweetheart mode. But, in her bitchy one, watch out.

Parts of this type of person are pleasant and enjoyable. But remember that you must consider the entire package when getting into a relationship. I really enjoyed having Marsha as a friend or buddy. In fact, we continued to be casual buddies over the next two years. You can avoid friends when they are in their bitchy moods. However, in a relationship, it is difficult just to leave town for two days when the unpleasant personality comes out. If you are already involved, or get involved, with a person with two personalities, it is imperative you talk about emotions. Look at his handwriting for talkativeness. This person has internal struggles within himself about what he wants. Therefore, the other partner gets mixed messages and might be hurt. If you talk about all his emotions, dealing with the strange variations in emotions can be much easier. People with this trait need to be with a mature, understanding partner who is willing to try to understand their changing feelings.

It is now a fundamental rule of mine not to date women with the trait of dual personality. In fact, even in my friendships with males, I am wary of this trait. That is why it is a Hell Trait.

Hell Trait #2
Lives for the Moment

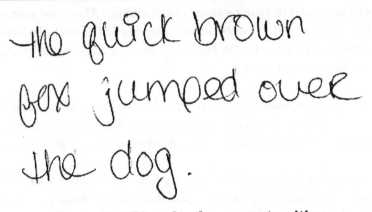

Figure 10.4: Lives for the moment writing.
Notice very limited upper zone strokes.

The "lives for the moment" person can also be typecast as immature or irresponsible. This person does not consider the consequences of his/her actions. Therefore, this person will do things because it feels good at the moment, not considering the long-term effects.

If you recall the three zones in handwriting, the middle zone is the "today/ mundane zone." It is in this zone that the daily activities take place. Any writing that goes above the mid-zone penetrates into the philosophical / ethical / future zone. "Lives for the moment" handwriting never penetrates the upper zone, therefore they are incapable of planning into the future or drawing their own ethical conclusions. These people depend on the daily environment for their ethical decisions.

This writer is not dangerous, just immature. This handwriting is common in 12-18 year old girls. During this time frame, they are not forced to plan ahead. They are allowed to live in the moment.

It is also the time they get in trouble: try drugs, get pregnant, party, skip school, etc. They simply don't plan ahead. This behavior may seem common among young boys too. However, as a handwriting analyst, I found the "lives for the moment" trait predominantly in young women's handwriting. Also, most people outgrow this trait. I rarely find anyone over thirty with the lives in the moment trait. On the other hand, a majority of young females display the trait.

Just like a sailboat, if you have no rudder or sail, you are subject to every change in current which comes by. This writer is subject to whatever, or whomever, seems like the best for her at the time.

I remember dating a girl during my high school years with this trait. Her name was Michelle and she was very beautiful. Her ethics changed with the wind! As I was visiting her house one day, I noticed a photo of her and some guy in a gondola in Venice, Italy. Inquisitively, I asked if she dated that guy while she was there. She said, "No. we were just friends." I persisted and asked, "Well, did you sleep with him?" She said no. About a month later we were playing some silly drinking game and the topic of where was the strangest place you ever had sex? Quite humorous answers came up. My answer was in a trolley car with her. Her answer was in a gondola in Italy! Did she lie, or what? People who live for the moment do or say whatever serves them the best at that time. The first day we met, she told me a long fabricated lie about her non-existent boyfriend and how they had just broken up. We stopped seeing each other when she decided she wanted to make out with another guy at a party when we were supposed to be together. After all, I suppose he was what she wanted *at that moment*.

You may think that it is not unusual for a girl to lie about who she has slept with. Perhaps this is one of those "acceptable" fibs for either gender to tell. However, when I looked, she did not have lying loops in her handwriting. As I found out, she did lie on more than one occasion. So the fact she had no upper loops throws out

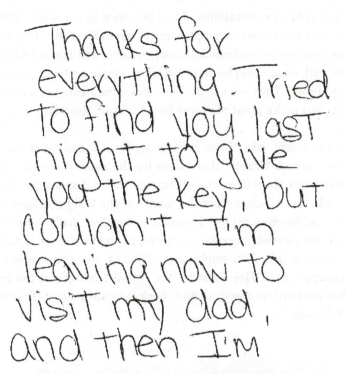

Thanks for everything. Tried to find you last night to give you the key, but couldn't I'm leaving now to visit my dad, and then I'm

Sample 10. 5: 22 year old female that lacks the ability to plan ahead. Although mostly printed, notice size of middle zone compared to upper zone.

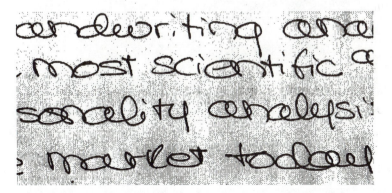

Sample 10. 6: 16 year old female. Childlike, immature, lives in today.

much of the predictability of her behavior because she actually believes whatever is most pleasing to her at the time. People like this are very unpredictable, undependable, and can be lots of fun. After all, what could be more fun than someone who lives to enjoy right now? They are not the best choice for a long-term relationship, but make great partners for a night on the town!

On the bright side, if you are looking for a one-night stand, this writer is your ticket! If she lives for the moment and has large lower loops, she will want it all, immediately! Because she likes to try whatever feels good at the moment, she will be willing to try new and different things. If you are dating one, don't be surprised if she does something completely stupid and then says, "I just felt like doing it." You might say, "Didn't you think about the consequences?" Her answer, "No. It just felt right at the time." That is when you check out and check in to the nearest clinic to get a V.D. test !

Hell Trait #3
Fear of Success

This is one aspect of a personality that you might never know about a person until years have passed, unless you look at the handwriting. The fear of success is shown in the lower loops such as y and g when the returning line of the lower loop turns downward, away from the baseline. It is easy to remember if you picture the lower loop like a race track. The race driver must make one full loop in order to complete the race. As the loop reaches toward the finish line,

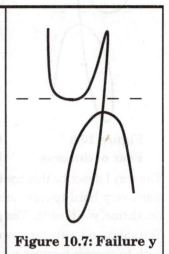

Figure 10.7: Failure y

the baseline, it turns away from the checkered flag. This same analogy applies to a person completing projects or goals in life. Whether you call it change directions, abort the mission, or just plain failure, this writer doesn't finish. He has a fear of success. Therefore, if the turn-away hook is severe, you know she really screws it up good. (Figure10.8)

If the loop crosses the baseline (the finish line), it changes the trait significantly. The person will finish the job and succeed, but she will have remorse and dejected feelings associated with the success it brings. Look carefully to notice if the turn-away hook actually crosses the baseline before it turns away. (Figure 10.9)

If it just doesn't complete the loop, it simply means something is incomplete in her physical life, it must have a turn-away hook to qualify as *fear of success*. (Figure 10.10)

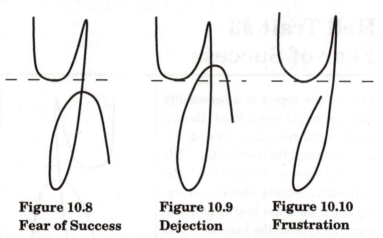

Figure 10.8   **Figure 10.9**   **Figure 10.10**
Fear of Success   **Dejection**   **Frustration**

The way I describe this trait to a person who possesses it is, "You work very hard toward success. Yet, when you get close to the finish line, you blow it. You give up, change directions, or just quit. You subconsciously turn away. Your subconscious sabotages your path to success because you are afraid of the changes that being successful might bring. You might have a resume and references as long as my arm that says you are a hard worker and very competent. But no one could explain why you never worked out like they expected you to."

This behavior applies to personal life, as well as professional life. Every time life is flowing smoothly, these people will find a reason (like an argument or conflict) that creates turbulence and problems. One of the most common reasons for this behavior is a pattern of being rewarded for failure, usually developed during one's childhood. A simple story illustrates this point. A little girl plays on the Little League softball team. She tries very hard to play well. But she strikes out all three times at bat and drops the fly ball. After the game, her parents take her out for ice cream and tell her, "It's all right, we love you, etc. " Then, when she comes home from school with an "A" on a test, her parents say, "That's nice, Dear. Did you clean your room?" As this story illustrates, a pattern is set that rewards failure more than success. For the child, the choice is very clear. "If I screw up, they will give me attention and console me. If I succeed, nothing special happens." So, the child develops the fear of success/desire to fail complex.

This analogy isn't the only way the fear of success develops, but it is one of the more common scenarios. I find this trait much more common in women than in men. My speculation as to the reasons for this is that a traditional upbringing places more emphasis on competition and winning in a boy's childhood than in a girl's. Therefore, there is more positive reinforcement for succeeding in a competitive environment for a young boy. Sometimes, a little girl who is assertive, competitive, and successful gets mixed messages. On one hand it is nice that she won, on the other hand, it's not lady-like to dominate and win the competition. Not to mention the fact that the little girls who act more vulnerable, helpless, and feminine get more attention from the little boys (big boys, too). After all, "The boys won't like you if you beat them while playing games." Perhaps this socialization process is one reason why this trait is more common among women.

This trait also has something to do with the fear of change. Success brings change. If a person's self-esteem isn't very high and successful change has brought unwelcome circumstances in the past, one could easily associate success with more unpleasant changes. If

Sample 10.11: Fear of Success

your entire network of friends are wanna-be's and wish-I-could's, then your success would create a change in your relationships. You might make them look bad!

This is a tricky trait to deal with successfully. Although the trait may present itself consistently in the handwriting, it doesn't always show up in short-term behavior. But when it does appear, it could ruin an entire project unless you jump in and bail it out. In a relationship, she could decide that the relationship is going too smoothly (it is successful) and decide to start a fight. When dealing with this person, you should always keep moving the carrot one step further than her reach. If the relationship is going perfectly, tell her there is room for improvement. If she works for you, don't promote her to manager as a reward for being successful, promote her to manager because you want her to prove herself on a different level. You aren't satisfied she is giving it her 100%. In other words, keep moving the finish line from her reach so she doesn't get close enough to turn away in fear.

Sample 10.11 is from a woman who has a severe fear of success combined with an incredible perfectionist quality (straight baseline). Her t-bars indicate tremendous enthusiasm and humor. If she didn't have the failure y, her personality would be without major flaws. However, she is a bit ostentatious and perfectionistic, although stable. Because of the good self-image and enthusiasm, I don't think the failure trait is prevalent in her everyday life. She probably just screws up the real important things in a very big way!

In conclusion, I would never hire someone with this trait. Likewise, I would not choose a girlfriend who has this trait. However, if you are already in love with a person with this trait, you can deal with it effectively, but it won't be easy. I suggest you avoid the fear of success trait if you can. If you or someone you love has this trait, you can discover how to eliminate it quickly by listening to audio tapes using modern NLP techniques. (See appendix C)

Hell Trait #4
Low Self-Esteem

This is the one trait that is perhaps the most common problem in the United States. In relationships, it sticks up its ugly head and will cause you problems. In handwriting a low self-image is shown by a low t-bar. The cross of the letter t is on or below the top of the middle zone. A low self-image is also revealed by a very small personal pronoun I. Since capital letters indicate the strength of one's ego, a small letter I reveals the writer doesn't have a

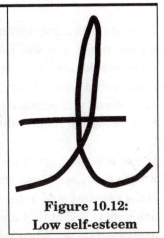

Figure 10.12:
Low self-esteem

great amount of ego strength about himself. Look for the personal pronoun capital I. To confirm any indication of self-esteem, look to the height of the cross on the letter t.

The person with a low self-image fears failure and fears change that could bring failure. Consequently, she doesn't set high goals or plan very far ahead in the future.

When I explain this trait to a woman who has it I usually say, "When you look in the mirror, you see all the imperfections. You think so many other women are prettier than you. You're constantly questioning your self-worth."

It is a self-critical evaluation that degrades one's sense of personal value. If you are dating someone who doesn't hold himself in high value, how is he going to treat you? Usually two scenarios reveal themselves. The first one is pleasant. He respects you and idolizes you for having so many things that he doesn't possess. In the process of valuing you, a person with low self-esteem will often go out of his way to do things to make you like him. But don't be fooled by the niceness in the beginning. The person with a low self-image always wants a payback.

Someone with a low self-image lacks personal power. If you don't love yourself, you will look for confidence and esteem through other people, instead of from within yourself. Therefore, in a relationship, you will not only have to possess enough courage, self-esteem, and personal power for yourself, but you will have to have enough to support that person's fragile ego, too.

If you are male, don't make the mistake of assuming that all women with low self-esteem are bitches. That's not the case. Some of the sweetest girls in the world have low self-esteem. What this amounts to is that they are so sweet because they want others to approve of them. When someone's internal references state that she is not approved of, she looks elsewhere to find approval. The approval will have to come from you. But as soon as you forget to approve, that person has no foundation to stand on. Thus she reacts like a rabid dog trapped in a corner, she must fight her way out. This fight usually includes biting you.

Often, you will find their lovers treating them like dirt, and they think they deserve it! Remember, if someone allows himself to be treated like dirt, he will have no problem treating you like dirt.

I like to describe self-esteem in handwriting with an analogy. At the state fair, there is always a tall pole with a bell on top. People take turns swinging a huge hammer that propels a metal cylinder up the pole toward the bell. Only a few men can actually make the bell ring. The letter t is much like that game at the fair. The stem is much like the pole. The cross of the t is where the metal cylinder stops after the hammer is swung. If the t-bar is crossed on the very top of the stem, the bell rings and "We have a winner!" Alternatively, if the t-bar is crossed on the lower side of the t-stem, we have someone who isn't very powerful (low self-esteem). The height of the t-bar also correlates exactly with the goals. A low t-bar signifies low goals. A high t-bar signifies high goals.

There are advantages to dating a person with a low self-image. He or she will bend over backwards, literally, to get your approval. People with a low image of themselves will usually stay in a bad situation much too long. They lack the courage to leave. Therefore, your lover won't leave you as quickly. Also, they tend to take more abuse than people who respect themselves. If you are abusive and want a partner to be totally dependent on you, perhaps you need a partner with a low self-image.

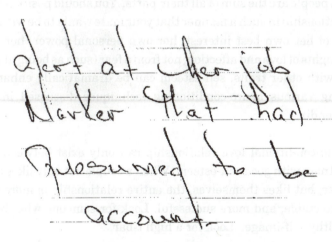

Sample 10:13: Low t-bars: low self-image/ low goals
(Notice the tall stems of the letters d and t indicate pride and vanity. This is false pride because it is not supported by a good self-image. This woman displays strength and ego to the world, while inside, she is weak and insecure.)

In almost all the cases where a woman has been abused, I find low self-esteem. (I don't know whether the abuse caused the low esteem on the low esteem allowed the abuse.) It reminds me of a 19-year-old girl who had terribly low self-esteem. She was living with a man who beat her regularly. He was also addicted to drugs. She had a very low self-image that caused her to feel that she deserved the violent treatment. Although she said she didn't like it, she didn't leave him. Why would someone put up with that? She was so insecure, she wasn't sure she could find someone better. She wasn't sure she had the strength to make it on her own. She kept thinking thoughts like, "No one else would want me, I am stupid and ugly, etc." (By the way, she wasn't ugly.)

A person with low self-esteem may be attractive in the beginning because the person is extra sweet, humble, generous, etc. Remember, people are the sum of all their parts. You should position your relationship in such a manner that your mate wants to be with you out of her own best interest, her own personal power, her own thoughts of love and affection, not from a fear (such as being alone). As with other traits, self-esteem can be dramatically enhanced using various neuro-conditioning techniques discussed in the appendix.

An unconditional love relationship can only exist between two partners with good self-esteem. When a couple not only likes each other, but likes themselves, the entire relationship is more fun, more stable, and more successful. Look for someone who has a healthy self-image. Look for a high t-bar.

Hell Trait #5
Needs a Challenge

This trait is very common in both men and women. It has been described as the trait of manipulation, anger at the opposite sex, or the need for a challenge. It probably fits slightly into each of those categories. I should warn you that although it is one of my hell traits, it is so common it is difficult to avoid.

It is shown in the letters c, a, and d. It is a hook-like shape that forms the top circle of those letters. It has been called a Stinger because of its resemblance to a bee's hook-like stinger which hurts very badly if you get stung.

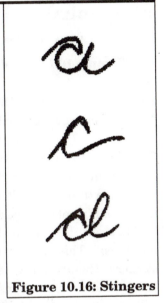

Figure 10.16: Stingers

People who have stingers in their handwriting usually get a thrill out of stinging others. It is usually directed at the opposite sex. Depending on the other traits in the handwriting, it could just be a game or malicious behavior.

The bottom line in a relationship is that the person who possesses the stinger trait needs a challenge to remain interested. These people will often seek out very tumultuous people, just to have a good fight. These are the game players. It is this type of person who says, "I hate playing games," and then proceeds to act in an inconsiderate way to give the impression that he doesn't like her too much.

In any case, these people are rarely satisfied with nice-guys or nice-girls. They are attracted to the rebel, the wild beast, the untamable. It is the thrill of the chase, rather than the prize, that

[handwriting sample]
reek development a great deal
More people were in a position
what was going on. Many invol

Sample 10.17: Needs a challenge. Notice stingers.

keeps them interested. This is the trait that says about a woman "Don't be too nice, I am only attracted to assholes."

Therefore, if you first meet a person who has a stinger in his handwriting, know that the most self-defeating move you can make is to throw yourself at him. Because he needs a challenge, he will only want you if he gets to chase you down. So, act as if you couldn't care less whether you go out with him or not. Act indifferent. This same attitude works with women who have stingers. This attitude is usually accepted as an effective strategy to take under most circumstances, but it is the only attitude that will attract people with stingers. The simple play hard to get strategy falls under the category of the economics of love. The need for a challenge is a different animal, but utilize that strategy as well.

What the subconscious mind is saying in a woman's stinger is that there is an underlying resentment at the male gender. The man's stinger shows an anger at the female gender. It reveals itself in a predatory attitude. The bigger the prey, the greater the feeling of conquering. Relationships become a game. Love becomes tumultuous and unpredictable. The entire movie *Dangerous Liaisons* was about a man with very big stingers. He manipulated the women into bed in a most dangerous game. If you aren't sure how stingers are revealed in relationships, go see that movie. How do you win? I don't think anyone ever wins that game. But the way to keep a stalemate going is never give in completely. If you date a person with this trait, never give up total control.

Hell Trait #6
Prevarication

Honesty is one of the most sought-after personality traits. Unfortunately, honesty or dishonesty is a result of many variables, least of which are the person's integrity and the specific situation. However, some people have so much internal confusion that they lie when the truth is better. The worst case scenario is the letter o shown here. This is the

**Figure 10.18:
Lying loops**

pathological liar. He will make up stories and is basically not trustworthy. He probably does not know what the real truth is. Luckily, I do not see this trait very often. I hope you don't either. However, if you ever see this trait consistently in someone's handwriting take my advice, "Run, don't walk, to the nearest exit!"

This trait and other levels of communication are shown in the lower case letter o. The letter o is a communication letter. You will notice that you can also see the other traits in the letter o such as: secretiveness, self-deceit, talkativeness, and frankness. The lying loops, as I call them, are a combination of a large secretive loop and a large self-deceit loop. It is shown by two huge inner loops in both halves of the letter o that cross. Together, this writer is deceiving others and himself! He simply forgets what the truth is! If you see this occasionally, in one out of ten, don't assume he is a pathological liar. He does lie, but not to the severity that the name implies. As you know, many basically honest people tell white lies in different circumstances. Ethics, integrity, and opportunity are also factors in honesty. You must take the entire writing into consideration.

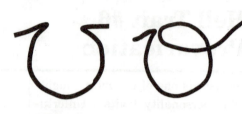

| Self-deceit | Talkative | Secretive |

Figure 10.19a: The Letter O Loops

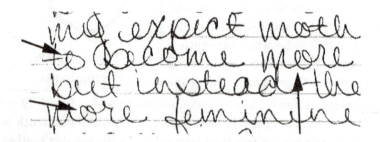

Sample 10.19b: Prevarication shown in double loops in o.

If you find two small inner loops in the letter o, you have a person that prevaricates (lies) occasionally about small details. A secretary often has these small loops when she says "The boss is in a meeting, may I take a message?" All the while, the boss is standing next to her saying, "I don't want to talk to him!"

If you recall the discussion about the three zones in handwriting, I mentioned that any loop, wherever you find it, is imagination. Therefore, if a loop is in the upper zone, one might imagine things associated with philosophy, religion, or ethics. If the loop is in the lower zone, the imagination might be physical or sexual. If the loop is in the middle zone, like the letter o, the writer imagines things pertaining to daily events. Since the o is a communication letter, you get imagination as to what someone tells you. The bigger the loops the more he lies or the more secrets are being kept.

Hell Trait #7
Resentment

Resentment is one of the most self-destructive personality traits anyone could possess. It is a burning anger rooted in a sense of unfairness. We have seen resentment come to a head each time we see a riot in inner city neighborhoods. Often, this violent display of aggression is a result of years of perceived unfairness by a system over which people have no control. The reality of the system is irrelevant because the resentment is

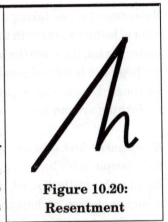

**Figure 10.20:
Resentment**

a perceived feeling of unfairness, not necessarily reality. The major victim of a person's internal resentment is himself. Each day he blames others, feels angry, suppresses emotion, and feels out of control building up such emotional tension inside that it invariably destroys his happiness.

When someone feels like he has been treated unfairly, it gives him an excuse to treat others with the same degree of unfairness. Just like in a city riot. Normally, men and women wouldn't run around burning and looting their own neighborhoods. However, given a specific incident which states very clearly that there is no justice for them, it gives those people an excuse to inflict a lack of justice on others. That incident is on a large scale with society in general.

The same mental justification works inside one's mind in a one–on–one relationship. If the husband comes home from work feeling resentment at his boss, he is likely to want to vent this frustration. Usually, resentment is not directed at the cause of the problem. Therefore, the husband gets angry at his wife for burning the meatloaf! Depending on the level of aggression and temper the husband possesses, the resentment could be the root cause of violence.

Resentment is like taking a very angry situation and putting it in a pot of boiling water with the lid sealed closed. The longer it stays under the lid, the more the pressure builds. Soon, the inside of the pot begins to bend and possibly even melt because of the pressure and heat. Eventually, the lid blows off with terrible force, affecting everything around it.

Resentment first eats away at the person inside. Studies reveal that people who have high degrees of anger and resentment become physically ill much more frequently than those who report a higher degree of happiness and contentment. In fact, one psychologist suggests that resentment could be a root cause of certain types of cancer. He did an informal study on his clients who had cancer. He told me that every one of the cancer patients showed the resentment stroke in their handwriting. It seemed logical to me that after getting cancer, a person might develop a sense of resentment and think life wasn't fair. However, he informed me that the resentment was in their handwriting long before any diagnosis of the cancer was formed. Therefore, the cancer may have been nature's way of telling them to lighten up. Resentment is not a healthy trait. After eating away at the person internally (psychologically and physically) it begins to affect his external environment: family, friends, and work. If you get involved with a person who has a high degree of resentment, you will be affected by that anger.

The trait of resentment is shown by an inflexible beginning stroke at the beginning of a word. It must start at or below the baseline and remain rigidly straight. This person is harboring anger at someone or some situation. It is an anger that is unresolved. Each frustration builds up more tension. Resentful people tend to be very intolerant of the frailties of life. They often think things are unfair. They have a built -up sense of hurt or injustice. They have a lot of dangerous stored energy. It is stored in the form of hate.

| **Figure 10.21:** | **Figure 10.22:** |
| **Temper t-bar** | **Resentment in "j"** |

Temper is the release of anger. (Temper is shown in the letter t. Therefore, if a person doesn't have a temper, the resentment will come out in other ways. This resentment is compounded if the person is a deep writer. Remember, the heavier he presses on the paper, the more he harbors emotions. If resentment is harbored for a long time, it could explode like a volcano. Avoid a romantic involvement with a person who posseses a large degree of resentment.

Sample 10.23: Resentment is revealed in an inflexible beginning stroke.

The young man knew and he was u
yet that fact neither consoled hir.
He was lost and the beauty and pe
He longed for an answer, shouting to;
to be answered only by the hollow
He wanted to understand the loss but.
flowed through his thoughts and pear
He fell to the ground, screaming in an.
tortured his mind and the pain

-- Michael F

**Sample 10.24: Jealousy in Michael's handwriting.
Notice tight loops on capitals signifying jealousy.**

Hell Trait #8
Jealousy

Webster defines jealous as being resentfully suspicious of one's rival or a rival's influence. It also says jealousy is being very watchful and careful in guarding or keeping one's possessions. Both definitions are accurate in defining one of a relationship's most detrimental emotions. I simplify these definitions and simply say jealousy is a fear of losing someone's love.

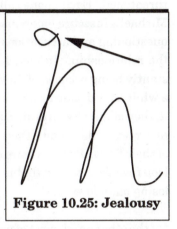

Figure 10.25: Jealousy

There is a trait for jealousy in someone's handwriting. However, you should note that many emotions we label jealousy could also be labeled as insecure, worried, overly affectionate, concerned, or simply valid concern for one's future. The jealousy handwriting reveals is the kind of constant jealousy which is unwarranted and stems from a deep fear of being unloved.

The sample of handwriting shown here is from a man named Michael who was obsessed with feelings of jealousy. One of Michael's means of expressing his affection for his girlfriend was through poetry. In almost all of his poems, Michael chose phrases that expressed his fear of her leaving him. He used phrases such as "I can't live without you. The pain of losing you would be so intense" and "Don't ever leave me." As you can hear, Michael's emphasis in his poetry was his fear of losing her, not his love and appreciation in having her. As the classic Napoleon Hill book *Think and Grow Rich* illustrates, whatever the mind dwells upon it turns into reality. Therefore, it was no surprise to me to discover that Michael's fiance left him after only four months. And yes, he was heartbroken, just like he had written about so many times before. He didn't just have pain and heartbreak after she left him. He had pain all during the relationship. He hurt at each moment he felt threatened. Each phone call, glance, or male visitor would cause Michael's insecure emotions to spring into action. His constant questioning and accusations of her created immense problems in the relationship. In fact, I have known women who were constantly being accused of having affairs by their husbands. After a while they decided since they were already getting punished for it, they might as well do it. So, these women had affairs which they never would have had if their husbands hadn't made such an issue of their fears. People's fears usually become reality. The jealousy loop reveals a person that is obsessed with the insecure feeling of losing one's love.

On the other hand, most of us will feel an emotion labeled jealousy at one time or the other. Because you occasionally feel insecure about losing the one you love does not automatically label you a jealous person. I remember when I expressed emotions some could call jealousy, but I thought they were valid insecurities. I had been seeing a particular young woman for about four months when she and her best friend took a ski trip one holiday weekend. I couldn't go, but honestly wished her a wonderful time. Since I have never been a jealous person, I didn't say, do, or feel, any insecurity about her spending the weekend skiing and partying with a bunch of horny men hitting on her. I figured she was an adult and could (and would) do whatever she wanted.

Up until this incident, we had never labeled our relationship. When you attach labels and names to emotions, those labels change the meaning of what you experience. Therefore, we were happy being best friends and lovers. But, we never used the boyfriend or girlfriend label and the L-word (love) hadn't passed our lips. In other words, there wasn't a verbal commitment. It wasn't until the Monday she returned that I felt the pain of the fear of losing someone so dear.   Something happened during the weekend that hurt my feelings upon hearing it.

As we sat at lunch talking about her trip, she told me she had met someone she liked. She said she might see him again and since she was very open and honest, she told me she had sex with him. My heart sank. Although we had talked about seeing other people, I never expected her to do it.   My body had definite physical reactions: no hunger, tight throat, pain in the chest area. Emotions do create physical responses. Although I was hurt, I don't think I was being jealous because my pain only started after I had been given proof there was a threat of losing my relationship. Jealousy is the imagined fear. However, I think jealous people live daily with the physical sensations of hurt, rejection, and betrayal that I had that day. Sad. Can you imagine the defense mechanisms that must be working to function under that level of daily stress? They can be intense. The defense mechanisms exhibited by jealous people can be as severe as violence, rage, introversion, neurosis, psychosis, temper, etc. It is for this reason I highly recommend you avoid anyone who possesses jealousy as a trait.

Hell Trait #9
Paranoia

This is one of the most significant of the Hell Traits that it is worth reviewing. As you recall, Sensitive to Criticism is an over-awareness of other's perceptions about oneself. It is the fear of disapproval. It is the overbearing need for approval. It is a fear that is shown by a loop in the lower case d and t stems. The amount of sensitivity as it relates to the personal self is shown in the stem of the lower case d. The amount of sensitivity as it relates to ideas

Figure 10.25: Paranoia shown in letter d

and philosophies are shown in the stem of the lower case t. The bigger the loop, the bigger the amount of sensitivity. The Hell Trait of paranoia is present when the loop in the "d" is inflated like a balloon and/or flat on top.

Anyone that has a big looped d also has developed some powerful defense mechanisms to guard such an open wound. Criticizing this person is like pouring salt into it. When these people feel betrayed, watch out for their defenses. If these loops are inflated to a disproportionate size, you know that the fear of criticism is unreasonable and you will see vicious sarcasm, resentment, aggression, etc., to protect the ego. Huge flat-topped looped d's that do not return to the baseline signify this fear doesn't return to reality (the baseline). Many allow their fears to hinder relationships, considerably. Invariably, you will be the victim of their feelings of mistrust at one time or another.

A truly paranoid person often has built up so many defenses, they might tell you, "I don't care what other's think." Their defenses are so strong, they may actually not feel the pain of that open wound anymore. If they have a huge looped d and say they don't care what other's think... you *know they are really in a lot of pain.*   If you choose to get into a relationship with a paranoid person, realize that he is subject to unreasonable fears. It can be a real challenging situation.   I have found when having a close friendship or relationship with a borderline *paranoid* person, as shown in handwriting, he will eventually feel you have turned against him and he will turn on you. A person who feels trapped in a corner will react like a trapped animal. He will fight. His exaggerated fear of persecution makes him feel trapped and you might be his victim.

If you must deal with this Hell Trait, let him know you approve. Give frequent compliments, but don't patronize. Since they are searching for approval, let her know you like what she is wearing. If you give sincere compliments to these oversensitive people, you will have them eating out of the palm of your hand because you are supplying what they need the most: approval. When the sensitiveness turns to paranoia, the niceness disappears very quickly.

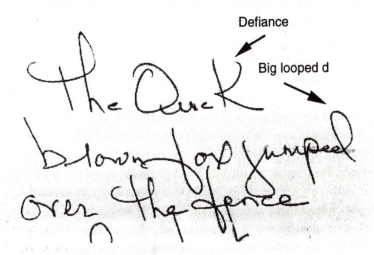

Sample 10.26: Extremely oversensitive to criticism.

Hell Traits
Closing Thoughts

The previous pages listed the personality characteristics that I think make a Hell Trait. Your list may be completely different. You may not like men or women who are sweet, kind, and generous. I have certain likes and dislikes that you may not share. However, from my experience, you should carefully consider dealing with anyone with a Hell Trait. It will be challenging in one form or another. I suggest you take inventory of your past relationships and make a list of the traits that bothered you. You should be able to compile quite a list of your own Hell Traits. Then, ask yourself what personality characteristics contributed to the behavior that you hated so much. You will probably find that the majority of those characteristics can be found in the handwriting. Then, simply avoid those traits in your next mate.

When you review the Trait Dictionary in Appendix A, you might find traits that you feel should have been mentioned in this chapter. There are a few traits you should be warned about. However, they aren't serious enough in all people to constitute a Hell Trait designation. Some of these Difficult Traits are: domineering, defiant, impulsive (E+ writers are often manic depressive and very moody), aggressive, temper, sarcasm, and an FA slant.

It is easy to avoid many of the worst Hell Traits. However, it is not as easy to avoid all the other traits that make a person human. After all, nobody is perfect. You may be forced to deal with one Hell Trait. But, you don't have to live with five. In return for putting up with one, you might also get a trustworthy, funny, and loyal mate. I don't think you can pass on all the people you see who have small idiosyncrasies, but you can afford to pass someone with a plethora of Hell Traits. My experience shows most people can learn to live and adapt to someone with one of the lesser Hell Traits. However, I suggest you search for someone without any of them.

Chapter XI

Would You Date This Person?

It is important for you to have some hands-on experience with some samples of handwriting before you embark into the dating scene armed with such a high powered weapon. If I were right there beside you helping you choose your next relationship, what would I say? This final chapter shows you a week's worth of dates and how I would rank them based solely on their handwriting. Over the next few pages you will find samples of some handwriting and a brief summary of the personality characteristics. I am confident you will be able to look at these samples and come to a conclusion whether or not you would want to start a relationship with that person. Since I don't know you, I can't tell you what you are attracted to. What I can tell you is the highlights of the personality that the handwriting reveals. I can also point out parts of the personality which I generally like in a person and the parts I generally find irritating. I have summarized my conclusions in a brief comment section and a simple star system rating. The star scale is zero through five. Zero signifying the worst possible personality for a relationship and five signifying a beautiful human being that anyone would be proud to call one's significant other. You have an opportunity to date a different person every day this week. Take it one day at a time and be selective. So, would you date...

Monday's Date

Personality Highpoints

Dual personality	Variable slant
Practical/ good self-image	High t-bars
Exaggerated enthusiasm	Long t-bars
Temper T-bars on the right side of stem	
Sense of humor	Wavy t-bar
Intense sarcasm	Pointed t-bar
Warped code of ethics	Unusually shaped h stem
Large imagination/ huge sex drives Large lower loops	
Irritation	Slashed i dots
Philisophical interests	Many upper zone loops and extensions
Extreme pride/ vanity	Very tall d and t stems, over 3 times the middle zone.
Scattered mind	Bouncy and unpredictable baseline

Comments: This guy may be a little strange and far out for most people. He is quite fun (humor and sarcasm) but, this same humor can turn to malicious intent when he feels threatened. (looped d's and big imagination). His enthusiasm and unpredicatable emotional outlay might be too far to an extreme for some people. Positive traits: enthusiasm and good self-image. Negative traits: irritation, temper, and dual slant.

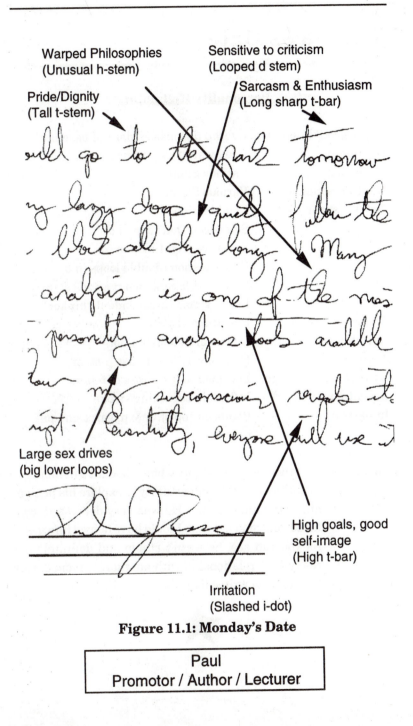

Figure 11.1: Monday's Date

Paul
Promotor / Author / Lecturer

Tuesday's Date

Personality Highpoints

Depression/ Pessimism Overall downward slant of baseline
Dominant   Downward tilted t-bars
Confusion   Various Slants
Dual Personality   Various Slants
Not Trustworthy   Combination of:
                        Self deceit (left loop in o)
                        Secretive (right loop in o)
                        Prevarication (double loops in o)
                        Scattered & confused (various slant/size)
                        Low d-stems (independent thinker)
Failure Complex   Downturned y
Irritated at himself   Downward slashed i-dots
Argumentative   Break-away lower case p-stem
Low/ Med Self-image   Low/med hieght cross of t-stem
Resentment   Inflexible beginning stroke
Impatient   Points on top of m & n, sarcasm, and
                        temper.

Comments: Dave was a homeless guy whom I bought a hamburger
          in exchange for the opportunity to explore his person-
          ality via handwriting. He was very depressed, con-
          fused, and angry. I wish I could have helped him more.
          As you can see, he wasn't stable and definitely not
          ready for a relationship with another. Avoid dating
          anyone who writes like this.

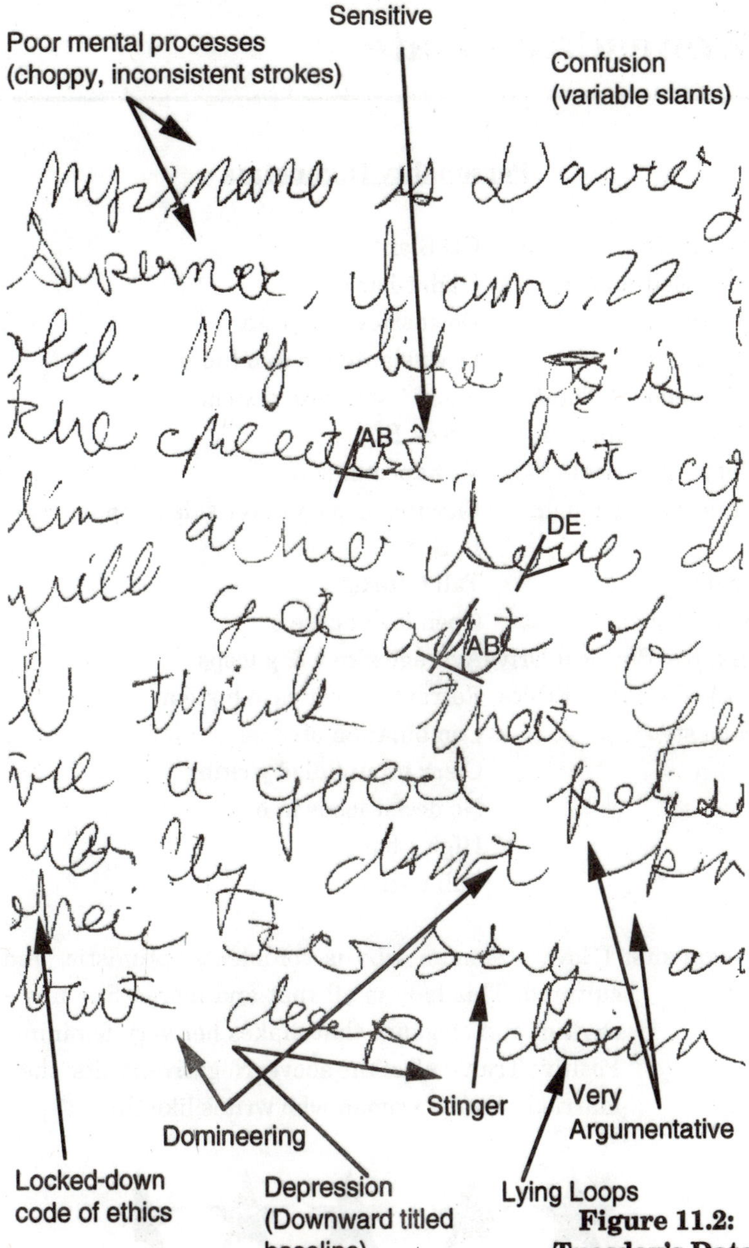

Figure 11.2: Tuesday's Date

Dave - Age 22 - Homeless Male

Wenesday's Date

<u>Personality Highpoints</u>

Ambivert	CD Slant
High Self-image	High t-bar cross
Direct	Downstroke on letter t
Diplomacy	Downslanted m & n humps
Independent Thinker	Short lower case d-stem
Desire for Culture	Greek E
Very Analytical	V-shaped m & n
Fluidity of Thought	Flowing loop on lower side of upper case B, S, & D
Pride	Tall t-stems
Frank/ open/ honest	Open lower case o
Healthy Physical Drive	Average size y & g loops
Locked Code of Ethics	Retraced lower case h-stem
Honesty	Combination of:
	Clear unmuddled writing
	No deceit loops in o
	High t-bar
	Tall t-stems

Comments: I love a woman who is confident, optimistic, and cultured. This lady is all that and more. She has a rhythm and elegance that makes her very feminine. Positive Traits: all of the above. Negative Traits: she's married. Find a woman who writes like this.

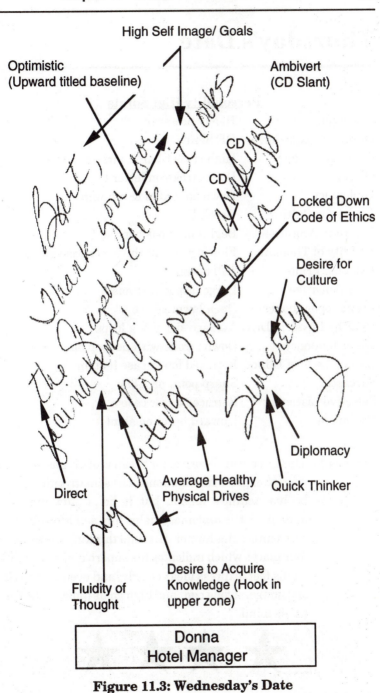

High Self Image/ Goals

Optimistic
(Upward titled baseline)

Ambivert
(CD Slant)

Locked Down
Code of Ethics

Desire for
Culture

Diplomacy

Direct

Average Healthy
Physical Drives

Quick Thinker

Fluidity of
Thought

Desire to Acquire
Knowledge (Hook in
upper zone)

Donna
Hotel Manager

Figure 11.3: Wednesday's Date

Thursday's Date

Personality Highpoints

Passionate	Heavy pressure
Outgoing Expressive	DE Slant
Good Self-image	High cross t-bar & large capitals
Direct	Downstroke on letter t
Diplomacy	Downslanted m & n humps
Desire for Culture	Greek E
Desire to Acquire	Beginning hooks on i & f
Fluidity of Thought	Flowing loop in the lower case g & y
Extreme Pride	Tall t-stems
Very Sensitive	Large looped d-stems
Frank/ open/ honest	Open lower case o
Healthy Physical Drive	Average size y & g loops
Loner tendency	Down stroke with no loop on y
Locked Code of Ethics	Retraced lower case h-stem
Sarcastic	Sharp point on t-bar
Selective Listening	Retraced lower case e
Optimism	Upward baseline slant

Comments: This is a natural-born actor because of his passion and need to express his emotions. His sensitiveness could be his Achille's tendon but it helps him read his audience. His diplomacy helps him sell himself. His sarcasm creates humor. His fluid thinking shows up in four places which indicates his superb ability to think on his feet, express ideas clearly, and even write. His self image, strong ego, and high goals indicate success in his mind.

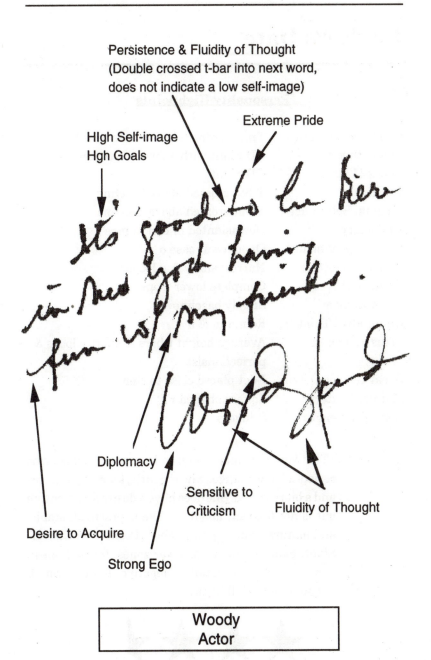

Persistence & Fluidity of Thought
(Double crossed t-bar into next word,
does not indicate a low self-image)

Extreme Pride

HIgh Self-image
Hgh Goals

Diplomacy

Sensitive to
Criticism

Fluidity of Thought

Desire to Acquire

Strong Ego

Woody
Actor

Figure 11.4: Thursday's Date

Friday's Date

Personality Highpoints

Good Concentration	Tiny writing (size of three zones)
Sympathetic	CD Slant with a few DE strokes
Poised/ Logical	CD Slant
Practical	T-bar crossed above baseline
Medium Self-image	T-bar crossed above baseline
Diplomacy	Downslanted m & n humps
Frank/ open/ honest	Open lower case o
Socially Selective	Narrow size y & g loops
Healthy Drives	Complete lower loops
Perfectionism	Steady baseline
Cumulative Thinker	Round m & n
Likes Sameness	Average height t-bars & short y loops & perfectionsist
Great Eye for Detail	I-dot placed close to stem
Manual Dexterity	Square shaped r's
Likes Challenges	Stingers

Comments: This young woman tends to be a perfectionist who resists a lot of change. She is gentle, kind, diplomatic, and a bit reserved. She does have a desire for attention but is not flagrant about it. She is practical, stable, and mature. She is predictable. Positive Traits: CD Slant, balanced upper & lower zones, frank, honest, and good eye for detail. Negative Traits: Small stingers (only Hell Trait).

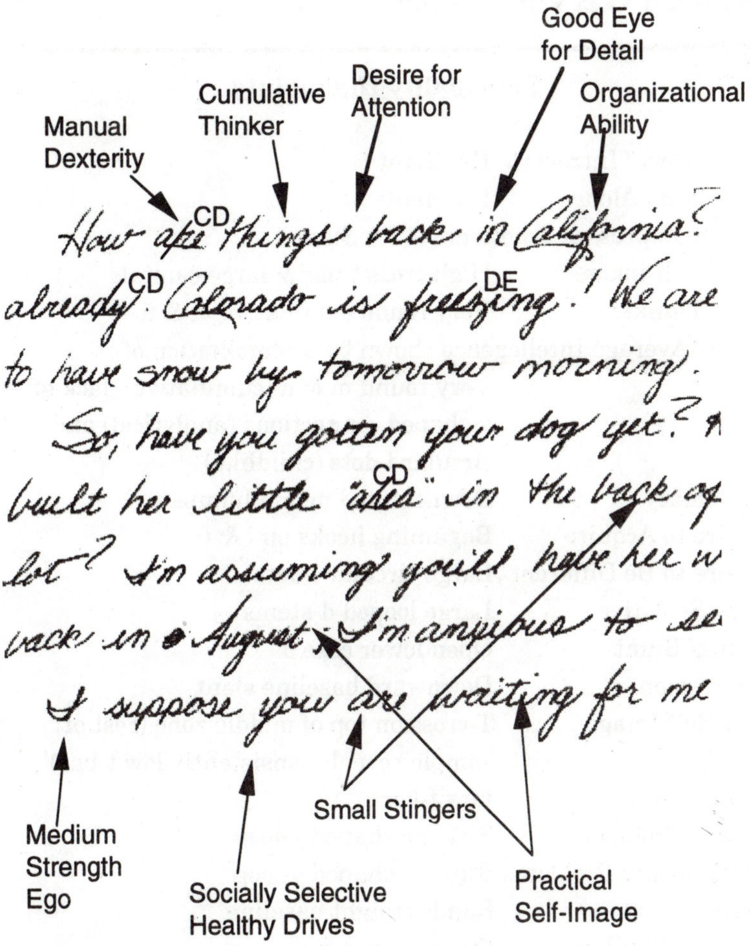

Manual Dexterity

Cumulative Thinker

Desire for Attention

Good Eye for Detail

Organizational Ability

How are [CD] things back in California? already[CD]. Colorado is freezing[DE]! We are to have snow by tomorrow morning. So, have you gotten your dog yet? I built her little "area[CD]" in the back of lot? I'm assuming you'll have her w back in August, I'm anxious to see I suppose you are waiting for me

Medium Strength Ego

Socially Selective Healthy Drives

Small Stingers

Practical Self-Image

| Wendy |
| College Student |

Figure 11. 5: Friday's Date

Saturday's Date

Personality Highpoints

Withdrawn/ Introvert	FA Slant
Like to Be Alone	FA Slant
Rarely Expresses Emotions	FA Slant
Good Self-image	High cross t-bar & large capitals
Slow Thinker	Very round cumulative m & n
Below Average Intellegence shown by a combination of :	
	Very round m & n (cumulative), lack of v-shaped connections (analytical) and circular i-dots (childlike)
Diplomacy	Downslanted m & n humps
Desire to Acquire	Beginning hooks on i & f
Desire to Be Different	Large circular i-dots
Very Sensitive	Large looped d-stems
Frank/ Blunt	Open lower case o
Depression	Downward baseline slant
Low Self-Image	T-cross on top of middle zone (rest of sample reveals consistently low t-bar)
Fear of Change	Low t-bar
Sexual Problems	Strange shaped y-loop
Relationship Problems	Strange shaped y-loop
Perfectionist	Rigid straight baseline
Needs a Challenge	Stingers in d & c
Anger at Men	Stingers in d & c

Comments: This woman is very introverted. She will be frustrating to any expressive person. Her social/people skills are minimul. Mentally, she is slow. She also has a lot of sexual confusion. I avoid anal-retentive introverts.

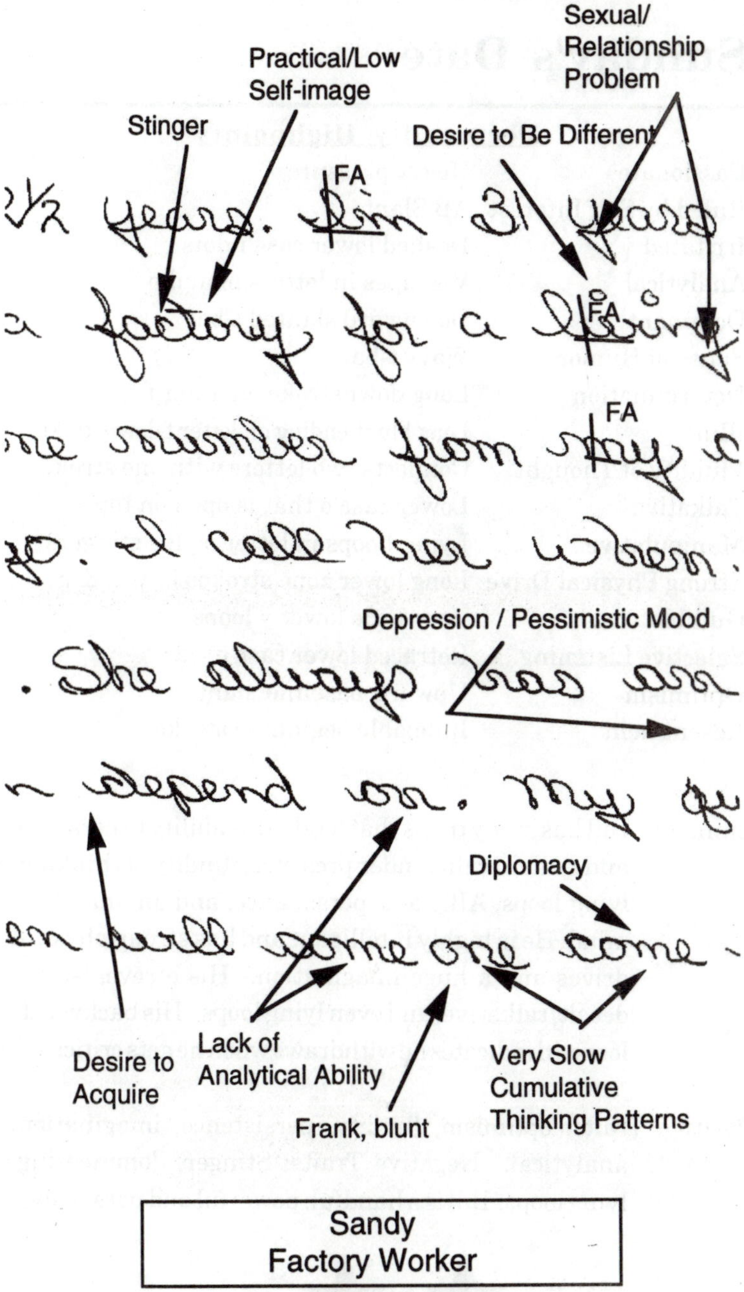

Figure 11.6: Saturday's Date

Sunday's Date

Personality Highpoints

Passionate	Heavy pressure
Ruled by Self Interest	AB Slant
Irritated	Dashed lower case i-dots
Analytical	V-shapes in letters m and n
Dominant	Downward slanted t-bar
Sense of Humor	Wavy t-bar
Determination	Long downstroke on letter f
Bluff	Long blunt ending on letter f downstroke
Fluidity of Thought	Connects two letters with one stroke
Talkative	Lower case o that is open on top
Manipulative	Lying Loops in letter o plus stingers
Strong Physical Drive	Long lower zone strokes in y, f, & g
Gullible	Very wide lower y loops
Selective Listening	Retraced lower case e
Optimism	Upward baseline slant
Resentment	Inflexible beginning stroke

Comments: Bill has many traits that lend to his ability to persuade and remain calm under pressure; fluidity of thinking, lying loops, AB slant, persistence, and an analytical mind. He is highly intelligent and has strong physical drives and a huge imagination. His o reveals self-deceit, talkative, and even lying loops. His backwards looped d indicates he withdraws when he gets criticized.

Positive Traits: optimism, fluidity, persistence, imagination, analytical. Negative Traits: Stinger, domineering, lying loops. Bill is a handful: powerful and persuasive.

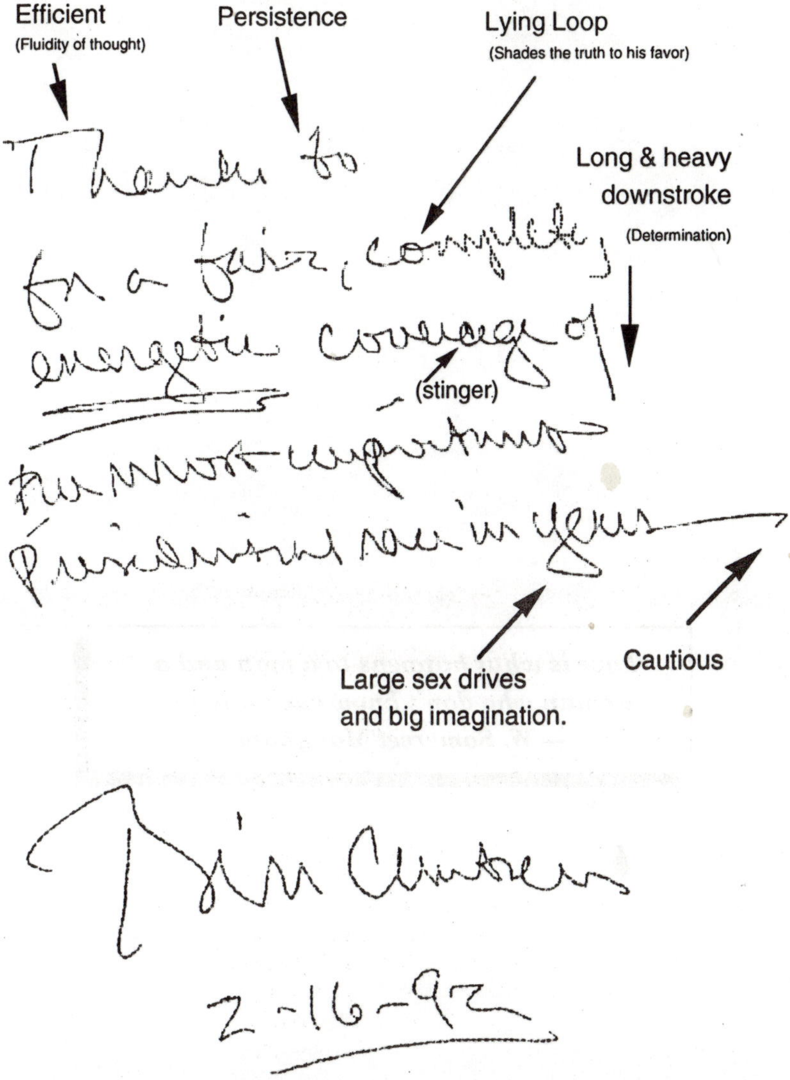

Efficient
(Fluidity of thought)

Persistence

Lying Loop
(Shades the truth to his favor)

Long & heavy
downstroke
(Determination)

(stinger)

Large sex drives
and big imagination.

Cautious

| Bill |
| President of the United States |

Figure 11.7: Sunday's Date

"Love is what happens to a man and a woman who don't know each other."
— W. Somerset Maugham

Section XII

Final Secrets

When I reflect on all the women I've gone out with over the years, I feel both pride and embarrassment. Although most were pretty, intelligent, or at least charming, some didn't stack up. In fact, I've often wondered what my mom would think of me if she really knew! Don't get me wrong, I've never gone out with total trash. But I have dated trashy! Some people you just wouldn't want your mother to meet.

On the other hand, occasionally you have a date with a person and you immediately feel like your mother would be proud. This is the kind of person with whom you want to be seen. A few years ago, a friend of mine asked me to her parents' corporate Christmas party because I was the only guy she knew that wouldn't embarrass her! It seems there are certain traits in young men that all fathers hate. Fathers usually hate guys who are sarcastic, defiant, irresponsible, disrespectful, wear earrings, and ride motorcycles! Likewise, moms usually like diplomacy, sincerity, respect, good manners, generosity, and being on time. There is no guarantee that because a person possesses one or more of the previous traits that your mother will like him or her. However, I have found that when I choose my friends that have many of these "bring home to mother traits", the probability of my mom (and me) liking them is very high.

It is entirely possible you have no desire to date someone sweet and kind. Just because someone isn't sticky sweet doesn't mean he won't be the perfect husband in your eyes. Everyone has different criteria for the ideal relationship. Some women want a man with money, fame, or a great body. Some men want a woman with money, fame, and a great body, too. Some men don't.

The following list contains the traits I consider very positive when found in a person. To avoid repetition, the location of where each trait is found in handwriting is in the Appendix and is not included in this chapter. Refer to Appendix for details.

As you look over the Bring Home to Mama Traits, pay special attention to your own personality. It might do you good to adopt some of these traits in your own personality. I have adopted many in my own life. Both I and my loved ones are glad I changed!

Bring Home To Mama Traits

Ambivert -This particular emotional outlay has the best of both worlds: emotion and logic. This person tends to shy away from extremes, but that doesn't mean boredom, just stability. The Ambivert has a good balance between the head and the heart. "The sign of an intelligent people is their ability to control their emotions by the application of reason" said Marya Mannes

Diplomacy - Diplomacy is the ability to communicate in a kind and gentle fashion. A diplomatic person can tell you that your cat just died and you'll thank them for being so concerned. It is a wonderful trait to have because diplomatic people handle difficult people well. Jane Austen once said, "I do not want people to be too agreeable, as it saves me the trouble of liking them a great deal."

Enthusiasm - Enthusiasm is the zest for life. It is the drive that moves mountains. The enthusiastic person is a leader of people. Enthusiasm turns ideas into reality. The great Harry S. Truman quoted, "A leader is a man who has the ability to get other people to do what they don't want to and like it."

High Self-Esteem / Visionary - High self-image produces confidence in all areas of life. People who like themselves, like other people more, thus treat them better. Also, they set high goals and tend to contribute to society. Robert Browning said, "Ah, but a man's reach should exceed his grasp, Or what's heaven for?"

Humor - Laughter is the best medicine. Norman Cousins cured himself of cancer by laughing. If it works for cancer, don't you think it would work to make your life healthier? Ethel Barrymore said about humor, "You grow up the day you have the first real laugh at yourself."

Optimism - The optimistic person has a positive attitude which is essential to success. It is nice to be around someone who finds the good things about any situation. Always look on the bright side of life. James Branden Cabell said about optimism, " The optimist proclaims we live in the best of all possible worlds, and the pessimist fears this is true."

Persistence - Persistence is an essential factor in the procedure for turning desire into reality. Most truly successful people have overcome obstacles to reach their goals. Without encountering obstacles, rejections, or failures, one never has the opportunity to be persistent. Persistence is an integral quality of successful people. Therefore, welcome obstacles as a means to getting closer to success. M.H. Alderson said, "If at first you don't succeed you're running about average."

Pride & Dignity - This is one aspect of the personality that is imperative to trust, honesty, and self-respect. It is a good trait as long as the pride doesn't turn into vanity. Didn't the Bible say that pride sent the devil to hell? Regardless, it keeps people honest. The wise old Ben Franklin once said, "Alas, I know if I ever became truly humble, I would be proud of it."

Metaprograms

Have you ever wondered why someone sees a glass of water half full or half empty? The answer can be explained by a person's metaprograms. Metaprograms help us understand why people focus on certain experiences in life and delete, overlook, or exaggerate other aspects of the same experience. Our behavior comes from the way in which we represent things in our minds. It is much more than attitude. The answer lies in the various ways that we process information. The answer lies in our individual metaprograms.

There are many different metaprograms that deal with various aspects of our life. Here, we are going to focus on a few particular metaprograms that will have an immediate effect on your relationships.

Metaprograms are the filters that sort through the tremendous amount of information you are exposed to every day. When you are driving, you might notice the car in front of you. But, there are hundreds of cars and people all around you that you barely notice because your mind is preoccupied. One person notices the billboard, while another notices the helicopter flying overhead. Why do two people focus on one aspect of life while having the same experience? This is one example of how we delete certain information and focus on other information.

This process of sorting information is imperative to your love life. By understanding a person's metaprograms you can predict human behavior in any given situation. Also, you can develop tremendous rapport by communicating and focusing on what he or she perceives as important in the world.

The Direction Metaprogram

Motivation can be boiled down to two strategies. People either move toward pleasure or away from pain. Most of us are motivated by both motives at one time or another in our life. Why are you reading this book? You either want to gain pleasure by learning more about how to create love in your life, or you want to find a way to end the pain of bad relationships. Most people take action when presented with the right motivational strategy. They tend to take no action when presented with an ineffective motivational style. Are you motivated more by gaining pleasure or by avoiding pain? I met a waitress the other day who said she was working twelve-hour shifts because her rent was due in two days. She was obviously moving away from pain, the pain of being evicted. She was working from a necessity metaprogram. I met another waitress that evening who looked equally as tired. When I asked her why she was working so hard, she told me she was saving money for an upcoming vacation to Europe. This woman was obviously moving toward pleasure. She was working from the perspective of possibility.

This relates to motivating your lover in many areas. How about getting a date? Have you ever wondered why a person declined the opportunity to go out with you after you presented all the benefits of having a date with you? Next time try a different approach. My brother Brett used to date a very pretty girl that sold mens' clothing at a department store. One day I asked her why she decided to go out with him. She told me that he was shopping for clothes just like hundreds of other guys do every week. After meeting casually a couple of times, he asked her out. Her first response was to decline the offer, but, he persisted. He said "You will be missing a great opportunity. I am one of the most fascinating guys you will ever meet. If you pass up this opportunity, you will be missing out on a lot." She stepped back, thought about it, and gave him her phone number. The initial approach didn't work. He could have talked about himself for days and she wouldn't have changed her mind. However, when he mentioned what she would lose if she declined, he got her attention. At the time, I didn't understand that a woman would actually be motivated to like someone after such a pompous statement. What I didn't realize then was that according to her metaprograms, he wasn't being pompous, he was appealing to her motivational strategy.

To establish someone's primary motivational strategy ask the following question, "What's important to you in a relationship?" If the answer contains phrases such as: not to cheat, give me space, or not be lonely, then you know that person moves <u>away from</u>. If the answer contains phrases like: grow together, be happy, have fun, love, then you know that person <u>moves toward</u>. Use the motivation that gets the best response. That may not necessarily be what motivates you.

The Frame of Reference Metaprogram

Does a person judge his behavior on the basis of his or others' opinion? What frame of reference does he use? Does he have an internal frame of reference (self)? Or, does he have an external frame of reference (others)? You discover this by asking the following question, "How do you know you have done a good job?" The person with an internal frame of reference will say "I just know," or "It just feels right." The person with an external frame will say, "When other people tell me, when I get rewarded, by my year end bonuses, etc." Many people have a balance between the two. It is the ideal situation that you have a strong internal frame and take external feedback to constantly improve your performance. Do you know anyone who is at one extreme or the other? Some people spend every hour of every day trying to gain approval of others. This isn't healthy. Likewise, it isn't fun to be around someone who knows from deep inside he is always right.

In handwriting, there is a correlation to this metaprogram. Someone with a large looped d tends to have an external frame of reference. Likewise, someone with a totally retraced d and short d stem tends to be completely internal. Both these tendencies will be increased if the slant supports it. In other words, if a person writes with a looped d and E+ slant, you know she will respond quickly to external feedback. Therefore, to make a happy lover, you must give positive feedback often. Likewise, an AB writer with no loop in her d will not care what you think. She will not take feedback or constructive criticism very well.

In a relationship, you need to find someone with a similar frame of reference as yourself. In any case, I recommend you find someone with a balance.

The Relationship Metaprogram

This metaprogram determines how people make sense of the world. Before you read on, do this experiment. Take three coins and spread them out in front of you. Ask yourself "What is the relationship between these three coins?" Write down your answers now.

The relationship you see between various items determines your relationship metaprogram. There are two different styles of understanding things. Some people match things, others mismatch. Did you write down that the three coins were all money, all round, all American? If you did, you are a *sameness* person. Perhaps you first noticed the similarities, but then noticed there were some differences. In that case you are a *sameness with exception* person. Did you notice all the differences in them? Did you say they were all different values, different sizes, different colors? If you did, you are a *difference* person. The difference person is also called a mismatcher. These people are not happy until they find the exception in a given situation. The difference between things is the way they make sense of the world. Perhaps you noticed that they were all different values and different colors, but were all round and money. In that case, you are a *difference with exception* person.

There are four categories in the relationship metaprogram: sameness, sameness with exception, difference, and difference with exception.

These categories are important for you to understand why people do what they do. You will use this knowledge to develop rapport. As we learned in chapter 6, rapport is the feeling that someone is just like us. If a difference person constantly mismatches (does the opposite, finds the exception, etc.) he is going to have great difficulty keeping rapport. The only exception is with another mismatcher. The two of them would find the exception to everything, do the opposite, and then feel connected because they operate from the same metaprogram.

What happens if a matcher and mismatcher go out on a date. She says, "I think this movie was a lot like that movie..." As she points out the similarities, he disagrees. He says "This movie was nothing like that movie." And goes on the list all the reasons. Neither person is wrong. However, no rapport is being developed. In fact, both probably feel uncomfortable because there is no agreement. Sameness people are great at developing natural rapport. They are looking to agree or find similarities. In essence, that is what develops rapport. On the other hand, a good detective couldn't be primarily a sameness person because his job is to find the exception, the clue, and what is missing. There are different roles for different people. You should date a person with a similar style to your own.

Sameness people see only sameness. They might say, "It all comes down to this." They always try to determine what is the same in any given situation. The sameness person ignores all the differences and just focuses on the things in common. They see the three coins as all the same. According to Anthony Robbins, this category represents about 10% of the population. He goes on to say, "Sameness people, in a desire for stability, will typically stay in a job for fifteen years to life. They see no reason to change what they are doing. (They are the people that resist change and stifle new ideas.) They can easily stay in a monogamous relationship over the long term because they like things to stay the same."

The sameness with exception person represents the largest group of our population at about 55% of the people. They like similarity but like a little variety. Studies show they typically stay in a job five to seven years. In relationships, this type of person can stay in a monogamous relationship for long periods of time as long as there are some differences. They need some variety in location, daily activities, sexual activity, etc. They must have some exceptions to the same day- to-day pace.

The difference person focuses on only the differences. These people overlook all the similarities. They see the three coins as all different. It is difficult for this person to see patterns or common trends. This person can go into a new job or situation and tell you exactly what is wrong, not working, or out of place. Robbins says, "They comprise about 10% of the population. Studies show they last in a job only eighteen months or less. Difference people have tremendous difficulty developing long term relationships. They have got do things differently all the time because they are looking for variety. In a relationship, they are always asking why they must do things in the same way. They want creativity."

The difference with exception person notices the differences then notices how things are the same. Robbins says in a job, this person will last eighteen months to three years. In relationships, they want variety and changes, but like a certain foundation, therefore providing a longer relationship than the total mismatcher, but a shorter term union than the sameness person.

In a romantic relationship, it is necessary to understand what type of person you and your mate are in order to be happy. If you are primarily a difference person, you must create variety. If you are sameness people, don't vary the schedule. You will have much more success in a relationship by choosing a partner with similar metaprograms to your own. If you are both mismatchers you might be happy dating for just a short period of time because neither one really wants the boredom a long term commitment represents. On the other hand, if you require a stable foundation of sameness, you will want to search for someone who likes commitment and long-term relationships. How do you find out? Ask the questions mentioned and ask about their past relationships. The answers will usually give you a hint of what they need. Although the past does not indicate the future, it gives us clues.

Do You Feel Loved?

To discover the final metaprogram simply ask, "How do you know you are loved?" The answers will give you the formula for feeling loved and making others feel loved the rest of your life. Some people need to <u>see</u> that you love them. These are the visual people that need to be shown by doing things, giving flowers, or taking them places. Some people are more auditory. They must <u>hear</u> that you love them. Therefore, if they don't hear the words, "I love you," they don't feel loved. The tonality is important. Tonality involves *how* you say "I love you." Is your voice soft, loud, fast, slow, etc.? Other people are more kinesthetic, they need to <u>feel</u> you love them. This person must be touched, caressed, kissed, and held. Otherwise, the feeling of being loved is not present. You must establish which method in your lover is the most important and use it often. Most people have a combination of one or two that are necessary to feel loved.

In the beginning of a relationship, people tend to use all three. When we start dating, we go places, buy cards and flowers, and often tell each other how we feel. As relationships progress, this constant 3-pronged approach at showing our love decreases. We get lazy and just use our own primary metaprogram to express our feelings. If the man needs to hear, "I love you," he will probably use that same program to express his feelings. If she needs to be touched to feel loved, he can tell her he loves her until he is blue in the face and she still won't feel loved. You must communicate in your partner's primary communication style, not your own. Make your partner feel loved and you will probably feel loved in return. If you don't feel loved, tell your lover what it takes to make you feel loved.

How Long Will Your Relationship Last?

Some people define success or failure in a relationship as the length of time they were together. Others define the success or failure by the quality of the time they had when they were together. I have known people to stay in a miserable marriage twenty years longer than the day it should have ended. My father was a marriage counselor many years ago. He told me he quit because his job was to save marriages that should have been ended. Some couples had no business being involved in a relationship with each other. They were totally incompatible. He changed careers because he didn't want to contribute to keeping bad marriages together. Furthermore, traditional wisdom says a marriage counselor should fix the marriage, not end it.

You have to ask yourself what constitutes a successful relationship. Does one weekend of intense romance with no disagreements fulfill your definition? Does a commitment meet your requirements? Do you have to be married to be convinced the relationship is a success? Metaprograms may help provide the answers to how you perceive relationships.

Conclusion

The quest for love will be a lifelong process. No matter whom you are with or how much love you have, you will always crave more. Love is not like candy, too much won't make you sick. In fact, the lack of love can make you ill. Recently, I heard a statistic on the radio that I found very interesting. The newscaster said single people with no significant others or family tend to suffer from disease, sickness, and even death at a higher rate than people who live in a family or committed relationship. That statistic means love contributes to good health and the lack of love can make you more susceptible to illness.

There is much more material that I wanted to include in this book. However, even if I could write all there is to know about love, you would be reading for the next century. Besides, there is no substitute for experience. Each relationship you encounter will teach you something if you are open to learning. Learning is much more fun in a live, three-deminsional, full color, touching, seeing, hearing, classroom called life than from a book. There is so much great information, I've just scratched the surface of the process of human communication. Neuro-Analysis can go much deeper than what I have covered here. I am already excited about digging deeper into the fields of human behavior psychology, neuro-linguistic programming, time-line therapy, graphology, and even hypnosis to write *more ways to make love happen.*

Even as I write this conclusion, I am learning about the trials and triumphs of love. Each time I skirt the fringes of love, I can also feel the power of a possible heartache. One thing that frustrates me greatly is the fact that each time my heart twinges with anticipation, love, or even infatuation, my logical side asks me to check out all the references. And invariably when I do, I realize that everything in the book is accurate. The handwriting never lies. Every Hell Trait eventually shows its ugly head. Every fear has its time and place when it shows up. Therefore, everytime I embark on a new relationship, I have to take an honest look at what I am willing to accept. Based on the material in this book, I have the ability to know what to expect before I get involved. This means that each time I get involved, I'm not surprised when the personality I saw in the handwriting on day one shines through in full color on doomsday. It leads me to reiterate one of the most important secrets in the art of making love happen. BE SELEC-TIVE. You must be patient, critical, and very choosy of the people with whom you get emotinally involved.

I know from experience, once your heart starts calling the shots, there is no turning back. Your heart is much like an employer who interviews one hundred candidates for a position. Once he chooses to hire that one person, firing him is a long, expensive, painful, and sticky situation. If you get into a relationship that is wrong from the start, it will be just as painful and sticky when the ax drops. However, if you choose the right lover from the start, an ending may never have to come.

For many, the ideal relationship might only come after years of imperfect ones. For a lucky few, the first one may last a happy lifetime. However, it can be much like a football team. A championship season is only realized after years and years of tough games and hard losses. Each mistake is a learning experience.

Bandler and Grinder make a terrific point in their book *Reframing* about success and failure, "Typically people think that success is good and confusion is bad. Actually, success is one of life's most dangerous experiences, because it keeps you from noticing other things and learning other ways of doing things. That also means that anytime you fail, you have an unprecedented opportunity to learn about something you otherwise wouldn't have noticed. Likewise, confusion is the doorway to reorganizing your perceptions and learning something new. If you were never confused, that would mean everything that happened to you fit your expectations, your model of the world, perfectly. Life would simply be one boring, repetitive experience after another. Confusion is a signal that something doesn't fit, and you have a chance to learn something new." Therefore you might want to think about your past relationships differently. What you used to see as a failure, you now can see as a learning experience. Likewise, each time you feel confused or unsuccessful, you are actually learning and growing. As you think about it, it is a good feeling not to have all the answers.

If I had been one of the people who fell in love with their high school sweethearts and lived happily ever after, this book would never have been written. In fact, in doing research for this book, I found very few of those couples who could explain the secrets to their success. Most of the love at first sight people had no idea what made their relationship work. I suspect they have a sameness metaprogram in high gear. It is a wonderful thing for them, but it doesn't help you or me. However, those people who had a variety of past relationships had much more insight into the success of their current relationships. Experience is the best teacher.

Don't be afraid to get your feet wet. Get excited about love sweeping through your life and carrying your heart away. You may come down one day, but it will be a sweet ride.

> *"Love is a many splendered thing."*
> *— Shakespeare*

Appendices

Trait Dictionary

**Personality Characteristics
As Revealed in Handwriting**

Appendix A

Acquisitive

in the way they

Shown by tiny hooks at the beginning of words. If hook is in the middle zone, this is a need to acquire material things. If in upper zone, it is a need to acquire knowledge, ideas, or education.

Aggressiveness

Shown by hard right upstrokes that replace a lower loop. The aggressive person pushes forward into the future asserting himself physically. Often this person needs physically aggressive outlets such as competitive sports or even violence.

Ambivert

CD Slant

Middle of the roader
Emotional but logical

Shown by a person's slant that is midway between a vertical and a hard right-slant. This person relates to both introverts and extroverts while keeping a level head even amidst the existence of emotional feelings such as empathy, sympathy, and even passion. Falls into the middle-of-the-road catogory on many issues.

Analytical Thinker

Shown by natural "V" formations at the base Iine, usually in m's and n's. The analytical person analyzes everything. This person has a strong reasoning ability to sift and weigh the facts.

Anti-Social

Shown when the lower loops of y's , g's, and sometimes j 's are retraced completely. The anti-social person does not trust anyone and rarely lets people get close enough to really know him. He fears getting hurt emotionally. This is a roadblock to intimacy.

Argumentative

Shown by the break-away p with a high beginning stroke. This person likes to argue. The trait will be increased if the writer is also analytical, irritated, sarcastic, stubborn, and/or impulsive.

Attentive to Details

Revealed by the dots on the i and j being placed close to the stem. The closer the dot is to the stem, the more attention the writer pays to details. This trait contributes to a good memory. Notices everything.

Cautious

Shown by long final strokes or a dash at the end of a line. This writer is inclined to be careful in order to minimize risk. This cautious tendency reduces any impulsive behavior and causes one to look before leaping.

Comprehensive Thinker ─────────

comprehensive thinking

Revealed by needle point strokes on the top of the n and m, also in the h or i. These people have lightning fast minds that are able to size up situations instantly. They are curious, impatient, intelligent and usually in a hurry.

Concentration─────────────────

it is very small writing that means good concentration ability.

Extremely small writing. People that write tiny have the ability to shut everything out of their mind and fully concentrate on one thing at a time. Often, on a first impression, these people seem reserved.

Cumulative Thinker ─────────

m   n   n   m

Round or even flat-topped m's and n's forming smooth letters. These people need all the facts before making a decision. They may take longer to learn, but they will remember. They can be very creative and good with their hands.

Curious & Investigative ─────────

men are thinking

Sharp points on the top of the letters m, n, r, and/or h that penetrate the upper zone. A quick, investigative, and exploratory thinker sizes up people and situations instantly. Gets irritated by slow talkers.

Defiance ————————————————

coke quick crack

A large lower case letter, especially k anywhere in the writing. This high buckle k is often referred to as the "go to hell K". The defiant person resists other's authority. Seen as resentment at being told what to do and as rebellion in young people.

Desire for Attention ————————

lips   *look*   *is*

High ending strokes that go up in the air much like a child raising his hand in class for attention. This person needs to be the center of attention and is always looking for ways to get noticed. This person needs lots of recognition.

Desire for Culture ————————

∂ $\mathcal{E}$ ∂ Σ

Lower case d's that go up to the left but never returns to the baseline. Also, the greek letter Σ. These writers have a desire for cultural things such as travel, adventure, music, and fine food.

Desire for More
Physical Activity

p   *p*   *p*

Shown by average to large loops in the lower case p. The larger the loop the stronger the desire is for more physical activity. This could include any physical activity such as exercise, travel, or sex. Verify this tendency by looking at the y loops.

Desire for Responsibility ─────────

Shown by a large round loop at the beginning of a word, usually in capital letters like W or M, but also found in the S. This person has a desire to be needed by a large number of people and will need to be in a leadership role.

Diplomacy ─────────────────────

Downslanted humps toward the right on m's and n's. This person has the ability to say things in a way that other people want to hear. He can also phrase touchy subjects in a nice inoffensive way.

Directness ─────────────────────

Beginning vertical strokes on the lower case t that go down and curve to the right (no beginning upstroke). This person wants people to stop beating around the bush and get to the point. Direct people don't like to be slowed down.

Dominant ──────────────────────

Down slanted t-bar, to the right, with a blunt ending. The dominant person tends to be in control and likes it. He takes charge making people follow directions without angering them.

Domineering

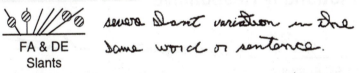

Down-slanted t-bar, to the right, with a sharp ending. The dominant person tends to fight for control. He takes charge, insisting people follow him. The sharp t-bar signifies sarcasm, whining, griping, and possible cruelness when he doesn't get his way. An unpleasant trait.

Dual Personality

FA & DE
Slants

severa slant variation in the same word or sentence.

Shown by an obvious slant variation from left to right in the same sentence. This person has trouble making decisions because the head and heart are in conflict. He withdraws into the introverted personality when he feels insecure. Unpredictable mood swings.

Ego Strength

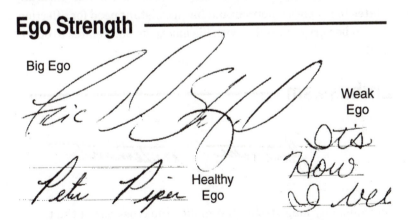

Big Ego

Weak Ego

Healthy Ego

Shown by the size of the capital letters. Capitals 4-5 times the middle zone indicate a writer with an inflated importance of himself (ego). Likewise, capitals within the middle zone indicate weak ego strength, thus affecting self-esteem.

Emotionally Withdrawn ─────────

FA / AB
Slants

Shown by a consistent leftward slant. The upstrokes and slant are a minimum of 90 degrees from the baseline. An introvert. This person keeps his own counsel, rarely expresses feelings, and makes logical unemotional decisions.

Emotionally Responsive ─────────

DE/ E+ Slant

The hard rightward slant reveals the heart-ruled, moody, impulsive person. The farther the writing slants to the right, the more this person is subject to emotional stimuli. This writer naturally relates to people's emotions and has a constant need for affection. He can be very expressive with his emotions and relates to others easily.

Enthusiasm ─────────

An unusually long stroke that makes the cross bar of the t. This writer bubbles over with enthusiasm and excitement. Enthusiasm is a key ingredient to success in leadership because it motivates others toward action.

Extravagent

Revealed by wide letter/word spaces *and* long final endings or ostentatious strokes. This person tends to overdo things. One may first notice this trait in the style of clothes she wears. It is a combination of desire for attention and generosity to one's self.

Fear of Success

Shown by a down-turned y or g that doesn't cross the baseline. The closer it comes to the baseline the closer the person will come to success, then turn away. Often a feeling of dejection occurs near success, thus this person gets very close to success, then fails.

Fluidity of Thought

Shown in the figure eight shape anywhere in the writing. Most commonly found in the lower loop of the g or in the capital letters of a signature. Signifies the ability to follow and change thoughts smoothly. Often a good conversationalist, speaker, or writer.

Frankness

σ σ O a σ σ

Shown in the letter o that has no inner loops and is relatively wide. This person will be honest and blunt when asked her opinion. If the o is open, then she will volunteer her frank opinion without being asked.

Generosity

give away stuff

Shown by long final strokes extending to the right at about a 45 degree angle and/or wide word spacing. This person will be eager to share. This writer derives attention and personal reward from being generous to others.

Goals

low t , practical t , high t

Shown by the height of the crossing of the t-bars on the stem. A low t-bar signifies low self-worth, fear of failing, and low or no goals. A t-bar crossed three-fourths up on the stem signifies practical goals. Ambition and high goals are signified by t-bars on top of the stem. T-bars crossed above the stem reveal the dreamer and goals too high to be practical.

High Self-Esteem

I have a strong self esteem

High crossed t-bar and large personal pronoun I. This reveals confidence, ambition, the ability to plan ahead, high goals, high personal expectations, and an overall good self image. This is the key to personal success and happiness.

Humor

My wit Very funny

Shown by a wavy t-bar and/or flourishing wavy beginning strokes in the word patterns. This person has a sense of humor and can become witty if the stroke ends with an angle (analytical) or a sharp point (sarcastic).

Imagination

you go jogging

Large and wide lower loops in the y, g and j reveals strong physical imagination, gullibility, and a tendency to exaggerate the tangible aspects of life. Has great ability to visualize and see things clearly. Big loops in the h reveal the philosophical imagination.

Independent Thinker

good cards doing

Shown by a short d or t-stem with a restricted or no loop. This person has his own ideas about the way life is. He thinks independently of what others' believe. His dress and choices in life tend to be made without regard to the norm.

Individualistic

es ist ein zu sein.

Shown by a circle i-dot. Most common in adolescent writing when a youth is trying to stand out from the crowd. In adulthood, she has a fear of being ordinary and must call attention to herself by being different. Also, it can indicate artistic creative expression.

Intuition

bread in words

Shown by breaks between letters and found often in part printed/ part cursive script. These people have a developed a sixth sense or psychic ability to feel situations very accurately, often before they occur.

Irritability

irritability

Slashed "i" dots. The longer the slash, the more irritated the writer is at the time of the writing. Slash down is irritation at the present situation. Slash left is irritated at themselves. Slash right is toward other people. Anger is usually present.

Jealousy

m T W Y

A tight beginning loop that is small and almost square. It must make a completely closed circle. This person fears the loss of somone he loves. Can be very possessive.

Likes Variety

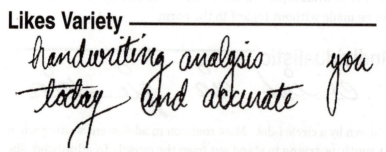

Shown by long wide lower loops that extend deeply into the lower zone. This person will get bored easily and needs variety in life. The physical drives are strong and deep, providing lots of energy.

Lives for the Moment

Shown by no upper zone strokes. Writing that stays in the middle zone. Immature. These people get into trouble because they live for today and fail to foresee the consequences of their actions. This person's philosophies and ethics change frequently.

Low Self-Esteem

Shown by the t-bar crossed very low on the stem. This person fears failure and fears change, thus sets goals with low risk. He remains in bad situations much too long and finds imperfections with himself. He is rarely successful in his own eyes.

Loyalty

a thing in marriage

Shown by a picture-perfect i-dot with no tail in any direction. Loyalty is a commitment to stand by those people or ideas that they consider worthy.

Lying

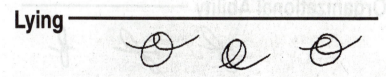

Shown by a combination of loops in the right and left side of lower case a's and o's. Huge inner loops that cross signify a person that lies pathologically. These people are not trustworthy.

Manual Dexterity

Square formations on top of the "r's" and/or "h's". This person has the ability to take things apart and put them back together. This writer has good manual dexterity and often good coordination. They are very mechanically minded.

Needs A Challenge

Shown by a stinger-like hook in the middle zone letters c, d, or a. This person has an anger at strong members of the opposite sex, while only being attracted to those who are a challenge. Once this person feels totally in control of the relationship, he/she will become bored.

Optimism

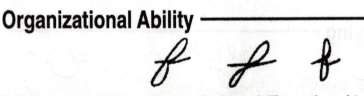

Revealed by a noticeable upward slant in the entire baseline and/or the cross bar on the letter t. The higher the incline, the more optimistic she is. She is sure tomorrow will be better and always looks on the bright side of life.

Organizational Ability

Balanced upper and lower loops in the letter f. The two loops bisect the entire letter. This writer will have the ability to create order out of chaos. Even if her desk appears messy, she will know what is in each pile. She is organized.

Perfectionist

I came in to the a early this morning so ran to pick up some km late just stayed to eat a bee your mother delicious c noodles. This a real goo

The baseline will be straight and even. This handwriting is that of a person who spends time putting everything in its place and reviews work trying to make it precise.

Persistence

t f f t t

Strokes that double back over the letter and end toward the right. Usually located in the t and f. This person has the quality of not giving up when confronted with temporary setbacks. He will persist until he completes the task.

Perversion

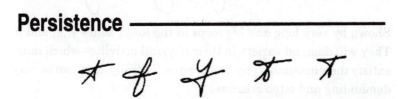

Lower zone loops that are not shaped normally. These bizarre lower zone loops signify the sex/relationship aspect of the writer's life is unusual. If the loops are large, as shown, the sexual appetite crosses the line into sexual behavior outside the norm.

Physical Frustration

Lower loops that are incomplete. This signifies the presence of frustration in areas such as relationships, exercise, or sexual activity. Something is incomplete in this person's life.

Physically Experimental

Shown by very long *and* big loops in the lower zones y ,g, and p. They will demand variety in their physical activities which must satisfy their insatiable physical desires. Sexually, they can be very demanding and often creative.

Positiveness

A t-bar that is blunt and not pointed on the end. This writer makes statements with confidence and conviction. He will act like he knows the right answer even if he is not sure.

Procrastination

A t-bar that is crossed predominately on the left side of the stem. Procrastinators will put off until tomorrow what could have been done today. This trait is one factor of laziness.

Pride & Dignity

pride and dignity

Shown in the t and d-stems that are retraced and taller than normal. These writers will demand respect and expect you to treat them with dignity.

Resentment

m h t a d

Inflexible beginning strokes at the beginning of a word. The stroke must start at the baseline or below and remain rigidly straight. This person is harboring anger, resentment, or hate toward something or someone.

Sarcasm

t l t t

Revealed by sharp-pointed t-bar. Sarcasm is like a verbal dagger defending the ego. Sarcasm is forming a dual meaning to whatever is said and is often mixed with humor. Sarcastic people have a sharp tounge that can hurt others' feelings. If the t-bar is crossed from right to left, the sarcasm is directed toward self, instead of toward others, creating a tendency to be self-critical.

Secretive

a a o o e

Circles within circle letters on the right hand side. The larger the inner loop is, the more secrets this person will withhold from others. If the inner loop is huge, this person will try to avoid giving you a complete answer.

Selective Listener

retraced "e's" and "r's"

Retraced e's that are usually found with narrow or closed a's and o's. This person can tune other people out. He has his own ideas and will only agree with you if you agree with him. In other words, this person can be closed-minded.

Self-Castigation

But what about

Shown by the backward crossed t-bar (right to left). This signfies the need to punish oneself. If the t-bar shows sarcasm (pointed), the writer tends to be critical and sarcastic of himself.

Self-Concious

m m n m

Shown by the increasing height of the humps on the m's and n's. When the second hump is higher than the first, this person has a fear of being riduculed and tends to worry what others might think when around strangers.

Self-Control

t t t t

A t-bar that is curved in a concave shape, much like a shallow saucer. The stronger the curve, the more self-control is being implemented. An umbrella shape signifies the person is obsessively controlling an action.

Self-Deceit

Inner loops on the left side of the circle letters. This person is deceiving himself about something that is happening to him at the moment. This person may not be consciously aware of the things in his life that he is refusing to face.

Self-Reliance & Leadership

Revealed by an underline below one's signature. This person possesses strong leadership qualities, relies on himself, and has a great amount of inner strength.

Sensitive To Criticism

Shown by the looped stem in the lower case d or t. The bigger the loop, the more painful criticism is felt. If the loop is really inflated, this person will imagine criticism. The d-loop relates to personal self and the t-loop relates to sensitiveness to ideas or philosophies.

Socially Selective

Long narrow loops usually in the y or g. The size of the lower loop reveals the amount of trust and imagination as it relates to people. The narrow loop reveals some trust, but they are very selective of whom they allow in their inner circle of friends.

Stubborn

Revealed by t and d- stems shaped like a tepee or upside down "V". The more this letter is braced, the more this person is braced to his own ideas. Stubborn people rarely admit they are wrong, and don't want to be confused with the facts after they have made up their minds.

Surface Thinker

Wedge-shaped "m's" and "n's" that do not penetrate the upper zone. This person is a quick thinker. He tends to depend on other people's views rather than on personal investigation. He often makes decisions based on others' opinions.

Talkative

Open circle letters such as a's and o's. The less connected the upper part of these letters are, the more they must move their mouth. Sometimes they will talk just to hear their own voice.

Temper

Shown by a t-bar that is crossed predominantly on the right side of the stem. The more it occurs, the easier irritation will cause them to lose control of their emotions. If combined with a heavy rightward (DE,E+) slant, they will blow up quickly.

Tenacity

tenacity

Shown by ending hooks on the right side of letters. This person tends to hold on to what is hers. If the hook is in the upper zone she will cling to his ideas and beliefs. If in the middle zone, she will be tenacious about material items.

Too Many Irons In The Fire

going in to many directions at one time making my writing, run into the writing below!

Long lower loops running into the writing below. This writer has too many projects going on at one time, thus having confusion of interests.

Will Power

strong thoughts

Shown by heavy pressure on the t-bars. This person will be able to follow a set course and display strong powers of the will. Will power tends to intensify all other personality traits.

Personality Inventory

with Handwriting Indicators

Appendix B

Personality Inventory

Me Mate

Emotional Outlay
Keeps feelings inside *(FA/AB writer)*
Expresses emotions impulsively *(DE/E+ writer)*
Internalizes some feelings, expresses others
Middle-of-the-road expressiveness *(CD writer)*

Emotional Intensity
Passionate. Intense: remembers emotional experiences for a long time. *(Deep writer, heavy pen pressure)*
Lets emotions go easily, forgives and forgets quickly *(Light pen pressure, light writer)*

Thinking Patterns
Procedural, slow, cumulative *(Round/square m & n tops)*
Sharp, quick, impatient, takes in everything at once *(Needle point, sharp edges, v-shaped m & n's)*
Digs deeply and thoroughly for all facts *(v-shapes)*
Makes quick surface decisions, based on others' investigations. *(Pointed tops with shallow dish-like connecting lines of m & n's, and/or dish like t-bar)*
Intense ability to concentrate *(Tiny writing)*
Can do many things at once, easily distracted *(Big loose writing, lower loops into lower writing, disproportionate f)*
Intuitive *(Breaks in handwriting, half printing/half cursive)*
Just the facts, logical *(AB writer)*

Goals
Ambitious *(High t-bar on top or above stem)*
Practical *(T-bar crossed 3/4 the way up on t-bar)*
Afraid of change *(Low t-bar cross, in middle zone)*

Persistent *(double crossed t-bar)* Determination: *(long heavy descending downstrokes)*
Gives up easily, lazy *(Combination of light pressure on short t-bar, and/or procrastination: t-bar on left)*
Fears success *(downturned y)*
Fears failure *(low t-bar)*

Prefers to follow *(low t-bar)*
Prefers to lead *(underlined signature, downslanted t-bars)*
Takes the initiative *(sharp upstroke, see trait dictionary)*

Me	Mate	
☐	☐	**Self-Image**
☐	☐	Vanity, cocky *(very tall d stem)*
☐	☐	Humble *(diplomatic & short d and t stems)*
☐	☐	Pride and dignity *(tall & thin d & t stem, thin/ no loop)*
☐	☐	Lack of self-respect *(low t-bar & short d-stem)*
☐	☐	Confident, self-assured *(High t-bar)*
☐	☐	Feels good about self, sees limitations *(Medium t-bar)*
☐	☐	Views self as average *(Average height t-bar)*
☐	☐	Views self as below average *(Low t-bar)*
☐	☐	Insecure–questions self-worth *(Low t-bar & looped d)*
		Social Skills
☐	☐	Outgoing *(Rightward slanted writing, CD, DE, E+)*
☐	☐	Quiet, shy *(FA,AB, uphill m & n humps, or tiny writing)*
☐	☐	A natural born salesman/actor *(DE writer)*
☐	☐	Self-conscious, fears rejection *(Uphill humps on m & n)*
☐	☐	Diplomatic–good with words *(Down hill humps on m & n)*
☐	☐	Generous *(Long ending upstrokes, spaces between words)*
☐	☐	Extravagant *(Flourishes all over writing)*
☐	☐	Wants to be center of attention (long ending upstrokes)
☐	☐	Cautious *(Long straight ending stroke on the baseline)*
☐	☐	Gullible *(Huge width in lower loop of y, g, and j)*
☐	☐	Socially selective *(Narrow loop in y, g, and j)*
☐	☐	Reluctant to trust *(Small loop in y, g, and j)*
☐	☐	Anti-social *(Retraced loop in y, g, and j)*
☐	☐	Aggressive *(No lower loop, sharp return of y, g, and j)*
		Reaction to Criticism
☐	☐	Doesn't care what others think (Retraced d-stem)
☐	☐	Independent of others' thoughts (Short, retraced d-stem)
☐	☐	Slightly sensitive, but independent (Short, loop d-stem)
☐	☐	Cares what others think (bigger looped d-stem)
☐	☐	Needs approval from others, hurts deeply when criticized (Bigger looped d and t loops)
☐	☐	Oversensitive, worries about what other people think
☐	☐	Paranoid (Huge looped d stem that doesnt return to baseline)

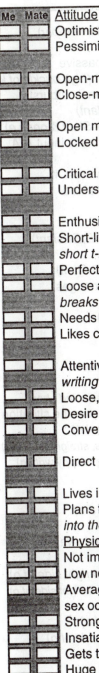

Me Mate Attitude

Optimistic *(Baseline slants up to the right)*
Pessimistic *(Baseline slanted down to the right)*

Open-minded *(wide open a,o,e and loop in h)*
Close-minded *(narrow/closed a,o,e and loop in h)*

Open mind to philosophies *(Loop in stem of h)*
Locked down ethics and philosophies *(Retraced h stem)*

Critical of others *(Sharp t-bar, open o, & sharp m & n's)*
Understanding/supportive of others

Enthusiastic *(Very long t-bar)*
Short-lived excitement, no follow through *(Light writing, short t-bar on left)*
Perfectionist *(Perfectly straight baseline)*
Loose and versatile *(Loose, bouncy baseline with breaks in the writing)*
Needs stability
Likes change *(Y loop long and tilts toward the right)*

Attentive to detail, structure, procedure *(copybook writing with i-dot close to stem)*
Loose, unstructured, detail secondary importance
Desire to be different *(Circle i-dot)*
Conventional *(Copybook writing)*

Direct - gets to the point *(t starts with downstroke only)*

Lives in the moment *(No upper zone strokes)*
Plans for future, philosophically probing *(Lots of strokes into the upper zone, sharp m,n, and h's, high t-bars)*
Physical/ Sex Drives
Not important *(No lower loops in g, y, and j)*
Low need for activity *(Small lower loops)*
Average sex/ physical drives – needs physical exercise/ sex occasionally *(Average size lower loops)*
Strong drives *(Long lower loops)*
Insatiable physical drives *(Long and wide lower loops)*
Gets too many irons in the fire *(Loops into writing below)*
Huge sexual imagination, average drives *(Wide loops)*

Me	Mate	
		Relationship Roles
☐	☐	Dominant; needs control *(Heavy Downslanted t-bar)*
☐	☐	Passive; likes mate to make decisions
☐	☐	Prefer neither partner is too dominant/passive
☐	☐	Defiant: resists authority-others' control *(high buckle of k)*
☐	☐	Temper–displays uncontrollable emotional outburst *(t-bar crossed on right side & DE,E+ Slant)*
☐	☐	Listens to others' concerns *(CD,DE,E + Slant & open e)*
☐	☐	Absorbed in own problems, closed to other's input *(FA, AB Slant & closed e & braced t-stem)*
☐	☐	Always looking for a challenge: loses interest if someone or something is too easily obtained
☐	☐	Distant, cold, self-centered *(FA/AB slant)*
☐	☐	Warm, friendly, open, expressive *(CD,DE,E+ slant)*
☐	☐	Makes logical thought-out decisions *(AB Slant)*
☐	☐	Subject to whims, emotions, and sudden urges *(E+ Slant)*
☐	☐	Jealous *(Tight squarish beginning loop)*
☐	☐	Sarcastic *(Sharp point at end of t-bar)*
☐	☐	Sense of humor *(Wavy t-bar)*
☐	☐	Resentful/angry *(Heavy inflexible upstroke)*
☐	☐	Dominant–controls situations well *(downslanted t-bar)*
☐	☐	Domineering–must be in control of others or the situation *(downslated t-bar with sharp sarcastic point)*
☐	☐	Organized, perfectionist *(Balanced f loops, straight baseline)*
☐	☐	Sloppy, scattered *(Unbalanced f loops, big, sloppy writing)*
		Communication
☐	☐	Frank, open, honest, and blunt *(Open o & a)*
☐	☐	Talkative *(Open o & a)*
☐	☐	Reticent–withholds information until asked *(Narrow o)*
☐	☐	Secretive *(Loop in right side of o)*
☐	☐	Slightly secretive to others *(Small loop in right side of o)*
☐	☐	Extremely secretive to others *(Large loop in right side of o)*
☐	☐	Deceitful to others *(Loop in both sides of o)*
☐	☐	Deceitful to self (denial) *(Big loop in left side of o)*

Appendix C ———————

Further Explanations,
Scientific Documentation,
& Other Books, Tapes, Products, and
Home Study Courses by Bart Baggett

Further information and explanations on Handwriting Analysis and Neuro-Analysis

Getting To Know Your Secret Weapon

As you may know, if you read a lot of business publications, handwriting analysis and the related neuro-sciences are some of the fastest-growing business and management tools for the 21st century. One futurist predicts by the year 2010, the majority of American businesses will be using handwriting analysis to help match potential employees with the job that best fits their psychological makeup and to assist in management, employee relations, and motivation. This is easy to believe since it's already true in Europe. *The Wall Street Journal, 1988*, published the following fact: In France, Spain, Holland, and Israel, approximately 80% of the top 500 companies either have a handwriting analyst on staff or hire one as a consultant to analyze every potential employee before hiring them.

In many parts of the world, leading psychologists and business people have been using handwriting analysis (also called graphology and grapho-analysis) for years. Almost all European Universities teach it in their psychology departments and now more and more U.S. universities are offering courses in handwriting analysis. But of course, American business doesn't wait for *Academia* to catch up; American businesses are already using handwriting analysis to discover the specific personality traits of business associates, employees, and potential employees. The advancement of modern technologies such as computers and fax machines has brought neuro-analysis within easy access of any small business or individual. In fact, companies can simply fax a sample of the person's handwriting to an expert handwriting analyst and receive a computer-assisted five-to-eight page analysis back within the hour. These reports contain very specific descriptions of this person's personality. One can also get counseling in person or over the telephone. Bart Baggett has taken this concept one step further. Any individual who has a question about a prospective lover, date, employee, or partner who faxes their handwriting can get the same report or verbal counseling that a corporation would receive. There is now no reason to date or hire a person who is incompatible, considering the solution is just a phone/fax call away. With the popularity of handwriting analysis continuing to grow, as it has in Europe, you will continue to hear even more about this fascinating science and its vast business and personal applications. You can hire Bart or locate a professional handwriting analyst near you by calling Empresse Publishing at 1-800-398-2278 or visiting the web page at www.myhandwriting.com.

Supreme Court Ruling On Handwriting Analysis

Handwriting analysis has proven to be so accurate and psychologically revealing that the U.S. Supreme Court was forced to make a ruling regarding whether it could be considered an invasion-of-privacy. The Supreme Court, in 1977, *United States v. Sydney Rosinsky* (FRP249) ruled: "What someone's handwriting looks like is considered <u>public</u> information—similar to, for example, how someone dresses or their body language, and the psychological analysis that can be extracted from that information is <u>not</u> considered an invasion of privacy."

Modern handwriting analysis (neuro-analysis) is one of those sciences that is so amazing, so revolutionary, and so accurate that some people who are uneducated in these areas find it hard to understand or hard to believe its accuracy—that is, until they have their own handwriting analyzed by a qualified analyst. Since becoming a skilled analyst, Bart has proven the accuracy of neuro-analysis to hundreds of experts such as psychologists, behavioral scientists, human resource specialists and numerous conservative top business executives. The initial skepticism invariably turns to curiosity and fascination when they hear the details of human behavior that handwriting reveals.

Accuracy According To Traditional Psychological Tests

Traditional psychologists who specialize in personality testing using more standard/accepted tests have worked with handwriting experts. One study revealed that the correlation between handwriting analysis and the standard MMPI psychological test was incredibly high. Not only is the accuracy of handwriting analysis as high as any other accepted personality test, in many cases it is far higher because it is neurologically based and not subject to the interpretation of what the subject thinks the question is supposed to mean. What was significant about the comparison of neuro-analysis to the standard and accepted (another word for "old") means of personality testing was that neuro-analysis did not require the person to answer 350+ questions; in fact with handwriting analysis, the person doesn't even have to know they are being analyzed! In the appendix of this book is a bibliography of several of the clinical research studies, with summaries, that demonstrate the accuracy of handwriting analysis.

Neuro-Analysis...What Is It, Really?

Neuro-analysis is the combination of modern neuro-sciences with the empirical study of personality; over the years, behavioral scientists and handwriting experts have categorized neuro-muscular tendencies as they are correlated with specific observable personality traits. In simple terms; handwriting & NLP.

Each personality trait is represented by a common neurological brain pattern in every individual possessing that trait. Each common neurological brain pattern has an associated neuro-mechanical micro-movement tendency. Therefore, every person, regardless of sex, race, ethnic background, or language with that personality trait will share that neuro-muscular tendency.

In plain English this means that there are very small neuro-muscular movements that are the same for every person who has that personality trait. The movements are so tiny that they have to be graphically frozen to be identified; handwriting is an example of this graphically frozen movement. Analyzing and interpreting that data is the science of Neuro-analysis.

Scientific Documentation

There have been numerous clinical research experiments that validate handwriting as an accurate tool for personality assessment. The majority of the pioneering research was performed before 1929 in Europe. This notion was personally verified when I, Bart Baggett, worked with some of the leading graphologists in Spain and France in 1989. My background was in the scientific American form of handwriting analysis pioneered by Milton Bunker. Because European graphology is so widely accepted in the corporate world and taught in the universities, I wanted to know what system of analyzing handwriting it was based upon. Do the European analysts use the same principles that I learned? After my first-hand experimentation, I concluded that the material taught by Milton Bunker is the same information that European graphologists have used since the late 1800's. It is commonly called the French system. The German system is often associated with the famous psychologist Gestalt.

By the way, the handwriting portions of this book are based on the French foundation. Therefore, to find the original documentation of the development of handwriting analysis, you should begin your search in Europe. Because of the difficulty in locating and translating these original documents, I have listed some more recent studies that support the validity of handwriting analysis as a diagnostic tool. The books listed may also be helpful as reference for further documentation.

Researchers	Results

Allport & Vernon (1967) One of the first successful experiments by Alfred Binet w/ Crepieux–Jamin in 1904. Findings for age & sex were negative, yet positive for honesty and intelligence. Experienced graphologists obtained 61% to 92% success in their analyzation.

Harvey (1934) Tested for 22 measurable characteristics and concluded that graphically expressed personality characteristics are results of complex patterns of behavior. Analyst must consider the complex relationships of many signs instead of just an individual sign here and there.

Munroe, Lewinson & Waehner (1944) Three projective tests (Rorschach, handwriting analysis, spontaneous drawings) exhibited strong agreement with each other as well as agreement with clinical observations.

Eysenck (1945) Concluded that a skilled graphologist is capable of diagnosing personality traits from handwriting with statistical reliability in comparison to a psychiatrist and the patient himself.

Muhl (1950) Concluded that handwriting analysis is a useful diagnostic tool for the physician as it reveals the emotional component (instability) of the patient which may manifest itself in physical disorders.

Sonnemann & Kernan (1962) Evaluations of handwriting samples written several years apart were consistent and demonstrated reliability scores similar to other objective tests. The evaluations related significantly to actual job performance and to concerns of management.

Galbraith & Wilson (1964)   Skilled graphoanalysts achieved satisfactory reliability in their measurement of personality traits including attention to detail, domineering tendencies, self-consciousness, and stubbornness.

Frederick (1968)   Graphologists statistically exceeded chance in selecting genuine suicide notes from 3 times the number of control notes.

Drory (1986)   Employee ratings by the handwriting analyst and job supervisors were highly correlated for 10 of the 13 variables that were tested.

Rodriguez (1986)   Graphoanalysts' evaluations were compared to the personality dimensions of the California Personality Inventory. 2 dimensions, dominance and intellectual efficiency, were strongly correlated. The study concluded that Graphanalysis demonstrates potential as a personality diagnostic tool and that trained analysts measure these traits reliably.

Other References

Allport, Gordon. *Studies in Expressive Movement*. The Macmillian Company, 1933.

Bunker, M. N. *Handwriting Analysis-The Science of Determining Personality by Graphoanalysis.* Nelson-Hall Co., Publishers, 1974.

Currer-Briggs, Noel, Kennett, Brian, and Patterson, Jane. *Handwriting Analysis in Business - Use of Graphology in Personnel Selection.* Associated Business Programs, 1971.

De Saint Colombe, Paul. *Grapho-Therapeutics; The Pen and Pencil Therapy.* Popular Library 1972.

Hartford, Huntington. *You Are What You Write.* Macmillan Publishing Co. Inc., 1973.

Marcuse, Irene, Ph.D. *Guide to Personality Through Your Handwriting.* Arco Publishing Company, Inc. 1974.

Pulver, Max. *Symbolism of Handwriting.* Orell Fussli Verlag, 1931.

Roman, Klara. *Handwriting: A Key to Personality.* Noonday Press, 1952.

Sackheim, Kathryn K., *Handwriting Analysis and the Employee Selection Process: A Guide for Human Resource Professionals.* Quorum Books, 1990.

Saudek, Robert. *The Psychology of Handwriting.* George Allen and Unwin Ltd., 1925.

Sonnemann, Ulrich, Ph.D. *Handwriting Analysis as a Psychodiagnostic Tool.* Grune and Stratton, Inc. 1950.

Wolff, Werner, Ph.D. *Diagrams of the Unconscious–Handwriting and Personality in Measurement, Experiment and Analysis.* Grune & Stratton, 1948.

Discover The Secrets To Creating Chemistry
Mastering Relationships & Seduction
Using Advanced Neuro-Linguistic Programming Techniques

Imagine....
... Creating that state of <u>incredible connection</u>
INSTANTLY...with whomever you choose...
...Guaranteed!

Now you can attend Bart's $295 2-Day Creating Chemistry seminar without ever leaving your home... for less! Imagine spending two days with Bart Baggett unlocking the secrets to creating states of lust, passion, love, and absolute connection.

The whole concept of "chemistry" has been very, very, very misrepresented by all those "experts." Maybe they were sincere, but for sure they were misguided. See, there's actually a simple, predictable, CERTAIN method that you will master in just two days...This secret system combines the powerful technologies of N.L.P., handwriting analysis, and Bart's own unique special methods.

Can you imagine how good you would feel to be able to walk up to anyone you find attractive and instantly create that deep sense of connection, rapport, sexual excitement? If in the past, you have left "chemistry" to chance, you are in for a big surprise. Read on.

Sexual chemistry can be created at your beck and call. In fact, you can also create states of lust, commitment, intimacy, and even love. Bart has discovered the most amazing new developments in the field of human development, psychology, and persuasion that can release your power to finally have the kind of relationship you have always wanted. And now, you can learn it all in a two day workshop from your car or home on cassettes tapes.

Have you ever wondered, "Why do some people feel an uncontrollable magnetic attraction to someone, and others have no spark?"

The answer is the internal mental process. Now, you can control this process.

After years of studying the master persuaders, linguists, lovers, and therapists, Bart discovered the secrets to falling in love AND he can teach you the specific method for making others fall in love with you, (or just lust, whichever fits your agenda.) Much of the technology is based on Neuro-Linguistic Programming™ and the concept of Time-Line. Even if you have a background in either one of these fantastic methodologies for change, you've never seen or heard the specific outcomes that you can achieve using this specific system. It is truly a breakthrough is human behavior.

As you complete The Secrets To Creating Chemistry Seminar, you'll understand clearly— maybe for the first time in your life— how some people consistently create charisma, love, and passion in their lives. What's more... you will have the actual skills to do it.

What skills?

Sophisticated communication skills that create intense states of pleasure whenever you use them. In addition you will learn specific tools to control your present attitude, other's reaction to you, and even program your future. You will be able identify, explain, and use the following specific skills:

• Create an instant state of attraction within the first 1 minute of meeting.
• Identify someone's motivational strategy.
• The best opening sentences so that people to find you totally fascinating.
• Elicit someone's highest values in life.
• Make your prospective lover FORGET about his/her current one.

Order On-Line: mail@myhandwriting.com

- Lead your lover into a long lasting commitment.
- Discover how to lead your lover into the ultimate orgasm.
- Learn specific ways to seduce a person based on the individual's handwriting traits.

Plus...

- The Most Influential Words in the English language that create intense agreement with you as you speak. These words put people into an instant state of trance and you can give subtle commands that they will follow.
- Using your body to communicate and lead other's unconscious mind. This goes much deeper than body language. This knowledge teaches to use your body to control the internal states of someone, without ever saying a word about it! It gives you rapport at the deepest levels.
- Over Ten Hours of Live Seminar Recordings.
- A special Time-Line Programming Cassette that literally places the memory of your ideal mate into your future time-line on the subconscious level. You just relax.
- The 65 page Secrets To Creating Chemistry Seminar Manual / Workbook.

Guaranteed!

"That's right, guaranteed. I realize that taking many hours out of your busy schedule can seem like a risk at first. (Not to mention the money.) In order to encourage you to pick up the phone and order immediately, I have decided to take all the risk. If you are not completely thrilled and excited about the new ways you have to control your destiny, relationships, and love-life, simply return the course for a full refund...up to one year after you order. You have my personal money back, no questions asked, satisfaction guarantee." –Bart

Order the Entire Course Today!

Includes: 65 Page Seminar Manual, Over Ten Hours of Live Recordings on Cassettes, NLP Hypnosis Tape "Create Your Future Lover", & Unconditional Money Back Guarantee!

The Secrets to Creating Chemistry Course
Item # BBSCCC — Only $195

Here's Why Past Attendees Recommend Bart's Creating Chemistry Seminar...

"I was worried that this would be just another positive thinking-pump-em-up give them nothing real course. I'm very pleased to say that it was instead very REAL and chock-full of effective and usable means to build confidence and achieve interpersonal goals. " —William Stanley, Sacramento, CA

"In depth. Details. Thorough. This was just what I needed to fully understand and feel comfortable using NLP in the context of relationships. This was time and money well spent. Highly recommended. "
— Art Simkins, Ontario, CA

"I would recommend this course to my friends because it will promote power in his or her life using specific knowledge and techniques ."
— Merilyn Grosshans, Las Vegas, NV

"Excellent. Exciting. Obviously, one of the best investments in time and money I've ever made. I would recommend this course to anyone because the effective combination of handwriting and NLP establishes a coherent non-judgmental approach to changing behavior. "
— Tam Margraf, Las Vegas, NV

Get Excited About Moving to the
Next Level...
"How You Can Analyze Handwriting in 10 Minutes or Less!"
Basic Home Study Course

This course is the next step in your mastery of handwriting analysis. If you're not ready for the Certification Level Training, enhance your understanding of the sometimes complex and confusing revelations revealed by handwriting. This is the same program ordered by thousands of people off of radio and TV programs nationwide! This is Bart's most comprehensive introductory level program.

You'll be surprised at how fast you learn using this system. It includes the best tools available today about the science of handwriting analysis, presented for you in both a visual and audio format so you learn interactively! It even includes The Grapho-Deck trait cards so you can literally grasp these concepts quickly and easily.

When you follow this step by step program, people will swear you are an experienced handwriting expert in no time flat! This course even includes a special "upgrade coupon" you can redeem to move to more advanced level courses. And of course, you get Bart's Unconditional One Year Money Back Guarantee! No Risk.

Includes 7 Items:

One VHS Video "How You Can Know Everything About Anybody in 10 Minutes or Less" - Bart walks you through his easy to follow method with dozens of examples and live analysis.

• **Tape I:** Analyze Handwriting in 10 Minutes or Less - A quick and easy guide to using handwriting analysis.

• **Tape II:** How to Use the Grapho-Deck® - This 60-minute tape walks you through using the deck to meet and understand people with world renowned handwriting expert Phyllis Mattingly.

• **Tape III:** The Compatibility Tape - Explains how to predict how two people will get along in a relationship. 30-year handwriting veteran

Phyllis Mattingly shares her insights into love and handwriting.

• **Tape IV:** How to Use Handwriting Analysis in Your Business or Workplace - Improve employee productivity and compatibility.

• **The Special Report** "How Anyone Can Be Analyzing Handwriting in 10 Minutes or Less!" - This 60 page report gives you the down and dirty, fast and easy steps on how to instantly analyze handwriting.

• **One Grapho-Deck®** - The Original and Best-Selling Handwriting Analysis Flash Cards. Over 50 sturdy cards, actual playing card size, that illustrate each personality trait.

The 10 Minute or Less Home Study Course!
1998 Version Pictured above designed to be used with The Secrets To Making Love Happen book, duplicate copy not included with this special offer.

How To Analyze Handwriting In 10 Minutes or Less Home Study Program

ITEM# HAND5   retail $149.95

Special Offer Secrets Owner Basic Upgrade (duplicate book not included)
ITEM #HAND5 Sec-Upgrd
Save over 50% $69.95

The Handwriting Analysis Certification Home Study Course

This Course Can Be Your Golden Key to Unlocking Your Hidden Potential!

You can now enroll in our comprehensive home study course and graduate a Certified Handwriting Expert in a few fun filled short months!

That's right! You can take your enthusiasm about understanding human behavior to a whole new level by becoming a Certified Handwriting Expert. You can now get all the education you need, without ever attending a live class or traveling hundreds of miles for a boring intensive, expensive, instructional session at some highbrow university.

Bart Baggett has captured the highlights of live classes on over 16 audio cassettes and packaged them with easy to follow, fascinating lesson handouts. You can get a comprehensive education on handwriting analysis without ever leaving the comfort of your home or car.

This program has that personal touch at just a fraction of what it would cost to attend such a program live. If you are busy and you value your time and money, this is the best program available to advance your knowledge and move to the next level: a Certified Handwriting Expert.

Think About How Learning More Can Benefit Your Life:

- Increase your confidence and self-esteem.
- Set and achieve higher goals without a fear of failure.
- Make a difference in everyone you meet.
- Understand all the handwriting strokes beyond the basic books and cards and even learn how to evaluate and stack traits!
- Master the science of Grapho-Therapy!
- Earn recognition and respect by becoming a Certified Expert.
- Be invited to be a guest speaker all around town.
- Earn extra income... Upwards of $100 an hour!

"If you enjoyed this book, you will absolutely fall in love with this Home Study Course. Join previous students from around the world in taking this self-paced program for the mastery of handwriting analysis. Upon qualification, you can become a Certified Handwriting Expert. You even have my personal One Year Unconditional Total Satisfaction Money Back Guarantee! It's a great course!"
– Bart Baggett

It will teach you how to explain hundreds of traits in such a way that you can inspire others to live their dreams, rather than be discouraged by their differences, limitations, and possible shortcomings. It really is a remarkable sight to see a person's attitude transform like an awakening butterfly. Just think, you can be the catalyst to such optimism, hope, and transformation in others' lives. This course really takes you beyond where any single book can take you.

Some of the most rewarding events in our lives come when we can sincerely make a difference in other people's lives. After you learn to be a Certified Handwriting Expert, that satisfaction tends to be a common experience.

This course is led by expert instructors who explain all the many variables and exceptions of handwriting analysis. You will have a clear picture for understanding people by their handwriting.

Continued...

Order On-Line: mail@myhandwriting.com

The <u>Standard</u> Handwriting Analysis Home Study Course: Includes over 16 Hours of Audio lectures, Handout Supplement, Textbook, Video, Kid's and Adult's Workbook, Emotional Gauge, Certificate, and much more!

6 Good Reasons For You To Enroll Today:

1. Learn at your own pace, using audio cassettes and the home study materials. Remember, there is no time limit on the completion of your training.
2. Extra Income: Earn $50-$125 per hour analyzing handwriting in your spare time.
3. Expanded insight and advanced knowledge - Hundreds of insights not included in the Basic Course.
4. Rare Handwriting Samples: Dozens of celebrities, millionaires, psychopaths, politicians and criminals!
5. Master the Science of Grapho-Therapy.
6. Graduation Diploma. Upon your successful completion of your exams and passing an oral test, a frameable blue and gold diploma will be awarded to you. Issued by the Grapho-Analytics Institute of Handwriting Analysis and authorized by the signatures of the Directors.

Just imagine... You, the expert, having fun and getting paid for talking to people, just by looking at others' handwriting. If you really want to go for it, consider the option of investing in the Standard or Deluxe Handwriting Home Study Course.

The Standard Handwriting Analysis Certification Course Includes:

- 14 hours of classroom instruction on audio tape
- Special 70 page Handouts Supplement of Unusual Samples
- Dr. Ray Walker's Textbook
- Emotional gauge
- 21 Tests for Certification
- Complete Trait Dictionary and Review Sections
- Two Bonus Tapes: Grapho-Therapy and Common Questions
- Plus: The How Anyone Can Analyze Handwriting In Ten Minutes or Less Basic Home Study Program. (see page 289)
- And Change Your Life in 30 Days Adults & Kids Workbooks and Tapes
- Plus the bonus... One Hour of Live Consultation/ Testing Coupon $100 value
- Much, much, more...

Standard Certification Home Study Course
ITEM# HACERT-STD. **$598.95**

Call now to enroll or request more detailed course descriptions with current discount coupons, new products, and special offers!

How You Can Earn $100 An Hour
Or More Analyzing Handwriting
(In your spare time or as a new career)

Even the World's Best Handwriting Analyst Will STARVE TO DEATH without a steady stream of new clients.

You see, I'm not only a handwriting expert... I'm an entrepreneur. This is not just my passion, it's my business. The sad truth is most people in the handwriting analysis business haven't a clue about how to turn this valuable skill into ready to spend cash! But I do... I make hundreds of dollars a day in the handwriting business. (Sometimes thousands of dollars a day! And, you can too.)

You Can Now Use Private Never Before Revealed Marketing Secrets to Make Over $100 An Hour as a Professional Handwriting Expert!

That is what this Marketing System is all about. Now, you too can earn serious money using your handwriting analysis skills when you put these "Marketing Systems" to work getting new customers on Auto Pilot. Imagine having clients waiting in line for your service! It's possible, if you know the secrets.

I'm going to show you how I started, what I do, and how you can duplicate my success or achieve levels I have never dreamed of! Even if you are just a beginner, you can begin making money in the handwriting business using my proven marketing methods. (Yes, these are the same methods I've used to land myself on over 500 major radio and TV talk shows in the country and create a thriving business with thousands of satisfied customers... worldwide!)

Some Various Areas You Might Specialize In:

- Jury Screening
- Employment Screening
- Questioned Document Examiner
- Compatibility/Marriage Profiles
- Psychological Profiles for Counselors or Psychologists
- Grapho-Therapy for personal improvement
- Entertainment: parties, fairs, trade shows, happy hours, or demonstrations.
- Behavior Profiling
- Criminal Investigations
- Lectures and Training

Best of all... you can get started in your spare time, from the privacy of your own home, with no boss and totally risk free!

This "Marketing System" is absolutely brand new. Before now, I have never revealed how I was able to land myself on almost every major talk show in the country... how I have talked newspapers into running feature length articles on me without charging me a penny .... how I sold thousands of books and courses on handwriting... how my jam-packed seminars and lectures are still making me money for years after I've folded up the chairs... and why numerous companies won't make a hiring decision without my approval of their applicants handwriting. The secret is marketing.

In the System, I reveal my hard earned marketing success secrets. In fact, since this program is so new, you will still be among the very first few people in the world to own and implement these marketing strategies. Most of these golden ideas I had to dig out of the "mine of hard experience." I spent years saying the wrong thing, placing ads that didn't work, and often spinning my wheels perfecting this system. Ask any entrepreneur — it isn't easy making the phones ring day in day out without a steady, predictable system to work for you.

One Year Unconditional 100% Money Back Guarantee:

I'll guarantee that if you haven't gained at least 10 times the value of your investment in the next FULL YEAR... simply send the worn, coffee stained, used, and well read Marketing System back for a full and complete 100% Refund. Now, I know you might only make an additional $1,000, $5,000 or $3,5000 next year from my course... but what is that worth TOTAL over the next ten years?

For every dollar you invest with me, I'll guarantee a **tenfold return** in value. All I ask is that you listen to all of the tapes; follow the program. If it doesn't work for you, I'll refund every penny. Take up a year to make your decision that it is worth ten times your investment! That is how confident I am that this System works. The entire course costs just under what you will make in ONE 8-hour work day once you start the ball rolling earning $100 per hour. If you're not making 100 bucks an hour now, what have you got to lose?

Order On-Line: mail@myhandwriting.com

The Deluxe Course, pictured above, includes everything you need to become a certified professional handwriting analyst and learn the Secret Marketing System that can earn you over $100 per hour in your own business. Most items pictured are sold separately or available bundled together as the "Deluxe Course."

The "How to Make Over $100 Per Hour Analyzing Handwriting" Marketing System Includes:

• 5 Hours of Instructional Audio Tapes:
- Live interviews with successful analysts.
- Day-to-day operations and marketing methods.
- Inside Secrets on making money from every angle of your handwriting business... newspapers, lawyers, corporations, lectures, parties, magazines, and even radio interviews!
- Special interview with Phyllis Mattingly about Document Examining, Jury Screening, Public Speaking, and lots more!

Special Sections :

• How to get FREE Publicity from newspapers and magazines. This report alone can recoup your entire investment in this program. Includes over 15 actual articles and/or press releases for you to model and study so you can start writing your own.

• How to Successfully Market and Teach Handwriting Seminars. This includes handouts, flyers, class outlines, and even the option of teaching a certification course in your home town or your country.

• How Not to Waste A Nickel on $10,000 Worth of Advertising! Ads That Work and Don't Work - Save yourself thousands of dollars marketing your new business. This will show you how to use advertising to fuel your new business in every detail... step by step. What ads to place, which publications, word for word ad copy, and the single most costly common mistake to avoid when advertising.

• How to get hired by Corporations

• How to get booked at a party, bar mitzvah, happy hour or any other social function for fun and profit.

• How to prepare a comprehensive Written Analysis.

• How to give a radio or newspaper interview: Includes an actual transcript of a radio interview to guide you on how to field questions from the media and come out looking like a saint!

• The secret of using your fax machine, voicemail, and mailbox for your 24-hour new customer magnet.

• Jury Screening and working with lawyers.

• Grapho 1.0 Computer Software for Customized Written Handwriting Analysis Reports. (For Mac or IBM) You can earn big money working at home, part time, from your computer!

• How You Can Be Booked Solid as the Guest Speaker at Clubs and Organizations in your home town, Get A Standing Ovation Every Time, And Take Home a Pocket Full of Cash From Every Lecture! This section teaches you everything you need to know to create, market, and deliver a first class presentation and get paid handsomely for doing so. We literally "dumped out our files" and photocopied everything from flyers to class lecture notes for you to get a quick start in the lecture and seminar business.

• Worldwide Internet Advertising — One Year Free Listing on our web site (www.myhandwriting.com) This will get you business worldwide by being among the select few who get the privilege of being endorsed on the world's most visited handwriting web site.

Silver Marketing System: Investment Summary.
√ Marketing Training Written Course
√ Grapho Computer Software Program
√ One Year Internet Advertising
√ Marketing Consulting/Fax In Coupons

Silver Professional Marketing Course $748.00
ITEM# SLVRMKTG

Deluxe Course (Combination) $1346.95
ITEM# DLXHACERT   (4 Month Financing Available)

"Standard Certification Course" Sold Separately or together as the "Deluxe" System - Substantial discounts apply when purchased together - please call for current prices, bonuses, or other discounts.

Order On-Line: mail@myhandwriting.com

The Grapho-Deck® is to Handwriting what Cliff's Notes are to Books!
Simple, Fast, Portable, and Fun!

The Grapho-Deck Handwriting Trait Cards® show over 50 personality traits graphically displayed with a concise definition of each behavior. The Grapho-Deck is truly the Cliff's Notes® of Personality. It is not a complete course, but a great way to jump right in and feel great grasping the basics. Great for beginners.

People from all over the world started writing me with stories of how much fun it is to use the little deck of 50+ personality trait cards to make new friends and understand others' personalities instantly! It makes handwriting analysis so simple and easy; it makes total strangers feel like you've known them for years.

This little deck of cards will make you the center of attention wherever you go and instantly reveal the truth about anyone's personality. To make learning both easy and fun, the deck can be ordered with instructional cassette tapes that guide you through the best methods and techniques for using it. You can buy it separately, but save yourself some money and get more value by ordering the Grapho-deck as part of a the Starter Kit or the Ten Minute or Less Home Study Course. Ask for details when you call to order.

Remember, you can always buy The Grapho-Deck individually or by the dozen as gifts for your friends.

NEW VERSION!!

GRAPHO-DECK ONLY 51 cards Full Color
Item#BBGD...........................$15.95

GRAPHO-DECK Starter Kit —2 Tapes & Deck
Item#BBGDStrKit....................$29.95

Special price for a dozen or more, perfect for gifts:
Item #BBGD12............$96.00 per dozen

Order On-Line: mail@myhandwriting.com

Change Your Handwriting, Change Your Life.
New 30 Day Workbooks Make
Grapho-Therapy Fun for the Whole Family!

The concept of understanding human personality from someone's handwriting is beginning to be accepted worldwide. One psychological aspect of handwriting not so well understood is using handwriting to assist you in changing your personality and even eradicate bad habits. The concept of "change your handwriting, change your life" is very powerful. It is called grapho-therapy.

Years ago, before I wrote my first book, I taught personal improvement seminars nationwide. I used many methods to move people from a state of ineffectiveness to a state of "personal power." Through research and years of looking at handwriting, I noticed a trend of particular personality traits that successful people shared. Likewise, I noticed a trend that unsuccessful, unhappy, or ineffective people had in common.

It doesn't matter what your goals are: growing a rose garden or winning olympic gold, there are certain traits that support you in attaining your dreams. Knowledge and awareness alone don't seem to be enough to make the changes. How many people do you know who have spent years in therapy, know all their problems, and are still a mess? If the changes aren't "set" into the personality, the changes usually don't stick. If you have ever been to a "pump you up" motivational seminar, you know what I mean. As soon as the excitement wears off, so do the new habits

I found that creating a neurological connection (by changing the handwriting) and repetition were the best methods to assure a high percentage of

success. One particularly effective method is via your day-to-day handwriting.

To support these long term changes, I designed the "Change Your Handwriting Workbook." During the live seminars, the response was overwhelming. Seminar participants loved the structure, insight, and daily activity that the workbook provides. Also, the workbook assists you in charting your goals and objectives for the coming days, months, and years.

Instead of having you attend a full day seminar, I've condensed the most important information on a 45-minute audio cassette that is included with the manual. You get the down and dirty "meat" of the full-day seminar at just a "snack" of the cost!

As you write in the workbook, you can actually see the changes happen from your own hand! Each day, you will feel the difference as you analyze your life in all areas. You can achieve quick, permanent, and specific personality changes in 30 days!

You can easily:

• raise self-esteem
• eliminate being sensitive to criticism
• overcome self-consciousness
• develop trust
• improve your relationships
• overcome fear of success
• and grow in many, many more areas

If you are looking for a great way to kick-start the "New You," this 30-day workbook can make the next month the most important 30 days of your life.

Kids Version
Just Released

Workbook for Children Raises Grades, Boosts Self Esteem and Improves Attitude

If you think changing your handwriting works great as a self-improvemnt tool for adults... wait until you see the effect it has on your children! You can now take a PRO-ACTIVE role in choosing your child's attitude, personality, and character.

This workbook is designed for kids 2nd grade - 6th grade and incorporates writing skills, NLP, goals, beliefs, and of course, handwriting changes to guide them to a more positive, pleasant personality. As a bonus, most kids begin making better grades and actually enjoy the excercises!

The workbook was mostly fun, but sometimes it was hard. In class I'm doing great! My teacher can't believe how much I've improved. She asked me to bring this book to school to help other kids. Since I have been working on my handwriting, I have been getting along better with my Mom. She does not have to yell at me to do my homework...not! My favorite letter is T. I cross them on the top because I'm the best. Thank you for helping me.

-Ryan Waton, Age 10
- Plantation, Florida

Individual Workbooks

• Change Your Life in 30 Days Workbook (Age 13 and Up)
- ITEM# BB30............**$29.95**

• Change Your Life in 30 Days Workbook for Kids (Grades 2-6)
- ITEM# BB30KDS............**$29.95**

Each workbook comes with an instructional audio cassette. Discounts apply for combinations or multiple books purchases.

Order On-Line: mail@myhandwriting.com

NEW FROM BART BAGGETT...
MyHandwriting.com
International Handwriting Analysis Training

Sign up for your free weekly e-mail Newsletter written by Bart Baggett. Just visit our website and type in your e-mail. It's free.

myhandwriting.com/newsletters

Also visit:

bartbaggett.com/catalog

botmarketing.com
(Internet Marketing)

HandwritingUniversity.com

e-onlinepublishing.com
(put the dash after the e -)

mentalfitnessproducts.com
(Affiliate program for resellers)

SexSecretsRevealed.com

Discover sexual secrets that will drive your lover wild in bed. Besides anatomy techniques described in video, audio, and text, Bart teaches NLP and hand-writing tips to improve your love life.

Toll Free 1-800-398-2278 or 01-214-651-8880
mail@myhandwriting.com
Direct all mail to: Bart Baggett
c/o Empresse Publishing
POBox 720355
Dallas, TX 75372 USA